STALKING GERALDINE

Cover artwork Martin Squires
Text artwork Helen Turner
Book design Włodzimierz Milewski

Note for libraries: A catalogue record for this book is available from Library and Archives Canada at www.collectionscanada.gc.ca

ISBN: 978-0-9952778-0-9

BOOKS

MW Books
Garden Bay, BC
V0N 1S1
Canada
mwbookpublishing.com
info@mwbookpublishing.com

10 9 8 7 6 5 4 3 2 1

Ray Wood

STALKING GERALDINE

BOOKS

This book is dedicated to my brilliant, loving and adventurous wife Robyn for whom the next adventure never comes soon enough and who somehow remains optimistic when the lee rail goes too far under or both axles disappear in the mud.

They cannot scare me with their empty spaces
Between stars - on stars where no human race is.
I have it in me so much nearer home
To scare myself with my own desert places.

Robert Frost   DESERT PLACES

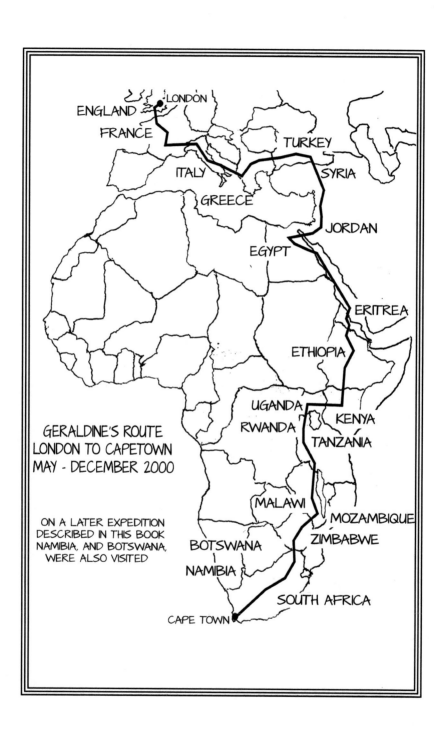

GERALDINE'S ROUTE
LONDON TO CAPETOWN
MAY - DECEMBER 2000

ON A LATER EXPEDITION
DESCRIBED IN THIS BOOK
NAMIBIA, AND BOTSWANA,
WERE ALSO VISITED

SOME AFRICAN VERNACULAR

Bakkie	A pickup truck
Bergie	A tramp
Biltong	Spicy sausage
Boeremusiek	Traditional Afrikaner music
Boma	An enclosure, esp. a fence of thorn bush
Braaivleis	A barbecue
Bwana	Important personage
Dagga	Marijuana
Donga	A fissure formed by soil erosion
Drift	A place to ford a river
Fundi	An expert
Ganja	Marijuana
Gramadoelas	The back of beyond
Kaalgat	Naked
Kloof	A gorge
Koppie	A hill
Matric	Final year of high school
Mekoro	A dugout canoe
Nagaapie	Galago. A small arboreal mammal
Nek	The ridge between two peaks
Pan	A lake, usually dry
Pap	Weak or soft
Quat	A soporific drug, usually chewed
Ratel	A honey badger
Stoep	A porch
Takkies	Canvas shoes, often worn without socks
Tsotsie	A habitual criminal
Ou	A man, probably white
Panga	A machete
Varkie	Little pig - a bottle of cheap wine
Veldt	Open space

CONTENTS

FIRST WATCHER

July 1966

Cape Town, South Africa (Departing North)

The 11.45 fromPaarl.

Since his transfer to the Mother City, he had made only three arrests. No charges were laid against the boys putting coins on the tracks at Rondebosh or the old bergie who continued to sleep under the signal box behind the abattoir. The remaining case took three minutes in court, the magistrate fining the old man two rand for spitting off the footbridge at Salt River.

The Cape weather was wet, windy and unpredictable. Damp pervaded everything. His uniform cloak - a shapeless affair of vulcanised rubber - leaked around his thick neck. The serge collar of his tunic was hopelessly distorted, the handcuffs were tarnished and his boots smelled like pilchards.

On Wednesdays he was assigned to the main terminus on Adderly Street. He preferred this to track work. The likelihood of apprehending a criminal was higher where there were crowds, and he could patrol the long platforms without getting wet. He appreciated shelter this Wednesday as a foul northwester hurled ragged sheets of cold water against the building and pounded the waiting trains. Mist obscured the mountain and muffled the sound of foghorns from the harbour.

The station had a littered utilitarian NON WHITE end and a better, well-maintained WHITE end that supported a cafeteria and a newsstand. There was no set routine. He walked the platforms from one extremity to the other. Most of the time he stood around, picking his nose, trying to look vigilant and important.

Racial divisions in Cape Town were as uncertain as the climate.

In Johannesburg you knew where you stood. The weather there was hot in summer with occasional thunderstorms, and dry in winter with regular frost. Persons in Johannesburg were white or black with few exceptions, and, generally speaking, the police were white and the crooks were black. Here in the Cape, the weather was unpredictable. There were few black people, and passengers came in a variety of shades. You never knew what they really were.

There were not many passengers on the 11.45 from Paarl. He suspected the woman was a non-white from the moment she disembarked from the front of the train. Frikkie the porter made no attempt to assist her with the heavy suitcase so was clearly of the same opinion. She made her lopsided way to the Adderly street entrance, where she sat on the suitcase watching the traffic outside.

She had no right to be where she waited near the newsstand and opposite the travel bureau. There might be a complaint and he would have forms to fill in. It was prudent not to have a confrontation with her, and experience had taught him that the way to handle these matters was simply to make a show of authority. He positioned himself opposite her, rattled the handcuffs by hitching up his pants and looked straight at her. She did not say anything and she did not move off. She looked directly up at him. She was one of the most beautiful women he had ever seen.

Twenty-five years old and about five foot seven, he estimated. Nice clothes. New *takkies*. Tiny gold watch. Skin copper brown. Oval face with freckles on the nose. Long eyelashes, high cheekbones and good teeth. Jet-black hair escaped a white headscarf. The mackintosh did not conceal her figure, and a slim ankle with a blue-beaded bracelet showed beneath the hem of her dress. There was a hint of a smile on her lips and clear rebellion in her dark eyes.

It was part of his job to enforce apartheid. He was conditioned not to think of women other than those of European extraction as attractive. The emotions he felt were unnerving and undermined his authority. He was uncertain what to do next.

A sodden pigeon pooped on the floor by his feet and she suppressed a smirk.

His quandary was resolved by events. A new-looking Land Rover with a canvas canopy pulled up in the loading area outside the entrance. The driver - a tall white man with dark hair and mirrored sunglasses - alighted and looked around. The noon gun boomed. The woman stood up with a defiant toss of her head and lugged her suitcase out of the station. The tall man greeted the woman, unlaced the canvas canopy, and shoved the suitcase inside. The cargo area was filled with boxes, and a spade was strapped behind the cab. It was a most suspect vehicle.

The woman removed her coat, lifted her skirt, climbed in through the sheltered driver's door and slid across to the offside seat. The man got behind the wheel and slammed the door. An astonishing thing then happened. The man kissed the woman. It was more than a quick peck and the action was obvious. The vehicle moved off.

He went directly to his telephone. Sarge answered. 'I just saw a one-five-seven here, sir. A white *ou* driving a blue Land Rover *bakkie* CA 16735. He picked up a coloured woman by the front door and I saw him kissing her before they drove off.'

There was silence at the other end of the line and he heard the captain sigh. Sarge was probably working on the Paarden Island boiler tube case.

'Jus' forget about it, Hennie, okay? It's *mos* not our priority. Forget about it.'

He consoled himself by smoking a *Texan* behind the newsstand and resumed his beat at platform three. *

Seven years after this event took place, a news item appeared on page five of 'The Bloemfontein Friend':

| the Corona-
Antonio Are-
... was able
... damaged
... at a mili-
... Cognac.
... on board

on board the
craft, Leon-
n, 59, who
... said: "We
... the port
aircraft. mv | **POLICEMAN KILLED**

The body of a white railway policeman, Corporal Henrik 'Klop' van der Merwe, was found Friday on the tracks near Aliwal North. Investigating authorities believe this death to be the result of a shunting mishap. Foul play is not suspected. | The British
his assistant
assassinated
a British de-
territory in
Atlantic. Sir
Sharples an
aide-de-cam
Hugh Sayers
killed as the
the grounds
ernment Ho
day evening
It was the n |

Corporal van der Merwe plays no further role in this narrative.

SECOND WATCHER

December 31, 1999

Greenwich, England

Flamsteed House built by Cristopher Wren in 1676.
The time ball has dropped since 1833.

The woman appeared to be acting on impulse when she rose suddenly from her seat and disembarked at Cutty Sark. She was far taller than the overweight man with the gym bag who almost lost her as he fought the closing doors, and was left stumbling on the platform with the whining train accelerating behind him.

Not pausing to look behind her, she pushed her ticket into the turnstile, strode through the echoing tunnel under the river and climbed up the spiral staircase on the other side. He followed at a suitable distance up King William's Walk. As she passed through St. Mary's gate, he had fallen a hundred yards behind. By the time he reached the teahouse on top of the hill, he was completely out of breath. His quarry had already purchased a cup of coffee.

It was a cold, overcast day and there were few people in the park. Keeping away from the tearoom window, he walked around the observatory building, peered up at the large ball suspended from a mast on the roof and pretended to be interested in souvenirs in the gift shop.

It was a quarter to one when she emerged from the tearoom and strode purposefully across the damp grass to sit on a bench close to a sculpture overlooking the river. On a second bench fifty yards away, he fiddled discreetly with the controls in the gym bag, turned on the digital camera and moved aside the flap. He zoomed in on the woman's head and she appeared crystal clear on the three-inch screen.

She could not be described as a classic beauty, but she was

striking, and exercise had brought colour to her face. Her dark eyes were restless and her chin determined. She wore a cashmere pullover and a duffel coat with horn buttons. He could clearly see a thin gold chain around her neck and a wedding ring on her left hand.

A maroon Daimler drove up and parked on the nearby avenue. The driver, suitably prosperous in a Burberry overcoat, alighted and stood by the vehicle talking on a cell phone while acknowledging the woman with a wave of his rolled-up newspaper. The woman rose and walked towards the car. The observer relocated to the bench she had just vacated and reset the camera. After pulling out a plastic bag of breadcrumbs, he scattered them to attract some pigeons. Adjusting what appeared to be a hearing aid in his left ear, he tilted the bag slightly downwards.

The man bent to kiss the woman but she turned her head, deflecting the kiss. However, she didn't resist him putting his arm around her shoulders. He held her affectionately as they walked up to the sculpture and stood looking towards the observatory, not talking. They made a handsome couple, both well dressed - he older, tall and blonde with broad shoulders, and she equally tall, dark and well proportioned.

A small crowd had gathered on the lawn close to the building, watching the time ball slowly climb the mast. The ball dropped and the crowd applauded before dispersing. The man removed his arm from the woman's shoulders to check his watch.

She turned to him and they began to talk. The observer could hear every word and his camera clicked repeatedly. His subjects were oblivious to his presence. The little tape recorder was running.

'Why here?' the man asked. 'We could have had lunch in a nice warm pub.'

'Don't say you've forgotten this too. You proposed to me here - eight years ago - right here next to this Henry Moore.'

'I haven't forgotten.' He pulled her closer. 'But that was summer, and this is winter and bloody freezing. I'm strapped for time too - I've got to meet with Gordon and there's the big bash tonight. You are coming, aren't you? You said you would.'

'I've changed my mind. I'm not coming. Look, no point beating about.' She paused, eyes downcast and scuffing leaves with her foot, then said, 'I asked you to meet me to talk about divorce.' He put his finger to her mouth, but before he could speak she pushed his hand away and continued.

'It's my millennium resolution. I've had enough of humiliation and public gossip. You're still carrying on the same way and I need to get on with my own life.' She drew in a deep breath and turned away from him.

'That bullshit again. Why do you always do this? What do you want to do - ruin my career? We've been over this time and again. You know I'm on the way up, damn it, I'm golden. We made a deal two years ago and I've kept my side of it -- '

She broke in angrily. 'I no longer give a shit about your career. And you no longer seem to give a shit about our marriage. Apart from when you trot me out to make yourself look good, we don't see each other. It's been two years since we've made love. You didn't even call me on my birthday and your little tart of a secretary sent me flowers two weeks after our anniversary.' She touched his arm. 'It's over. I'm sorry. I still care for you, but I'm not going to go on like this.'

'Come on! You never used to be unreasonable. We've given counselling a shot. I see the shrink every two weeks and unload my soul. This is something that takes time.'

She was clearly struggling with her emotions. 'Oh God, this is so difficult. It's so hard to let you go - but what's the point of pretending? You tell me, what's the point?' She was fighting tears. 'Just how long did you expect me to go on?'

'Oh, for God's sake - what is this about? Is it that you've found somebody else, then?' The observer saw his hand reach out and fasten on her wrist. The woman cringed and colour drained from her face.

'You can't expect me to live like this. We used to be such a team. I worked like a dog to help you get to where you are. When the gossip started, you didn't tell me the truth and you made me look like a fool. I've put off having children because it was never the right time for you. You've got the flat in town and I never see you. Avoiding scandal, you say - a trial separation. You just want a wife so you can show off to your bloody public and get your picture with me in the newspapers. I'm past caring what people think. What you've done is nothing new, and they'll get over it. Let go - you're hurting me!'

The man released her arm and she stepped back from him, ashen-faced. He leaned against the side of the sculpture, brushed leaves off the plinth with his gloved hand, put the folded newspaper on the damp concrete and sat down facing her. She put up the hood of her coat. The observer noted the imprint of the man's hand on her wrist and saw that she was shaking. A cold breeze caused the microphone to sing and he adjusted the squelch button.

'You know I love you,' the man was saying. 'I'm just confused, but I'm dealing with this the best way I can. I avoid you because every time we do get together, you start a bloody fight, and I'm buggered if I'm going to give you an easy divorce under these circumstances. Think of my mother! She's sick, and another divorce will kill her. All I'm asking for is time.

'I knew when you wanted to meet me here today that you'd make a scene. I've felt it coming. You're in one of your moods - I know you too well. When you make up your mind to do something, there's not a hell of a lot I can do to stop you.' He rose and took a few steps away before turning back to her. 'Look, I have a proposal for you; let's give our marriage a full ten years. If this stuff isn't resolved in the next eighteen months, I'll give you a divorce. Hell, I'll sell Oakmead and give you half and you'll be set for life. But I'm not giving up - given time, I think we can still work things out. And I promise you that if we do you can have a baby - all the kids you want. You're not too old.'

She sighed. 'I'm sick of all of this muck, and here you go again dangling the prospect of children. Right, I'm not too old now, but God knows when the time will be perfect for you. It's no good. I want out now.'

He moved closer to her and raised his voice. 'Go ahead, have it your way. It'll take you a year to get your legal ducks in a row and

I'll fight you every bloody step. You'll ruin any chance I have of the top job by raking up what you call "muck". The press will jump on it. Are you prepared for that? Your legal fees will be a small fortune. And don't think I don't know what went on with you and the guy at work. I'll bring that up, too. Trust me - waiting another year and a few more months is a very reasonable suggestion.'

A silence followed. The woman stood facing him, arms akimbo and face flushed. The man took his gloves off, uncrossed the woman's arms and unbuttoned the duffle coat. He put his hands under the coat and drew her to him. His voice was soft and cajoling. The observer caught the words *place*, *honeymoon* and *bridge*. She immediately escaped this show of affection, rebuttoned her coat, and stood facing the river for a few seconds before turning to confront him again.

'I'm not going to be sucked in. What would I get this time? Pearls? I'd be stupid to promise to meet you back in Africa. You wouldn't show up anyway.' She turned away and spoke almost in a whisper. 'I'll agree to your ten years, but only to keep it out of court. What's eighteen months more anyway? I don't have anyone else now. I'm going away. I've got Mum's money and you can't control how I spend that. Go ahead with your plans; make up more stories about me not liking publicity, being immersed in work and all that rot. No one will miss me.' She turned to face him, her voice firm now. 'I don't want to see you again. You frighten me. I'm sick of you spying on me, I know you've had people watching me - don't deny it. If I find someone else in the meantime, it will be your own stupid fault.' Melodramatically she pulled off the wedding ring, was about to give it to him, thought better of it and dropped it into the pocket of her coat.

'Don't do anything stupid,' the man said.

'Believe me, I won't. See you in 2002 and we'll sort out the legal stuff. Good luck with the promotion. Enjoy the party. Don't even think of following me. If I want to see you, I'll let you know.' As an afterthought, she added, 'You won't be able to find me anyway.'

She turned on her heel and set off down the path.

The man stood watching her for a minute with his hands in his pockets, then muttered, 'I wouldn't count on that, darling.' Then, whistling softly to himself, he put his gloves back on and returned to his car. He made an aggressive U-turn and accelerated downhill in a swirl of dead leaves.

The observer turned off his machine and zipped up the gym bag. He poured himself coffee from a Thermos, lit a cigarette and made a call on his cell phone. A lone pigeon pecked near his feet.

'Thanks for the tip, Reg. Perfect shoot. Not quite what I expected; it was wife trouble again, but worth something.' Twenty minutes later he bought a ticket and merged with the crowd riding the Docklands railway back towards the Tower. *

* *Fred Bigglesworth is a mid-ranking member of the U.K. paparazzi whose work can be seen in English tabloids. It is not known how he celebrated the last night of the millennium.*

THIRD WATCHER

June 2000

Plymouth, England (departing south)

Smeeton's tower in Plymouth was the Eddystone lighthouse
between 1759 and 1877.

The astringent, low-slack smell of exposed mudflats hung over the estuary. Waiting vehicles simmered in the heat and creosote oozed from cracks in the pilings. The beefy driver of a juggernaut removed his shirt to display a distorted collage of tattoos. A Swiss couple quarrelled in a Saab convertible. Gulls pecked at a Popsicle dropped by a howling child.

Ginger enjoyed his summer job 'sorting' in the terminal area of the Brittany Ferry, where his duties were simple and repetitive. When a vessel docked he guided disembarking drivers, making sure they kept to the unfamiliar left. He watched for signs of hidden migrants and concealed pets. He rearranged traffic cones and directed departing vehicles across the ramps.

Between waves of activity, regulated by the coming and going of vessels, the job was undemanding. He sorted arriving vehicles into appropriate lanes and scrutinized them for the hazards of leaking petrol tanks and unsecured gas cylinders. Once the waiting area filled, he had little to do but saunter up and down the lanes answering the occasional question. During these slack periods, he liked to examine the more exotic cars and the four-wheel drives. He also looked at girls. There were always lots of girls, and on days like this some wore very skimpy clothes. Ginger was obsessed with girls. He had never succeeded in attracting one, and spent his nights composing increasingly exaggerated accounts of himself on Internet dating sites.

The girls were captive in the holding area until boarding time. He was overcoming his shyness and had spoken to a few. It was conceivable that one of these girls might find him personable and manly. Inevitably the departure of the subsequent ferry would terminate such an embryonic relationship. This was a bummer, but he had downloaded a gaudy business card and added his name and e-mail address. The printing was somewhat smudged, but he planned to present it under favourable circumstances.

A big Land Rover rumbled into the parking area, and Ginger waved it into the 'over-height' lane. It was an older vehicle with faded green paint, but it was clean and free of dents. It sat high on its springs and was shod with aggressive tyres. The galvanized rack on the roof was fitted with locked metal boxes. There was an impressive drum winch over the front bumper and steel lifting rings. A coil of rope was held in the bonnet-mounted spare wheel with military webbing. Ginger was impressed.

He held up his hand when the Land Rover was the prescribed foot from the vehicle ahead. The driver was a woman, not old, but beyond his target age group. She alighted and stretched and he saw she was dark and tall. The front seat passenger was a thickset young man with close-cropped hair wearing well-worn khaki clothes. It was the girl in the rear seat who got his attention. She was a stunner - round, bouncy and blonde - wearing a tank top and frayed denim shorts. She was not much older than he was.

He retreated and watched from a distance. The burly man lifted the bonnet and fiddled with the engine. The tall woman shouldered a small pack and strode off. Ginger decided to make his move. He squeezed between the back of a Grenada and the front of a Deux Chevaux and circled round amongst the trucks.

He met the tall dark woman, walking in the opposite direction, in the narrow canyon between a pantechnicon and a wine tanker. The passage was constricted, but brightly illuminated by sunlight reflected off the cylindrical body of the lorry. They each made the mistake of assuming the other would pass on the opposite hand, stepped sideways twice in unison, then stopped facing each other. She was a good foot taller than he was. She was dressed in light green and had tied the lower front of her shirt in a knot, exposing her midriff. He looked up and saw she was younger than he had first thought. 'Excuse me,' she said. 'Is the loo down this way?'

He nodded, tongue-tied, and flattened himself against the side of the lorry. The woman eased herself past, holding her arms penguin-fashion and facing his way. The top two buttons of her shirt were undone. At eye level, inches from his face, passed a wedge of blue brassiere and a freckled valley of brown skin that glistened with a sheen of perspiration. 'Thank you,' she said over her departing shoulder, leaving a trace of perfume in the oily air.

The blonde was leaning against the sunny side of the Land Rover with her legs apart and her face turned up towards the sun. She wore dangly earrings, and a silver pin pierced the rim of her navel. Ginger drew a deep breath.

'Going far?' he inquired, trying to keep his voice gruff. The outline of her breasts showed clearly under the thin cotton.

She opened her eyes and appraised his long neck, pimpled face and attempt at a moustache. His uniform was too big for him and the reflective vest was stained. He did not close his mouth completely and his front teeth were crooked.

'Fifteen minutes to sailing,' he said earnestly, conscious of time slipping away.

'Wow,' she said. 'We cut it pretty fine. This old thing's so slow I thought we were going to miss the boat for sure. You work here?'

'Yeah,' he replied. He wondered what to say next and fell back on his stock question. 'Going far?'

'Africa, actually,' she said. His heart sank - that would take months. 'I'm going to see the animals and stuff.'

'"The dark continent,"' he quoted. What did people say to keep conversation rolling? 'Hot, isn't it?' he ventured. The gulls circled above him, calling plaintively.

'I've got a stone in my shoe,' she said. He had noticed the yellow sandals. She bent down and poked her red-tipped finger between the straps. The breathtaking view down her shirt weakened his knees.

The man in khaki slammed down the bonnet and joined the girl. 'Hi,' he said, leaning against the door with his muscular arms folded.

'Hi,' said Ginger, and moved off. When he reached the ramp, he decided to go back. He had to have another look.

The tall woman had returned and they were grouped in front of the Land Rover, sharing a tube of Pringles. Ginger walked with his hands behind his back and nodded officially as he reached them. He was rewarded with a dazzling smile from the blonde girl. 'Would you take a picture of us?' she asked, producing a little camera. 'You push this button.'

He took the camera and backed up several paces. They stood by the vehicle in a posed group - the man in the centre with his tanned arms around the waists of the women. The blonde, he noticed sadly, snuggled. The tall woman did not smile. He pressed the shutter.

He heard the boarding announcement, handed back the camera and hurried to his station. The Land Rover growled up to him with the man driving and hesitated at the top of the ramp. The tall woman waved, and the younger one blew him a kiss. The brakes squealed on the descent into the belly of the ship.

He had forgotten to give her his card. He never saw them again.

Late that evening, he lay fantasizing on his bed while the computer cooled under the sloping roof. He did not hear the yobs yelling by the pub. He had replaced the muscular man and was somewhere in Africa. The Land Rover was parked outside the tent.

Surprisingly, it was not the blonde girl who had shown him the rings in her nipples who accompanied him as he paid his tribute to Onan that night. It was the tall, dark woman with the sexy perfume and a now unknotted shirt who lay in his arms as he drifted off to sleep. *

* *George 'Ginger' Collins now writes code for Amazon U.K.; he is married with two children.*

CHAPTER 1

"We want you to find an old Land Rover."

Lowly freelance motoring writers seldom get to meet senior executives in multinational car firms face to face. I was surprised when the message appeared in my e-mail. I recognised his name immediately. The Americans had purchased the Land Rover Company less than a year ago, and he was rumoured to be a very exacting and hands-on new Managing Director.

```
Your editor has been kind enough to give
me your e-mail address. I would like to
invite you to our London office for a
chat. Would Monday at 4 be convenient?

                          Melvin Noor
```

I took the train to Waterloo and the tube to Green Park. With fifteen minutes to spare before the appointment, I walked once around the square in the afternoon sun, admiring the immaculately maintained Georgian buildings. There was a discrete *FORD* logo on a brass plate near the door of number 51. A gaffer booked me in and guided me to the lift. On the second floor, a well-groomed woman greeted me. Five minutes later I was sitting on a leather couch, and Melvin P. Noor was offering me a coffee.

He was younger than I expected and, fair to say, my complete opposite. Trendy suit (mine was six years old), hair impeccably cut (my salt and pepper was unruly and needed a trim), shoes obviously Italian (my Prospectors were Canadian and ingrained with the dust of three continents). Manicured nails, pressed shirt, gold tie clip. The discrepancies extended to height but not weight - at six foot five I was a good eight inches taller than he, but within a kilogram I'd bet we weighed the same.

He made the coffee himself, using one of those mini espresso machines in an alcove off the office. I looked around this centre of power in the international automobile industry. The walls were covered with photographs of teams of men and cars. A recent picture showed him with Peter Marsh, the new minister of transport, opening the motor show. There was a wonderful shot of an XJ120 at Silverstone - I could not make out the signature in the corner. On a credenza behind the desk, amongst papers arranged in orderly stacks, I saw a copy of my book *Solihull Story* with yellow notes protruding from the pages.

He had a midwestern accent and a matching informality. 'I'm pleased you were able to come in today, Giles. My schedule has been pretty hectic lately. This is an exciting time. We're launching seven completely new models, and there is a raft of details to keep tied together. You must be pretty busy with your writing; I enjoy your regular column in *Land Rover Aficionado*. We were pleased with the positive story you wrote about the new Range Rover we're working on.'

'Thanks,' I said. 'It's an outstanding vehicle. I'm not too sold on the phoney vents in the fenders, but overall I like the styling. The ride and off-road capability are amazing.' I nodded in the direction of the credenza. 'I see you've got a copy of my book.'

He laughed. 'Indeed. In fact, that's been compulsory reading around here. I took twenty copies over to Detroit and handed them out at corporate before the takeover. It's a dandy history of the company and a good read. You seem to have made a career out of writing about Land Rovers. No matter who I asked, I was told you were the expert on the company.'

'There's more to me than that,' I protested. 'I write on other British makes and do quite a bit of travel stuff; mind you, there is sometimes a Rover angle in that, too. I'm glad you liked the book. It almost wrote itself. Fascinating story. That small group of men, with access to tons of aluminium left over from the war, conceived of this rugged little truck and built a product that's a household word around the world today.'

'I've heard about your travel stuff,' he said. 'The people up at special projects told me you had driven Land Rovers on every continent and were the person to invite on any expedition. Too bad we don't do much of that anymore.' He paused. 'I detect a bit of an accent - reading your stuff, I expected you would be from around here.'

'Most of my readers are British and I live in Hampshire now. The magazines on English cars are mostly published here. I've developed a less North American style. I call a car a car - not an "auto", and a Land Rover is a Land Rover - not a "truck" as it is in the States and Canada. I was born in what's now Zimbabwe, so I have a mixture of accents.'

'That gives us something in common,' he said. 'I've been back in Europe for seven years.' He proceeded to put me at ease by telling me about himself. His mother was English and he had attended

Shrewsbury school as a youth. The family moved to the United States when he was eighteen after his mother married an American. He went into the motor industry straight from MIT. Recently he had been involved with Jaguar, Aston Martin and Volvo.

Eventually he turned to business. 'I've asked you here today because I think you're just the man to take on a project for us. I'd like to hire you as a consultant on a special mission. Not sure how long this will take. Could be a couple of weeks or several months.' He now had my attention, as special projects usually paid well. 'I think you're uniquely qualified to get results. My colleagues were surprised when I suggested approaching you, but all agree you're the man for the job.

'The project does involve some writing, but that's not the primary objective. Before I discuss this with you, I must stress that it will require some discretion - we don't want our competitors to know what we're up to. Our legal people have prepared an agreement here; if you'll look it over, perhaps we could get started.' He handed me a single typewritten page and took his coffee over to the window.

The document was simple. It was made out in my name so they must have assumed I'd be willing. I, Giles Jackson, agreed to undertake certain work as a consultant to the company. The period of engagement was for a minimum of three months with extensions as mutually agreed. I bound myself not to unnecessarily disclose the nature of my services to outside parties. The remuneration was generous, and travel (business class, surprisingly) was included.

I was intrigued; in my experience, global car companies don't hire freelance journalists. I wondered how much they knew about me. They'd asked around. The editorial people at *LRA* must have given me a good reference. Giles Jackson. Born 1952 in Bulawayo, Southern Rhodesia. Canadian citizen. Divorced. Social drinker. Compulsive traveller. And not very well off.

'Looks okay to me,' I said. 'I'm flattered to be approached. I take it that what we are discussing is - how shall I put it - above board?'

'Absolutely.' He looked momentarily pained. 'You can start immediately?'

'Couple of minor things to clear up, but yes.' It was hard to hide a grin. Summer is a slow time for freelancers and beating the bushes recently had not produced much work.

'Sign it, then,' he ordered. 'Keep one copy for yourself.' I borrowed the Parker from the desk set and signed. He put his copy into a green folder.

He leaned back in the swivel chair and put his hands behind his head. He had a boyish grin. 'You're going to enjoy this,' he said.

'We want you to find an old Land Rover.'

CHAPTER 2

Mrs. Stevenson got a postcard from Cappadocia.

'You want me to find you an old Land Rover?' I asked, puzzled. 'That won't be difficult. Pick just about any barn in this country and you'll find an old Land Rover in it.'

'Not just any old Land Rover. This is a very specific old Land Rover. Here, look.' He rose from his desk and went over to a stack of charts on an easel. He sorted through them and found a series of artist's drawings. He moved one to the front. The picture showed a familiar beast - a Land Rover - in an African setting. Game grazed amongst acacia trees and Kilamanjaro brooded in the distance.

'You know our *Defender* model, Giles. The classic Land Rover. Direct descendant of the original. As seen in hundreds of safari movies. Used by police forces, armies, aid groups and adventurers. The quintessential Land Rover. No other vehicle we make is as well known or as well respected. And yet the *Defender* is a big problem for us. You know why? Because it's old-fashioned. It's heavy, inefficient and uncomfortable. It's virtually hand built, so costly to manufacture. With the end of the cold war, the army no longer needs many. We've stopped selling them in the States - they don't meet federal regulations. Sales are dropping all the time. Instead of keeping it simple, we've added electronics. Hardly anyone drives them across the Sahara any more.

'There is a faction in the company that wants to drop the *Defender* models altogether. In the days of unibody construction, they say, *Defender* is an anachronism. It drags down the profitability of our whole product line. Discontinue it and good riddance.

45

'Then there is an opposing faction that argues passionately that without *Defender* the company loses its soul. Without these boxy-looking trucks - grunting over the mountains and ploughing through the deserts - Land Rover becomes just another mass producer of look-alike, boring SUVs.

'Last month I made a decision. We had a product planning conference at Solihull. I told them I appreciated all the input. I reiterated the opinions of the dealers, summed up the conclusions of the accountants and flattered the engineers. I was sympathetic to the production people. Eventually I showed them this.'

He placed a second drawing over the first. The vehicle was recognizably a Land Rover, but the body shell had undergone a transformation. I was not sure I liked it. The location appeared to be in Utah or Arizona. A setting sun glowed on a mesa.

' "We are going to keep on making *Defenders*," I told them. "'Only these are going to be better *Defenders*. We need a tough-image truck with a lot of capacity. I want you to redesign the damn thing from the outside, keeping the basic shape. The retro look is in. Look what Volkswagen has done with the *Beetle* and Daimler Chrysler with that *PT Cruiser* thing. GM is killing us with the smaller *Hummer*.

' "Get the axles and transmissions from Detroit and put in a decent engine. Fix the niggles everyone complains about. Spend money on soundproofing. Go totally robotic on that darn frame and get it past the Feds. Simplify it so the poor jokers in Cameroon can keep it going, fix the goddamn leaks, push the fuel mileage up and get the seats to move back for a change. Extend the bloody windscreen so the average American doesn't have to consult his chiropractor after a day of trying to see the traffic lights change!

'"Furthermore,"' I said, '"if we can't make it profitably in England, we will make it in South Africa - or anywhere else where there's a division happy to take it on."'

'They were stunned. I think everybody thought it as good as dead. I told them I had a gut feel that we could make it a winner. I approved a big budget and gave them a retail target of thirty-five thousand dollars on the long-wheel-base model.'

He paused. 'Tell me, Giles, have I done the right thing?' He looked anxious, waiting for affirmation. I considered my reply carefully.

'Personally,' I said, 'I'm thrilled. I would hate to see it dropped. But I'm not sure if it can be pulled off. It's going to depend a lot on the marketing - American acceptance will be crucial. And you have some dire quality issues to address - electronics and body corrosion for starters - '

'You're right,' he agreed, interrupting me. 'After America, other markets are secondary. I was there last month and spent three days brainstorming with the publicity people. This is going to fly. We're launching it as a concept at the Detroit Auto Show and the emphasis is going to be on pedigree. Pedigree, first-class engineering at an affordable price.

'This is where you come in, Giles. We decided that, next January at the Detroit Show, we're going to have an old Land Rover on the display next to the new concept model to demonstrate just how well these things stand up. Not just any old Land Rover but an old Land Rover that is the direct ancestor of our new *Defender*.

'Some people claim this is the 1956 Series One 107 station

wagon. Let's face it - that was an ugly truck. No, to my mind, the true progenitor of our new *Defender* is the 1959 Series Two Long Station Wagon. It's the same size as the *Defender* and has the classic shape with the crease running along the window line.

'I called the curator at the British Motor Industry Heritage Centre - we subsidize them some. Told him I was looking for a 1959 model Long Station Wagon. Turns out they don't have one. Said it shouldn't be too difficult to find one as they are not all that rare.'

'He's right,' I agreed. 'Those early units were very well built, and the metal in the frames outstanding. They suffer far less from the corrosion that has claimed the sixties and seventies ones.'

'So I'm told. But the curator also told me something that really got me excited. He said that the very first Long Station Wagon ever built had come up for sale just last year in very good condition. Chassis number 161900001. Only two previous owners, and it still had the original plates. An academic in Oxford was selling it. The curator wanted it for his museum. Bit of a premium price, but he went to look at it and made a pretty handsome offer. The owner said he would think about it.

'When the curator called back two days later - to put on a bit of pressure - the owner said it was sold. A woman called Sarah Oakes from London had bought it! She'd written a cheque for half the amount and was to return the following week to pick it up after MOT testing. The museum guy got the telephone number of this woman from the owner and called her up, thinking that she would let him have it for a few hundred pounds more than she'd paid. She turned him down. Said she was going overseas in the vehicle and had no intention of selling it.

'Giles, that truck is a dream publicity machine. The very first *Defender* type vehicle ever made! Still going strong after forty-two years! We can feature it at Detroit and tour it round the U.S. dealers afterwards. If I weren't so busy and didn't have a young family, I'd be on the track of it myself. You married?'

I shook my head.

'I love publicity, and took a personal interest in this. The guy at the museum still had the telephone number of the fellow who sold it and the number of the woman who'd bought it - Sarah Oakes. I called the seller and got his wife on the phone. She was downright rude and would not help.

'Sarah Oakes's number had been disconnected, but I got her address from last year's directory. It's on the on the Isle of Dogs. A couple called Wilds rent the flat. He used to work with the owner. The building manager, Mrs. Stevenson, told me that Ms. Oakes had gone overseas for a year or more, had left last June, driving the Land Rover. Must have got as far as Turkey, because she sent a postcard. She had no idea where Oakes was, but gave me the telephone number of a Richardson whom she was to contact if there were any problems with the tenants.

'I called Richardson; he turned out to be a solicitor. Very proper. Told him exactly who I was and that we wanted to buy Sarah Oakes' Land Rover at a premium price - would he give me a number where I could call her? He basically told me to bugger off. "Ms. Oakes has given me instructions that under no circumstances am I to reveal her whereabouts to anyone. Good day."

'We have some pull at the RAC, so I got a copy of her carnet - the passport for the vehicle. Useless. She could have gone anywhere with it - although it does list three other drivers who could possibly be traced. Here's a copy, along with everything else I know.' He handed me a buff document envelope.

'This is your assignment, Giles. I want you to track down this woman and purchase that truck.'

'What makes you think I can find it?' I asked. 'The world is vast. It could be anywhere and you've got an owner who doesn't want to sell.'

'She'll sell,' he said. 'After driving one of those things a few thousand miles, she'll jump at the opportunity for a sweet price. What convinced me you were the guy for the job was the story you wrote last year in *Land Rover Aficionado* about how you found the remains of the old centre steer prototype out in Anglesey. That took persistence. You dig, you don't get put off and you are an accomplished world traveller.

'I'm a friend of Peter Marsh' - he gestured towards the picture - 'you interviewed him last month. He spoke very highly of you. We're both on the government's *Select Committee for Establishing Minimum Consumption Standards in Passenger Vehicles*. Peter said you ask tough questions and don't get sidetracked. And your editor entertained me for half an hour with your exploits - not all of them complimentary. My gut feel is that you can crack this particular nut and get us some great publicity as well.'

He looked at his watch. 'Got to go. Find this Land Rover and interview every person you can who had anything to do with that machine - publicity will love it. Buy it. Get it in a container and get it back here so we can tart it up and have it in Detroit by the end of the year. I'll be back in this office next Friday. Call and give me a status report. Keep in touch by e-mail when possible.' He handed me a card. 'Here's the address.'

I stood up. 'You're on. Print me up some corporate business cards. That will open doors. And give me a temporary e-mail address on your server.'

'No problem.' He pressed his intercom. 'Veronica, please organize Giles some business cards and a corporate e-mail address. Also arrange him an advance of five thousand pounds.'

He shook my hand and picked up the file. As I left the office, he said, 'I don't know if it helps, but somebody told me that truck has a moniker - it's called *Geraldine*...' *

---

* *At the time of this meeting, in an alley many thousands of miles from Berkeley Square, a man with no front teeth spotted a thick jute bag printed with the words Coffee de Costa Rica protruding from under the lid of an overstuffed dumpster behind a trendy waterfront bar. He retrieved this prize under the sympathetic eye of a security guard and examined it carefully before doubling it over his shoulders. He walked up a mile of twisted streets until he reached a deserted lane.*

With little fear of being observed in the evening drizzle, he shinnied expertly up a gatepost. He padded the vicious fringe of rusted razor wire with the coffee bag and dropped silently down into the weeds in the yard beyond.

He ignored the rusty Mercedes Benz, which he knew to be well picked over, and concentrated on the second vehicle, which, although older, had not yet suffered from his attentions. He examined the tyres, making a little cluck of exasperation when he observed the unusual size.

Frustrated in his attempts to open the doors or the engine compartment, he contented himself with using his knife to unscrew the headlamp assemblies from the front grille. He stuffed these parts down the front of his jacket and made an agile departure back over the fence.

CHAPTER 3

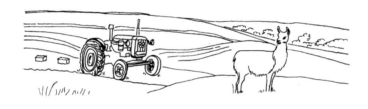

Ferguson tractor with admirer.

I live in a cottage on the edge of the New Forest. It used to be an apple-sorting shed and is on what remains of a large farm. The apple trees have gone at the behest of the bureaucrats in Brussels and most of the area is in hay. My landlords, Simon and Jean, are fanatical about hay and have won prizes at agricultural shows for the quality of this simple crop. Their reputation is such that some racehorse owners buy nowhere else.

The farm also supports a diverse and expanding number of animals, as Jean takes pity on any unwanted beasts and strays in the district. A recent acquisition is a male llama with a history of impotence. The llama acts as guardian to the herd of pygmy goats, and directs thinly veiled threats at me when I cross the paddock to reach my door.

I sometimes think Jean regards me as having the same problem as the llama. She makes attempts to mate me with stray females in the district.

The rent is cheap, as I did most of the conversion work on the cottage myself. Simon and Jean like to travel with their horses, and I become keeper of the other animals when they are away. It's an arrangement that works well for everyone.

The station bus dropped me at the end of the lane and I walked the half-mile home. It was warm enough to sling my coat over my shoulder. Simon was driving his old Ferguson tractor into the barnyard as I arrived at the gate. He loves to talk. He leaned down, shut off the engine and commented. 'Been to a funeral?'

'No. Got a job, minimum three months, good money.'

'Maybe you should buy a new suit.'

'It's not that sort of job,' I said. 'I think I'm going travelling.'

He invited me in for tea. Jean buttered scones and I gave them the gist of the assignment. They were intrigued.

'If your Melvin is a friend of our honourable minister of transportation, he's probably gay,' Jean said. 'If you were to believe a tabloid headline I saw in Tesco.'

'I don't think so. He mentioned his wife and kids. And I certainly didn't get the feeling Peter Marsh was gay when I interviewed him last month. He's just a regular guy. We spent half an hour talking about old Land Rovers.'

'Giles, you've been in the bush too long.'

Simon was not the least bit interested in the sexual preferences of business executives or cabinet ministers. 'I'm pleased they are going to keep on making the old bugger,' he said. 'Wouldn't seem right to stop after fifty years.'

Jean said, 'Unusual for a woman to buy an old Land Rover - she probably bought it for a man.'

'Where are you going to start?' Simon asked.

'I'm going to have to find someone here who knows her. She must have friends and relatives in England. And she had three other drivers listed on her carnet application - they may be traceable. There's probably an e-mail address somewhere. Chances are someone did expedition preparation work for her. I don't think finding her will be that difficult, and hopefully the Rover hasn't come to grief.'

I started work that evening by calling directory information. There was no listing for the Wilds, who were renting the apartment. I wasn't surprised, as many young people have cell phones and don't bother with a landline - especially if they are at a temporary address. Mrs. Stevenson, the superintendent, had a listing, but there was no reply when I called. It would be useful to talk to Wilds himself, as he had worked at the same place as Sarah Oakes. I decided to make another trip to London, but I had other avenues to explore as well.

Preparing for an overland expedition is not a simple process. Besides the paperwork involved, the vehicle must be sound and well prepared. Serious people get professional advice and have their vehicles prepared by experts. A number of firms in England specialize in this work, and it would be simple to call around and find if any of them had equipped a Series Two Land Rover for a Sarah Oakes.

The book *Overland Expedition Planning Guide*, written some years ago by my old friend Mark Franklin, is the long-distance driver's *vade mecum*. Mark is in his seventies now; he has explored the Sahara, crossed the Congo and was the first to drive a Land Rover into Kathmandu. Highly regarded, he's the logical person to call when looking for advice. I telephoned him at home in York. It was a lucky opening shot.

'I'm looking for a party that left England in a Series Two Land Rover last summer,' I explained. 'The owner is a woman called Sarah Oakes. I was wondering if you've heard of her?'

'Your lucky day,' he said. 'A woman called Sarah did call me up about a year ago talking about a Series Two. We had quite a long chat.

'She called late one evening, well-spoken gal, no-nonsense get-to-the-point type, bought a copy of my book and said that she had found it helpful. She was calling for advice. I get lots of calls like this and get a bit short with wankers. She took me by surprise by offering to pay me for my time. I told her I had dispensed so much free advice over the years that I could hardly start by charging her, but I appreciated the offer. And I thanked her for buying my book. Most people seem to borrow them from libraries.

'She said she was planning a trip down to Africa with three other people and had the opportunity to buy a 1958 Land Rover in top nick. She asked if this would be a suitable vehicle, and could I suggest anyone who would equip it for her as I described in the book.'

'So she was going to Africa?' I mused aloud.

'Yes, Africa,' he said. 'I liked the sound of her, so I was pretty liberal with advice. I remember she asked me to talk more slowly; she was making notes.

'Obviously I concurred that a good Series Two was suitable, but warned her to check it was a runner; the only way to be sure she was not being taken to the cleaners was to have an expert inspect it. She said she was buying it privately and that she trusted the man selling it - an older chap who could afford to maintain it.

'I asked how much she was paying; it was a bit much for a forty-year-old motor. I stressed that it was uncomfortable to travel in: slow, hard riding and bloody hot. I suggested she take it to be fitted out by Overlando Ltd. outside Colchester. I told her how to get a carnet from the RAC and gave her a contact there.

'I warned that the whole exercise would cost more than she probably thought, and that she should be choosy about her travelling companions - the farther you drive, the more obnoxious people become. I did not gloss over the risks, there are some rough characters out there, and things have changed a lot since I first started.'

'Did she say why she wanted to go? It seems something unusual for a woman to organize.'

'Very unusual. But she sounded confident on the phone. Didn't seem reckless or stupid. She accepted the risks and said she felt capable of handling the situations that might arise. By the time we finished the conversation, she had me convinced she could do it, and I didn't try to dissuade her. I was tempted to sign on myself.'

'I urged her to take the Nile route. Stay out of the Congo - too risky.'

He gave her health advice too, emphasizing the dangers of yellow fever, bilharzia and malaria. He told her to take lots of women's stuff, as it is impossible to find in many places.

He had not spoken to her again, although Sam Loos from Overlando had called him and thanked him for sending a new customer. Sam had said the Series Two was a good truck and she was spending a fair amount on it.

'A few weeks later she sent me a gift, a Peter Mathiesen book. It was damn nice of her - I'd never even met her. It came in a TNT parcel from a company called Electroport. Told the driver I hadn't ordered anything, but he made me sign for it. She wrote in the flyleaf, "Thanks from Sarah and *Geraldine*."*

After Mark hung up, I turned on my computer and logged onto the Internet. I tried *www.electroport.com* and found a company in California that made plugs and cables for computers. I tried *www. electroport.co.uk* and was told the page was not available. I pulled out my London directory again and found *Electroport Ltd.* with an address in Beckton.

The road atlas showed Beckton to be five miles from the Isle of Dogs. I was on track.

* *Writer and raconteur Mark Franklin published his autobiography* Beyond the Blacktop *in 2003. He shares his cottage near York with his wife, broadcaster Pamela Rogers. He remains as irascible as ever.*

CHAPTER 4

1960s Bedford Military Lorry converted to expedition use.

Noor was correct - tracking down *Geraldine* was akin to getting the facts lined up for a story. I needed to cast my net as widely as possible and talk to anyone who had known Sarah Oakes before she left. This included people with whom she had previously worked, including her tenant Wilds, who had no listed telephone number. Another trip to London was indicated, this time by car.

On Wednesday morning I took the telephone out onto the patio and sat under the honeysuckle making a series of telephone calls. I first tried Tony Morganter, thinking that Sarah might have told him her plans when she purchased the vehicle from him.

A woman answered the telephone. I gave her my name and asked if I could speak to Mr. Morganter.

'May I ask what this is about?'

'I'm trying to track down the old Land Rover he sold last year.'

'I'm confident he would not wish to talk to you about that,' she said. The line went dead. I called the number again. There was no answer. I reminded myself that not all people were forthcoming when approached by a total stranger.

Morganter is not a common name. On the Internet, I found an Oxford University faculty list that included an archaeologist Anthony J. Morganter. His college gave me a telephone number that connected me to an answering machine. His voice was measured and precise. I left a short message saying I had an interest in Land Rovers in general and his old one in particular, and asked him to call me back on my cell phone.

The solicitor, Richardson, was short with me and interrupted my introduction. 'I have no interest in who you are or what you want. I've told you people this before. The instructions from my client are very clear. Under no circumstances am I to give any person her address and I am not to forward any unsolicited correspondence. Good day.'

Sam Loos at Overlando Ltd. was more helpful. He knew of me from my articles in *Land Rover Aficionado*. I told him of my conversation with Mark and my interest in Sarah Oakes and her Land Rover. 'I think there's a story here,' I said. 'I'm interested in doing something on the expedition preparation industry for the magazine. Could you spare me an hour or so if I came up on Friday?' He agreed to that and I said I would be there by ten.

From what Mark had said, I knew Sarah Oakes had not set off on her travels with a group of old friends. She had sought out strangers who had the time, means and the interest to join her. I speculated on how she might have advertised what she was planning, but was devoid of ideas. The logical thing seemed to be to advertise on the Internet. An exploration of the possibilities proved daunting. There are hundreds of interest groups on websites devoted to adventure travel. Thousands of individuals are attempting to link up with others for a wide variety of foreign adventures. The destinations are frequently exotic, and the chances of anything ever really happening seem remote. To complicate the process, there are thousands of points where these sorties are organized and there are very specific age, gender and sexual preferences amongst the advertisers. Word searches using *Land Rover* and *Africa* in various combinations uncovered scores of possible connections, none of which led anywhere. If Sarah had found travelling companions on the Internet, her advertisements and the subsequent correspondence were deep in the memory of an unknown server and beyond my reach.

I opened one of those people-search programs and entered the names of the additional drivers listed on the RAC carnet that Melvin Noor had given me. The only Angela Barnes was sixty-eight and living in Malvern. There was no Gerhard du Plessis shown in the United Kingdom. There was an Adam Williamson listed in London with a U.K. e-mail address. I e-mailed him asking him if he would please contact me if he knew someone called Sarah Oakes.

Du Plessis is a South African name. There were seven G. du Plessis listed in South Africa. I ran a general search in Google, and something interesting turned up. A year previously, a Gerhard du Plessis had written a paper entitled *Field Identification of Rhodium in Gold-Bearing Ores* in the Journal of the Royal Geological Society. The Internet reference was from a discussion group, and the paper had provoked a debate amongst its contributors - all of it completely above my head. The author had not joined the discussion, perhaps indicating he was not connected to the Internet at that time.

I made a call to the offices of the Royal Society and asked if I could get a photocopy of the paper and the present address of the author. A Susan Minter told me she would 'see what she could do' and asked me to call back later in the week.

Bill Saunderson, a former employer of mine, owns a small fleet of ex-military Bedford trucks. He started his business, *'International Adventure Tours',* in the early 1980s, taking groups of young people on overland trips in the back of the Bedfords. He once hired me as a driver and guide, and I saw quite a bit of the world driving for him. One of his most popular itineraries is a twelve-week *Trans African Safari*. I conducted many of these expeditions. The routes taken down Africa change frequently depending on the time of year and political considerations.

He was pleased to hear from me. 'Want a job?' he asked.

'I'm getting too old for that,' I said, 'and besides, I'm employed.' Bill's constant challenge is finding suitable staff. It takes resourceful people to lead his expeditions. A good guide becomes mechanic, doctor, diplomat and psychologist. There is no time off for months at a stretch.

'How're the Bedfords holding up?' I asked.

'Can't kill 'em,' he said.

'I was wondering if any of your guys on the Africa run had bumped into a party heading south last summer,' I said. 'Four people in an old Land Rover station wagon. Probably went up the Nile, across Lake Nasser and down through Ethiopia. Heading for South Africa, I think. One of them is called Sarah Oakes. I'm trying to track her down. Bronze green truck. Nothing fancy but well kitted out.'

'I doubt they crossed Lake Nasser,' he said. 'The Egyptians and the Sudanese weren't getting along last year and the ferry wasn't running. One of my chaps might have seen them. You know what it's like. You meet so many parties. Half of them haven't a clue what they're doing. Nobody said anything to me about a group like that, but then it's nothing very unusual.'

'Oh well,' I said. 'I didn't think you would have heard anything unless there was some sort of disaster.'

'I'll do something for you,' he offered. 'We've got a training session next week for some new lads, and all the old hands are in town for that. Some of them did Africa last year. I'll ask them when we get together. I'll call you back if anyone knows anything.'

At nine in the evening I checked my e-mail and found a message from Adam Williamson.

```
I do know of a Sarah Oakes and may be able
to help you. Call me at 6574-764-7658.
```

CHAPTER 5

"We spent two days on Skye and hiked into Camasunary."

I called the number. He answered immediately. 'Adam Williamson - can I help you?' Plummy English; friendly but guarded.

'Thanks so much for getting back to me,' I said. 'I'm trying to track down Sarah. I knew you were on a trip to Africa with her last year. I did an e-mail search and found your name. There's no privacy anymore, is there?'

'I'm amazed,' he said. 'I wonder if there's any way you can take your name off those lists? But you're mistaken. I planned to go on that trip and was quite involved in the preparations. But at the last minute I had to pull out. How do you know Sarah?'

'I've never met her.' I said. 'I was talking to an old friend of mine who is an expert on wilderness expeditions and he told me about her. I write travel stories for a magazine for Land Rover owners and would like to interview her about her experiences. Sorry for assuming you had travelled with her.'

'How did you know I even planned to go?' He asked, puzzled.

'You showed up as an alternative driver on her carnet. Why did you pull out?'

'Quite a long story,' he said. 'At the time I agreed to go, I had just separated from my companion. We had been together two years. I was pretty cut up about it and depressed, and I felt I needed to get away. A friend saw an advertisement about someone who was planning a trip to Africa in a Land Rover and suggested this might be just the thing to get me away from the situation. I rather liked the idea of a trip down Africa in a Land Rover and I thought there would be opportunities to meet local artists and buy work.'

'You collect art then?'

'I own *Zimbabwa* gallery in Chelsea. African ethnic is really in. I represent several outstanding people in West Africa and Zimbabwe. I fly out there frequently and have a good manager who looks after things when I'm away. Excuse me a minute -' There was a muffled conversation in the background before he returned.

'You still there? I called the number I'd been given and Sarah Oakes answered. We had a long conversation and she sounded competent. She told me about her plans. I explained why I wanted to go and told her about my situation. Coincidence - she told me she'd just come to the end of a relationship, too. She mentioned how much the trip would cost - it seemed quite reasonable - less than I expected actually. We agreed to meet at her flat one evening.

'I went out there on the Docklands railway. Nice - in a great location overlooking the river. We sat on her balcony and talked. She has good taste - well-made Victorian cottage furniture, Denby china, and some stunning rugs that her family has owned for ages. Very tall for a woman. I really couldn't place her background - looks a bit oriental. Well-spoken, though. She has a degree in something technical from Bristol. We got on well. She had a nice cat, which jumped on my lap. We had some tapas for dinner at a place nearby and then a couple of drinks in a pub near her flat. At the end of the evening she told me I was welcome to join in.'

'Why was she going? Seems a funny thing for a woman to be organizing.'

'She didn't say. She planned to stay on in Africa for a while after the trip. She made it clear I would have to find my own way home. And perhaps it's not as unusual as you think. I know two woman who hitched through South America together.'

'My editor's particularly interested in that angle - there is some history of intrepid women heading off into the blue with Land Rovers. You must have been impressed with her. Was it clear she was leading the trip, or was it to be a democratic enterprise?'

'I didn't ask that, Giles. I think it was pretty clear that she was going to be the boss. I was pleased she was happy to have me along, I'm not exactly Richard Hannay.' Somebody laughed in the background at his end.

'Did you like her?'

'She's a very nice woman,' he said, 'but with a real temper.

'She'd already selected the other two people going with her and we met one evening in the back of a garage in Beckton where she was storing the Land Rover. There was a South African guy called Gert who didn't say much, and a girl called Angela who talked a lot. I loved the Land Rover. We checked over the equipment and rolled out a sun awning thing. There was a ladder you could use to climb on the roof. Gert started the engine. We all sat inside looking through the dusty windows at the junk piled in the garage and imagined what it would be like in the wilds of Africa. Then we walked a few blocks to a Punjabi restaurant to have dinner while we planned. By the end of it - disparate group though we were - I felt we made a good team.'

He went on to explain that they had decided to leave England in June the previous year. They agreed to a one-week excursion to Scotland together in May to make sure the Rover ran well and to test their equipment.

'Tasks that needed doing before leaving were divided amongst us. I was to plan what food to take and get a medical kit put together. I also volunteered to get a compact disc player; there was not even a radio in the Land Rover. I have a friend in the stereo business that helped install the player. There's no way I could have done it myself - we had to take the whole dashboard apart. He is very handy with tools and knew about electricity. Positive earth and stuff.

'The trial trip to Scotland went very well. We shared the driving, which I found a bit tiring, heavy on the arms. Angela was hopeless, but Sarah and Gert seemed to be able to go all day. We spent two days on Skye and hiked into Camasunary. We all got on and there were no problems. The stereo worked well - I took a lot of good music. We stopped on the way home in Colchester to have the Rover checked.'

'Sounds like fun. When did you discover she had a temper?'

'This won't make me sound good, but two weeks before we were to leave I bumped into my ex at a club in Notting Hill. I pulled out of the trip. What can I say?

'I called Sarah and told her about my reconciliation and the change in my situation. She just went ballistic. It was impossible to mollify her or defend myself. She called me a prick and a few other choice names. Really ranted on at me. Eventually when she paused, I managed to say, "Look, there's nothing I can do. You can have the CD player and the medical kit, okay?" My partner was listening in on all this and told me I was well off out of that situation. She came across on the phone as a really awful woman*.

That doesn't excuse what I did - it did leave her a bit in the lurch - but if she had been like that on the road it would have been pretty unpleasant. Sorry, excuse me again - '

Another muttered conversation in the background and a second laugh.

'Sorry, but I have a customer here. Look, if you catch up with her could you let me have her address? I'm generally a forthright sort and it has always bothered me how things turned out. I'd like to contact her and make amends.'

'I'll e-mail you if I find her. You never heard from her again?'

'Not from Sarah,' he said, 'but I do know they got as far as Africa. In December I bumped into Angela - she got as far as Egypt before getting sick and flying home. I was Christmas shopping in Knightsbridge. She works in that Scotch place near Harrods, where they flog kilts and shortbread.'

'Adam, you've been incredibly helpful,' I said. 'Not everyone is as forthcoming to a total stranger. One last thing. Is Oakes her married name?'

'No. Er...no, buggered if I know, really. Drop in and meet me in the gallery some time.'

* In another time zone with a different season, this awful woman saved her work and switched off the laptop. She usually stopped before midnight and turned on the water that took a long time to fill the stained bath. As the tub filled, she made herself tea and sat in front of the barred window looking down on the darkened city.

She never needed an alarm clock. She rose as the thin call of the muezzin summoned the faithful to the mosque. She had no compunction about an early run of two miles up and down the steep streets. On weekdays, she dressed well from a limited wardrobe and applied a small amount of makeup in front of the cracked mirror. She had recently started parking the rusty Mazda facing downhill as it needed a new battery and would not always start on colder mornings.

CHAPTER 6

Horatio was obviously a regular.

I made an early start on Wednesday and drove to London in the old Discovery, taking the M25 round to Waltham Abbey and cutting down to Ilford on the M11. I was in Beckton by ten and went down towards the river looking for Electroport Ltd.

There was a gate chained with a new brass padlock protecting a paved yard with rows of weeds growing in cracks between concrete slabs. A perimeter fence enclosed several brick buildings with curved metal roofs of the type that was popular in the thirties. No lights were on, and I could see the door to the main office was off its hinges under an old sign that read *Electroport Limited. Excellent Electrical Engineers*. Broken glass glinted in the sun.

I walked along the fence. At one point the wire had been pulled up, making it easy to duck underneath. Surrounding the front door were heaps of sodden office files. A skip was filled with broken desks and other junk.

Peering into the second building, I could see it had been a machine shop. Threaded bolts protruded from the floor and flexible cables dangled from the roof. The machinery was gone. An old gantry crane sat high on tracks with a chain hanging from the traversing mechanism.

At a third building, signs were posted reading 'Test Area. Authorized Staff Only' and 'Wear Hearing Protection.' It, too, was empty and vandalized. Nesting pigeons cooed in the rafters. A pink card lying amongst the droppings on the floor read 'Lot 439'. There had been an auction here.

Beyond the factory was the river. The tide was ebbing and ducks paddled amongst broken bricks in the mud. A tourist boat was moving slowly upstream. The Millennium Dome and the buildings of the Greenwich Observatory could be seen diagonally on the opposite bank.

I made my way back to the car. There was nothing to learn here.

As I reached the Discovery, an elderly man approached on a bicycle with a fishing rod tied to the crossbar. I waved him to a stop. 'When did this place close down?' I asked.

'Must be 'bout a year now,' he said. 'Closed down sudden like. They had this auction last summer. You could 'ave bought a computer for twenty quid if you knew wot to do wif it. One bloke got a big Record vice for a fiver. I still kick myself, as I should 'ave bid on it.'

A Fokker turboprop flew overhead, low on its approach to the city airport, I waited for the noise to subside.

Then I asked, 'What did they make?'

'Generators,' he said. 'They were 'ere when I was a lad and they made generators then, too. My dad worked 'ere. Fitter, 'e was.'

'It's looking a bit derelict now,' I ventured.

'Don' make no difference,' he said. 'It'll be coming down. Fancy flats here like they got up the river. See ya, mate.' He swung his leg over the saddle and rode on.

I made my way to the Isle of Dogs and parked in the visitors' parking spot at Mariners Walk. The flats were arranged in a semicircle with green space in the centre. Every unit differed from its neighbour, and the rooflines were staggered with balconies arranged to give a maximum of privacy. The paths were paved with red brick and the stairways curved. Nowhere were there more than three floors. There were no overhead wires or visible television satellite dishes. On the balconies I could see barbecue units, plants and mountain bikes. Off to one side was a pub called *The Reach*, which obviously predated the flats. It looked out over a backwater, which in years past must have had some industrial purpose. It would be a pleasant place for a pint, and was certain to be busy in the evenings.

Number fifteen had a green door and a fine view of the river. The place was untidy. The plants around the door still had last year's leaves in the tubs, and there were cigarette ends scattered about. A cardboard box labelled 'Child's stroller - made in China' had been fashioned into a small kennel. Someone had printed 'Horatio' over the door opening.

I knocked, and was immediately joined by a large tabby cat that waited expectantly with me. There was no response from inside the apartment, but the cat looked up at me and meowed.

An older woman appeared with a laundry basket. 'She goes to the market on Fridays,' she advised. 'You might find Gareth in the pub.' I wondered if this was Mrs. Stevenson.

'Thank you,' I said. 'In case I don't find him, you wouldn't have their phone number, would you? It's not in the book.'

'Well, I do,' she said. 'Who are you? We get all sorts here.'

I wondered what sort I was. 'I've just come from Electroport,' I improvised, 'where Gareth used to work.'

'Well, I suppose that's okay, then,' she said. 'Come along and I'll get it for you.'

We went to number thirty-eight, and she wrote down the telephone number. I declined tea. As I left, she said, 'If you're from where he worked, you'd know Sarah Oakes. Do you know when she'll be back? A man who claimed to be her husband was here looking for her a few months ago.'

'I'm afraid I don't,' I said. 'I think she's still overseas. Actually, I would like to contact her, too. Can you think of anyone else who would know where she is? What was the name of the husband?'

Wouldn't tell me, would he? She had another bloke - used to park a green Daimler in the visitors' parking lot - all night sometimes. She never introduced us.'

There were few people in the pub. I ordered a steak pie and a Green King. As the barmaid pumped the beer, I asked if she knew Gareth Wilds.

'Course I do. That's 'im over there playing darts.' She shouted, 'Gareth!'

Wilds was a tubby man of about thirty. He waved at me and held up five fingers. I sat down at the open door and waited for him. My lunch arrived. The tabby from across the way sauntered into the bar, arched its back against my leg in greeting, and accepted a scrap of steak from me and an ashtray of beer from the barmaid. Horatio was obviously a regular.

Wilds sat down opposite me. I extended my hand. 'Giles Jackson. I was just looking for you at number fifteen.'

'Oh, were you?' he said warily. 'What about?'

'Nothing too important - I just wanted to talk about Electroport. You worked there with Sarah Oakes? I'm trying to track her down.'

He relaxed. 'You're not the first one.'

I thought to appeal to him in a way he obviously enjoyed. 'Would you like some lunch? On me, of course. Pad the expense account.'

'Well, thanks,' he said. 'The cauliflower cheese.' I went to place the order and came back with another two beers.

'They tell me Sarah's overseas,' I said after we raised our glasses.

'Not due back until Christmas at the earliest,' he said. 'And don't ask me where she is. I don't know. And I don't think anybody from Electroport knows except maybe the Chief. What gives? You're the second bloke recently - that fat guy - is he a friend of yours?' He shouted at the barmaid. 'Don't forget the HP, Susan.'

I decided to be vague. 'Sarah's a friend of a friend, and I don't know the fat guy. What did you do at Electroport?'

'Got myself certified in CAD drawings at the polytech and was taken on as junior draughtsman, putting old drawings onto *Solidworks* in the computer.' His meal arrived and he drained his mug, indicating he might like another. I returned from the bar and he was still musing on my question. 'Rough going at first. Some of the older blokes really resisted. Sarah was brilliant. She was behind it, of course.'

'Sarah Oakes is an engineer?' I asked, wondering why I was surprised.

'B.Sc., AMIEE,' he said. 'Good pie, eh? I reckoned early on that she was a real go-getter - never missed a thing or put anything off. If a job needed doing, she just went out and did it. If I stalled anything or was working slow, she let me know straight off. She always wanted more views. She hated anything sloppy - said the machinists cocked up if you gave them half a chance.

'She was always flying off somewhere, sales, marketing, Q.C., patents, wasn't much she didn't have her hand in. The Chief really relied on her. Pretty smart cookie.'

'What is she like?' I asked. 'I've never met her. I'm trying to track her down because I want to buy her old Land Rover.'

'Well,' he said, grinning, 'the first thing you notice about her is that there is a lot of her - she's over six feet tall. Imagine a normal woman drawn to a scale of about 1.25 to 1. Boobs and hips in perfect proportion and quite slim waisted. And she always looks tanned. Right know-it-all, too. Bossy. She was not very popular - a moody type, you could say. Never told me her age but I guess a bit older'n me. She'd been married before, had a wedding ring when I first started, but she stopped wearing it after a while.' He laughed. 'I fancied my chances with her at one time myself and made a move at the Christmas party. Boy, that was a mistake. Not nasty, mind you, but I was not her fighting weight. You might have more luck.'

'What was the Chief like? How old is he?'

'Sir Harold Matthews? About fifty-five, I'd say. He got a gong - OBE - saw it in the paper. "Long service to the electrical manufacturing industry." Brilliant, but a slave driver. He expected us all to work as hard as he did. He often went all night, drawing and calculating in his office and messing around in the tool room. I think he sometimes slept in the chair in his office.

'Knew all of us by name and really took an interest in us. When he found out my girlfriend was expecting, he encouraged me to marry her and gave us a couple of hundred quid, although he didn't make it to the wedding.' He polished off his toffee pudding.

'Was he married?' I asked.

'Yeah. Two grown-up kids. Nothing to do with the company though. Scuttlebutt was that the son's useless. Daughter's married and lives in the States. The Chief lived in a stately home near Tunbridge Wells. Never seen it, of course.'

'Was it a successful business?'

'Well, I'm not an accountant, but I think it was. We had work from all over the world. We were known for the high efficiency of the alternators we made. They operated completely unattended for months at a time, you know.

'The business finished 'cos he had a stroke. Right out of the blue at work one morning. Ellie, taking the tea round, found him on the floor of his office. He didn't die, but he was never right again. Sarah carried on for a while but got into one of her moods and had a big blowout with McKay, the new manager. She resigned or maybe got fired. I saw her crying and clearing out her desk and after that she never came back. Soon after that they announced that the factory would be closing and we were all laid off.

'That's amazing,' I said. 'It just folded up?'

'The brand was sold to the Germans and the land to property developers.' He looked downcast. 'I'm having trouble finding work at the same level. London Transport will give me a job, but their wages suck.'

'How did you come to be renting Sarah's apartment?'

'She called me and offered it. She was going overseas. We jumped at the opportunity of getting a bigger place, and this is a very nice area. We promised not to smoke inside and to look after her cat. Horatio's a nice cat but he gives our baby sneezes. We've been trying to find someone else to look after him.'

'I know someone who would,' I said, thinking of Jean. 'But you might want to get his mother's - Sarah's - permission - and you've no idea where she went or why?'

'I haven't a clue,' he said. 'You think she'd at least call up to find how things are going. The Chief would know, I think. We used to get the feeling they were pretty chummy.' He tapped the table and winked. 'You get my drift...'

Before I could explore this relationship, a flushed young woman appeared at the doorway with an infant in a loaded pram. 'There you are, Gareth,' she said, ignoring me completely. 'Did you do the wash?' He downed his glass, thanked me for the meal and was led off.

I was collecting my thoughts when a squeal of brakes and a sickening crash outside emptied the pub. A leather-clad courier sat on the cobbles cursing, his machine on its side twenty feet away. A furry body lay on the pavement next to the outdoor tables.

We helped the rider to his feet. He was shaken but unhurt. The cat lay crumpled with a little blood around its mouth. 'Is 'e dead?' asked the barmaid.

A cardboard box was found behind the bar and I gently slid the furry body into it. There was no sign of life. 'I'll take him to a vet.'

I said. 'Tell Gareth about it.'

By the time I located a veterinarian, pitiful meows showed that Horatio was still alive. I jumped a queue of concerned pet owners and met Dr. Blake. Placing the cat gently on his examination table, he probed for injuries before listening with a stethoscope and examining the mouth. 'I see this all the time,' he said discouragingly. 'There could be massive internal injuries. As far as I can tell, the spine is not broken and the lungs are functioning. The best I can do is give him a painkiller and a sedative. Take him home like that and see what he's like when he comes round.' He administered the injections and the yowling gradually subsided. He checked something by lifting one eyelid with his thumb. 'About fifty-fifty, I would say.' I paid his receptionist and headed home with the cat wrapped in a towel provided by a sympathiser.

It was a long drive home and the M25 was slow and crowded. Dusk came near Basingstoke. Horatio lay warm but immobile under my hand. It was hard not to wonder about his mysterious owner. Tall, smart, divorced and thirty-something, she had interrupted her career, left her flat and her tabby cat and headed off to Africa in an elderly Land Rover. What was her motivation? There was something impetuous and romantic about this, and it was difficult to get her out of my mind.

I pulled into the farm well after dark. I took my patient in to Jean, who fussed around the inert body. She found a place for the box in her kitchen after banishing some indignant and curious residents to the yard.

'He's a beautiful cat. Where did you find him?' *

'He belongs to the woman who has the Land Rover. He was injured on his way home from the pub.'

She gave me a funny look. 'What's his name?'

'Horatio.'

'Hello, Horatio,' she said, stroking the cat. She passed me a beer. 'I bumped into Anna at the Ringwood pool today and she said you hadn't called her or answered her e-mails. I've invited her for dinner a week Saturday. Are you free?'

'I may be in Africa,' I said.

---

* *The owner of this unfortunate animal spent her day visiting a manufacturing plant situated miles from anywhere significant. She watched a team of hard-hatted men working in a cavernous shed, where furnaces glowed and a massive hydraulic press forged camshafts for diesel engines from bars of red-hot steel. She then attended a meeting in a Spartan boardroom, where a man with a thick accent discussed statistical process control. She learned that the quality of the forged camshafts exceeded the rigorous standards set by a group of engineers in Stuttgart, and that these same camshafts could be found in the heart of the engines of one of the world's most prestigious cars.*

After this meeting, she dismissed concerns for her safety and drove the coast road home as the red ball of the sun plunged into the dark Atlantic.

CHAPTER 7

"She got herself stuck in the duck pond."

Competitors envy Sam Loos. His business occupies a grain barn on a farm run by an educational trust. The trust charges him a minimal rent, and in return he maintains the early agricultural machinery displayed and used on the property. The farm extends over a large area near Colchester, and I found it without difficulty. Mechanics were working amongst Land Rovers undergoing reconstruction on the shop floor, and Sam oversaw the proceedings from his untidy office in a loft. Gears of assorted sizes acted as paperweights, and photographs of customers and their Land Rovers adorned the walls. Loos was a cheerful, nondescript, middle-aged man with dirty fingernails and a South African accent. We were drinking instant coffee. He was excited to hear I was writing an article and gave me a tour of his workshop so I could take some pictures. He liked to talk.

'I piss off easy with city people who drive off-road vehicles to look macho,' he was saying. 'I work on four by fours that get used where they're needed. Only about thirty percent of what we do is expedition preparation - most of it is foreign aid or charity stuff. That long wheelbase 130 there we are converting into a mobile eye surgery for Mali, and the one behind it is going to Madagascar for an Oxfam group. And I only convert older models. If it has any electronic circuits, I don't let it in the door. Too unreliable.'

This was dangerous ground. To keep circulation going at the magazine, we give extensive coverage to glossy new models, and write complicated articles on how to keep automotive electronics functioning.

'That's interesting,' I said. 'I'm surprised you can support a business working only on older models. That's an excellent point, though, and I'll bring it up in the article. I'm especially interested in the expedition preparation side. I'm amazed how much people will spend to get an older Land Rover fitted out to drive long distances. That 110 there, for example, with the special roof rack and tent - you say that will set someone back thirty thousand quid?'

'Easy,' he said, 'maybe more. 2.8 diesel, long-range tanks, differential lockers, expedition rack, roof tent, side awning, stove, shower, stowage, security, overdrive and air conditioning - it all adds up. That guy can afford it. He's a retired banker.'

'What about people who don't have that kind of money? Can you do anything for them?'

'Of course. Look at that woman you asked about. Sarah Oakes. I don't think she spent more than ten thousand, including the vehicle, and she got a pretty good package. Not as comfortable, of course, using an old Series Two.'

'I'm interested in that - the vehicle is over forty years old and she took it to Africa. That's fascinating, and readers will love it. Tell me about her.'

'Big woman,' he said. 'Took a bit of getting used to. Obviously smart and quite sexy. Not drop dead gorgeous, but something about her you don't forget.

'She drove it here on a bloody miserable day in February, directly from Oxford where she found it. Some grief on the way - kept cutting out on hills - it had been standing a long time, and the petrol stank. The heater was knackered so she was frozen when she arrived - her teeth were chattering. She came right in and sat on the radiator while I made her a coffee.

'She had some sort of severance package and wanted to take a couple of years off to see the world. Her folks had driven a Land Rover from Cape Town years ago and she wanted to do a similar trip. She went to a dealer in London - you probably know the place - big signs you can see from the Docklands railway. There was nothing there for her, although they tried to sell her a used Range Rover. She was boggled by the prices.

'Efficient woman. She did her homework. She read Mark Franklin's book, bought every magazine she could find and quickly figured out that she would be better off with a good used motor. She made a lot of phone calls and a few useless trips. Buying a Land Rover was like finding a mate, she told me - you have to kiss a lot of frogs to find a prince.

'She purchased the Series Two because it was in good condition and she liked the chap who was selling it. It had less than fifty thousand original miles on the clock. She'd been to Oxford to help him fix the brakes for an MOT.

'After she warmed up, we put the Rover on the hoist and spent an hour going over it. She was right there with me. I was amazed at the condition. It even had the original tyres still fitted, and the old side exit exhaust system that has been obsolete for years.'

'Pretty unusual getting a job like this from a woman?' I ventured.

'She's an unusual woman,' he said.* 'Here's the quote I gave her. If you want to write something about us and the work we do, this is a pretty good example of what it takes to equip an older Land Rover for an African expedition.'

He left me reading the quote while he dealt with a customer over the telephone.

'Impressive list,' I said, when he returned. 'And not cheap. Did she go for it? And no winch?'

'Questioned some things. Like the extra fuel tank, the parabolic springs and the Canadian overdrive. I justified it all and she told me to go ahead and do it. She gave me a cheque in advance. Mind you, she was cagey with her money. I would have liked to give it a coat of paint, but she said no to that. And it had a winch already - a humongous thing driven by a bottom power take off - I'd never seen one like it before.'

She returned once the upgrades had been completed, Loos said. They drove around the farm together and he showed her how to use the low-range gears, free-wheel hubs, winch and other equipment. She understood perfectly how the equipment functioned. She was a competent driver. Under his direction she had driven through a difficult ditch and up the bank of a coppice, leaving a blizzard of mud, twigs and leaves in her wake. She was flushed with excitement by the time she reached the top.

'She got herself stuck in the duck pond,' he said with a laugh. 'I told her to cross the edge just to get a feel for wading, but she charged in too deep and splashed the ignition. We pulled her out with the tractor. It was the only time I ever saw her agitated. She seemed to get really pissed off with herself in some way, and became angry with me too. It wasn't my fault.'

Loos saw her again before she left, when she returned for him to torque up the head bolts. She arrived with three other people who were going with her to Africa. He opened a file on his computer to show me a picture of the Land Rover and the crew. 'I'll e-mail you a copy,' he said. 'Use it if it's of any help to you. You should probably get Sarah's permission though.'

I asked. 'No e-mails, postcards or appeals for spare parts?'

'Nope.'

'Any news of how things went?'

'Nothing,' he said. 'Strange. They left at rather a bad time too. There was that war in Ethiopia and the kidnappings in Libya.'

'Did she have a boyfriend?' It seemed too personal a question, and I thought he'd baulk, but he answered amiably.

'She never mentioned any man, and it was pretty obvious the two guys with her were just there for the trip. She never flirted with me or played the helpless woman. All strictly business. But I tell you, if I wasn't spoken for, I would have jumped into that Land Rover and done the trip. Once I got to know her, I realized just what a woman she was, and the lads in the shop were pretty smitten, too. She did say it had been quite difficult putting the party together. Lot of totally unsuitable people had answered her advertisements - most of them had no money and were just wankers.'

There was nothing more to learn, and he had given me plenty of material for a worthwhile story. I thanked him and prepared to go. He followed me out of the workshop. 'Let me know if you hear anything about her,' he said.

At home that evening, I downloaded the picture he had sent me. It was an excellent shot - the Land Rover well fitted out and purposeful, the people happy and relaxed. Sarah Oakes was the tallest in the group, tanned with long, dark hair. Sunglasses were pushed up over her forehead. She wore an open-necked blouse, capris and red espadrilles. In contrast, the younger woman was blonde, petite and sunburned, wearing a tee shirt and abbreviated shorts. The two men were complete opposites. Du Plessis was tough looking with an aggressive stance, dressed in faded khaki with long socks worn South African-style to his knees. Williamson was thin and natty, his face shadowed by a Panama hat.

The picture was taken in high resolution; I cropped it to enlarge the image of Sarah. She stood at the front of the machine with one foot on the bumper. The sunglasses cast a shadow on her forehead and there were laugh lines at the corners of her dark eyes. She was not wearing any rings, and the watch on her wrist was clearly a Rolex. There were freckles on her arms, and her ankle was slim in the sandal next to the mean looking winch. The detail was so fine I could clearly see the cheese head screws holding the Land Rover badge on the grille. I saved the picture as a screen saver and went to bed.*

---

* *This same Thursday the unusual woman known to be a poor correspondent enjoyed a rare afternoon off. She spent two hours in a library. She delivered a pillowcase full of her clothes to a cheerful older woman in a laundry. She drove a Mazda to a garage, where she purchased a battery for a fraction of the price a similar one would have cost her in England. She went to an outdoor market in a poorer part of the city, where she bought fruit from an old man who greeted her by name. She found cardamom and garam masala in a covered bazaar, and looked at several Indian dresses but was unable to find her size. She collected her finished laundry on her way home.*

At six, three men in a small BMW collected her at her flat. They went out for a Greek meal, over which they had two bottles of good wine and argued extensively. She was in bed by ten.

CHAPTER 8

A black Labrador that was pleased to see me.

Sir Harold Matthews was friendly when I called to ask if I could come and see him. I told him I was a writer considering doing a story on the history of the Docklands, and was interested in what happened with Electroport. He seemed like a man with little to do, and agreed readily to a Friday afternoon interview.

The house was a mellowed Victorian mansion set on about ten acres with rolling paddocks, five miles from Tunbridge Wells. As I turned into the drive, a green Daimler driven by a woman with platinum blonde hair was pulling out. She waved as she passed.

Wisteria blossoms blew over the porch steps. My use of the big brass knocker provoked what sounded like a ferocious dog. After a minute Mathews opened the door. The house smelled of lavender and dog. The latter proved to be a black Labrador that was pleased to see me. Mathews led the way into a large living room with a picture window overlooking a stable yard and a meadow where a mare with her foal were grazing. He was skeletally thin with his clothes hanging loosely. His complexion was puffy and sallow. He waved me to the sofa but sat himself in a hard chair, explaining that he had difficulty getting up from a low seat.

The room was comfortably furnished with well-worn antiques that spoke of old money. There were hunting prints on the walls, and a Victorian Kirkman grand piano covered with sheet music.

I started by congratulating him on the OBE, and he nodded and thanked me. He listened attentively when I told him my yarn about the research I was doing for a book on the Docklands. He said his old father would have known far more than he did, but showed himself to be well informed about the area. As I made notes, I realized that my putative project might make an interesting book.

'All Electroport made was generator sets?' I asked. 'That seems a very limited product range.'

'We stuck to our knitting,' he said. 'I've seen good companies go to the wall when they tried to diversify into products they didn't understand. We were the best in the world at what we did, and there are thousands of our sets out there to prove it. Dad made his fortune during the war with petrol units for searchlights, and he made them for the colonies after that. Simple robust sets. Air-cooled diesel engines. You know anything about diesels?'

I told him I did, and that the sound of a single-cylinder Lister diesel evoked memories of my childhood on an African farm. Solid surly lumps of green painted iron, they were used extensively for borehole pumping and lighting on farms in Rhodesia. To keep them quiet, exhausts were often run into a forty-five gallon drum buried underground and filled with water. They made a burbling noise as they ran. They leaked a bit and you could smell spilled fuel from a mile away if the wind was blowing in the right direction.

'I've never seen Africa,' he said. 'I planned to go, but that never came about. I've travelled to America a number of times.'

He got back onto the subject of his company, and there was no stopping him. He gave me the whole history, how the business started, the bomb damage during the war, the cheap searchlight units, the hard times in the sixties, the acceptance of units by the U.S. military during the cold war and the needs of cell phone towers. He spoke slowly, with frequent pauses, short of breath. I noticed an oxygen tank near his chair, but he wasn't making use of it.

'Our units operated completely unattended for months at a time,' he continued. 'More efficient than everybody else's. That means that for every gallon of diesel you poured into the tank, you got a few more kilowatt-hours out of the other end. Great selling point in remote areas. The parts business kept us going too. We made very few changes over the years and kept things simple.'

'Rather like Land Rover used to do,' I remarked.

'You're familiar with Land Rovers? One of my employees just bought an old one.'

This might be easier than I'd anticipated. 'I know quite a lot about them. I also write for *Land Rover Aficionado*,' I said. 'Your employee - would that be Sarah Oakes?'

'The very one,' he said. 'How do you know her?'

'I don't, really. I do know she purchased that old Land Rover from an archaeologist, but I was surprised to learn she's an engineer.'

'She was working in Portsmouth, wanted to move to London for personal reasons; she applied for the job when I advertised that I needed an electrical engineer. Terrific girl.' He grew silent and stared at his clenched hands. 'Incredibly bright and objective. She identified critical issues within the company within a couple of weeks of starting. She defined targets for marketing and manufacturing. I sent her off to visit all our overseas accounts and she came back loaded with orders.' He gathered his thoughts. 'She's very tall and quite beautiful - tanned looking - her mother was a Cape Malay.'

'Somewhat exotic,' I ventured. 'But you obviously worked well together.'

'Amazingly so. The accountants were thrilled with the way the company took off. There was even some talk of taking it public. Flagging markets revived, and she got us involved in the cell phone business. She recognized the need there for reliable motor generator sets.

'In tropical climates, they use solar cells and, in some areas, windmills. But in most places where there is no grid, they need stand-alone generator sets. The potential market is massive. She persuaded me to address a conference in Boston on "*Efficient Long-term Base Power*". We went to America together - a very successful trip. Paid back the cost of a new suit.'

'A new suit?'

He laughed. 'Yes, a new suit. She wasn't complimentary about my wardrobe. She said I must have inherited it with the company in 1965.'

The stroke that felled him had come on a Tuesday in November. He recalled he was not feeling well on his way to work, and the pain hit him at about eleven in the morning. He was virtually unconscious for ten days, then found himself in a hospital room - a depleted man. Specialists came and went and he was subjected to a daily barrage of tests. The prognosis was not good; he had considerable paralysis. The consensus was that he should rest for six months and then undergo a course of rehabilitation to help him cope with his disabilities. He was sufficiently realistic to see that he would never work again. After a week of turning the matter over and over in his head, seeking an alternate solution for his staff, he called his lawyer and his accountant who persuaded him to put the business up for sale.

'I never went back to the plant,' he said. 'Those fellows who bought it were just after a quick quid. My solicitor told me that the day after the contract was signed, they put the property up for sale and started winding down the business. They completed the orders in hand and flogged the designs around the industry. A German company bought the rights to the products.* My father must have turned in his grave. There was a sale of assets that were not wanted and the staff were all laid off.'

'Including Sarah Oakes?' I asked.

'Hell, no!' he exclaimed. 'She went almost as soon as the City people bought it. They put in a manager with an MBA and without a clue. Two weeks later there was a flaming row. He told her that she had neither the qualifications nor the experience to run a business, and she told him that he wouldn't recognise an alternator if it bit his arse. Marks told me about it. She was laid off with three months' salary. Typical Sarah,' he smiled. 'Zero diplomacy, just straight to the point. I wish I'd been in on the meeting.'

He reached slowly over to a side table and passed me a silver framed photograph. The picture showed a couple in formal dress. A handsome man in his prime shook hands with Prince Charles. The woman beside him was a radiant Sarah Oakes.

'Us,' he said. 'Last year. We won the *Queen's Award for Innovation*. It was the highlight of my career...'

I sat staring at him after that. He was not all that much older than I, and was surrounded by luxury, with more money than he would ever need, yet I was much more fortunate than he. The dog leaned against his knee. It was quiet in the big house. I had no business delving into his private life, but I felt he knew where my quarry was.

'You were lovers, weren't you?' I stated.

* *This information is incorrect. The international corporation ALSTOM purchased the brands and patents of Electroport Ltd. The company's head offices are located in Levallois-Perret, France.*

CHAPTER 9

The place was expensive, but created the informal ambience of a Portuguese dockside café.

I expected a denial but none came. He looked down at the dog and fondled its ears. Eventually he asked, 'Is it that obvious?'

'I put two and two together when you were talking,' I lied. There was little point in telling him the suspicions of his junior staff or the observations of his lover's landlady. 'Tell me about her.'

'Would you mind joining me in a drink?' he asked. 'I'm not supposed to have it, but what the hell. In the cabinet behind you.'

I poured Scotch into crystal tumblers and added soda from the old-fashioned siphon on the sideboard. 'I've never told anyone about that,' he said. His hand shook. The foal cantered across the meadow outside on spindly legs. 'Funny that I should want to tell you, really. A fellow I have never set eyes on before. And I don't really know why you're interested.'

I felt a surge of sympathy for him. I leaned over and stroked the dog. 'Don't tell me anything you don't want to,' I said. 'It's a bit astray from my Docklands work but I like human stories and I've got all afternoon.'

'I'm dying,' he said. 'They've given me a year. I want to tell someone about her. Sure as hell she won't be mentioned in my obituary…'

He told his story with complete candour. Intimate details of his love affair embroided the fabric. I knew that a severe stroke could rob its victim of inhibition and this certainly seemed the case.

He had been married twenty-seven years and although he was disappointed in his relationship with his wife, it never occurred to him to be unfaithful to her. She cared for her horses rather more than she cared for him. She never showed interest in his work. They both had independent means, and she had her own circle of horsey friends. He regretted this absence of affection, and remembered fondly a warm wench who had been his lover in his Master's term. He spoke slowly, frequently pausing and sipping his drink reflectively.

When Sarah had visited Electroport for her job interview, he was stirred by her vitality. She told him she was single but he noticed she wore a wedding ring. He gave her the job because she was by far the most qualified applicant.

'She always looked nice, wore very little makeup - didn't need it - her skin was lovely. She was a valuable member of my team and I soon came to rely on her. Quite frankly, without her, the company would probably have gone under. Mind you, she could be a bit hard to get on with. She was sometimes short tempered and could be hard on her colleagues. When she was in one of her bad moods she worked like a fiend and we all steered clear of her. She could be impossible at times, but she got the job done.

'We got into the habit of having an extended lunch together every other week. I looked forward to those afternoons. She gave damn good advice - some I never asked for.'

When she proposed that he submit a paper for the *Boston Conference on Base Station Design* he had agreed, and when his paper was accepted they went out for lunch and shared a bottle of champagne.

Prior to leaving for America, she took him suit shopping.

'She told me that getting one off the rack on Beckton Main

Street was not on, and took me to a tailor on Clifford Street, where she helped me choose two new suits. We went on to Liberty and she selected shirts and ties for me. Talked me into a new pair of shoes as well. It was fun going shopping with a woman who knew about clothes.'

'My wife was put out. Furious really. She told me I looked like an old fool.'

He paused, deep in reflection.

'New colour brochures were printed and we gave ourselves titles. I became "Harold Mathews, MIEE Director," and I insisted on "Sarah A. Oakes B.Sc., Engineering Manager".'

In Boston, their rooms were on the fifteenth floor of a pretentious hotel near the conference centre. He gave his presentation in the late afternoon on the last day of the gathering. The paper was well received and the questions afterwards, coming from a very technical audience, were stimulating. At the cocktail party following, several people approached them, expressed interest in their products and gave them business cards.

'Quite a few men talked to Sarah - she was the best-looking girl there. She wore the white cocktail frock I insisted on paying for the day we went shopping in town. I was pleased when I heard her turning down invitations. That night, after it was all over, we went out for dinner - just the two of us.'

They shared a late meal at a seafood restaurant overlooking the harbour. The place was expensive, but created the informal ambience of a Portuguese dockside café. Two relaxed and competent engineers who enjoyed working together disposed of a litre of

Alentejo. The debris of their lobster dinner had been pushed aside and he was drawing a circuit for a better RF suppression unit on the back of the dessert menu when she took the pen away and put her hand over his. 'Hal,' she said, 'let's not talk about work.'

'There was a candle on the table in an enamelled holder, and the glow lit her face. She has a beautiful oval face. I noticed she had a bit of makeup on her eyes and she had her hair down around her shoulders with a green band holding it back. Her eyes sparkled. As I looked at her, I got this tight feeling in my gut. I couldn't meet her eyes. I looked down and she had a line of freckles across her chest, and those freckles formed a perfect isosceles triangle with the vee on the top of that darn dress...'

In the taxi back to the hotel, he recalled, she rested her head on his shoulder and put her hand in his. Back at the hotel, she led him to her room.

I sat quietly, not wanting to break the spell. He was not relating events so much as reliving them.

'I held her for a while and we didn't talk. Then she kissed me. She disappeared into the bathroom for a few minutes and I sat on the bed. She came out in a short nightdress with her hair hanging loose. She kneeled on the bed and undressed me, then folded back the covers, and we just lay there together...'

The old dog shook himself and settled at his feet.

'Don't think it was a wild night of passion,' he said ruefully. 'I was pretty out of practice.'

He was a confident leader, master of things electrical and mechanical, an excellent speaker, adequate horseman and a passably good cook. None of these things were the least bit of help to him that night. He lay with her, awed by the body he caressed, and humiliated by the inadequacy of his own response.

Eventually she fell asleep. He eased himself quietly from the bed and went over to the window, where he stood reflectively, knowing he had crossed his personal Rubicon. The other towers around were dark, and a solitary taxi idled on the street below. He gathered his clothes, went to the bathroom and closed the door gently before finding a switch. The red heat lamp came on, and he left it at that. He picked up her dress from the floor and brought it to his cheek, and as he did, the musky scent of her on his fingers moved him. He gave up all thought of leaving, went back to her bed and drew her to him.

'We didn't say much to each other on the flight home,' he recalled. 'I put my arm across her and tucked my hand between the seatbelt and her thigh. She went to sleep on my shoulder and murmured a little, but I didn't catch the words. She woke as the landing gear went down. Thirty minutes later we were in the Jag and I drove her home.

'Nothing has been the same since----

'You're a lucky man,' I said, and meant it.

The next week at work it was as though nothing had happened, except that there was a little pink Post-it note on his tee square which said 'XXX', and once he found her looking softly at him when they were in a crowded meeting.

On the afternoon of their next pub lunch, they had gone to her flat and not returned to work.

Despite being busy with the increasing production, and with her never far from his thoughts, he found he was more creative than he had ever been before. It was as if the seeds of ideas that had been lying dormant in the back of his brain had germinated and were thrusting themselves out of his subconscious.

'The crew in the tool room and the winding shop would groan when I came in with new prints,' he grinned. 'I would get them milling odd slots in stacks of laminations and making coils in unheard-of configurations.' This activity brought him closer to Sarah, as she was the only member of his staff capable of understanding the theoretical aspects of the work. The talk of flux density and power factor were beyond the grasp of his more practical workers.

'Essentially, what we did,' he explained, 'was find a way to get more ampere turns into the same size of slot and increase the gauss. We built an alternator this way, supervising a crew of sceptics in the shop, and clamped it to the test bed driven by an old synchronous motor whose characteristics we knew by heart.. The new machine was five percent more efficient than anything built before. I instructed my patent attorney to put Sarah's name above mine on the application.'

'It sounds like a wonderful relationship, you were a perfect fit," I said enviously.

He nodded. 'Inevitably, the subject of the future came up. Sarah and I had been out to dinner and planned to spend the night together. We walked along the embankment to her place. I was sleepy, but she made me sit up; she wanted to talk. I told her that if it was about work, I was not going to listen. "This is not about work - it's about us," she said, launching into what struck me as a carefully rehearsed speech. The enormity of it washed over me. I'm considerably older than she is and what she was suggesting came like a bolt from the blue. I saw her lower lip quivering and there were tears in her eyes.

'The short version is, she was going to divorce her husband - he'd been having a long-term affair - a really messy story and I won't get into it. But what she mainly wanted to say was that she wanted to have a baby with me.

'What could I say? I was stunned. I knew how devastated Belinda would be. I thought of my children's disapproval, having to sell this house, my friends thinking I was a fool, the uncertainty of it all.....'But there was only one thing to do. I kissed her and asked her to marry me....

'She didn't say anything. She was too choked up. I held her tight and could feel the sobs in her chest.'

Three days later he had the stroke.

When he recovered sufficiently to write, he composed a letter and had a nurse post it to her. 'I wrote that I loved her but knew - as she must know - that I was no longer the man she loved, and never would be again. I asked that she not come to see me - I was vaguely aware that she had visited me at the hospital. I told her she must try to forget about me completely, and find somebody else to make as happy as she had made me. At the end I wrote: "Remember me as I was, not as I am now. I am sending you a gift. Please do not refuse it."

'I instructed Richardson, the solicitor, to assign the new alternator patent completely to her.

'I heard about the trouble she was having at work and how she was laid off. She had just bought that Land Rover, so she must have seen it coming. She went to Africa and I've completely lost touch with her.' Tears were running down his face now.

I hardly knew what to say. 'I'm so sorry' I said in a weak attempt at commiseration.

We sat in silence for a long minute.

'It seems such an unusual thing for a woman to do,' I went on, hoping to distract him. 'She must have an adventurous spirit and be pretty independent. What beats me is how she can afford it - an expedition like that costs a fair amount.'

He grunted. 'When I sold the company,' he said slowly, 'even after taxes I had more money than I could ever use in this life. I sent gifts to the five key people who worked with me. I gave her twenty-five thousand pounds - "for the travel and future engineer account....."

'It means so much to me to know that she is putting it to good use.' *

---

* *Five months after this meeting took place, a brief obituary appeared in the Times recording the passing of Sir Harold Mathews (OBE, MIEE) of Tunbridge Wells. The notice gave a short summary of his professional life, listed his contributions to society and recorded that he was survived by his wife, Belinda, and two adult children.*

CHAPTER 10

Mount Sinai. "I thought I would never get all the way up, and I was quite chuffed with myself."

F inding Angela Barnes was not difficult. I walked the few blocks of Knightsbridge opposite Harrods, found the only establishment catering to people seeking something Scottish, and recognized her sorting cashmere scarves. I judged her to be about twenty-five, although she wore a good deal of makeup.

'Excuse me,' I asked, 'are you Angela Barnes?' She nodded, looking me up and down. 'I'm Giles Jackson. I write for a magazine called *Land Rover Aficionado*. I heard you just did a trip in a Land Rover to Africa, and I'd love to talk to you about it.' I gave her my *LRA* card.

'You work for a magazine? Yes, I went last summer - it was wild.'

'I really would appreciate if you could tell me a bit about it. Any chance you could meet me for a drink after work one day?'

'That'd be nice,' she said. 'We close at five-thirty. How 'bout today?'

I returned at five-thirty and waited in the entrance. She appeared wearing a knee-length green coat and high-heeled black boots. She took my arm as we walked down Sloane Street to a place she described as 'fab'. We got on well over our wine, and she talked almost incessantly. Then I suggested dinner. She liked Greek food, so we took a taxi to a place she knew in South Kensington near her flat.

She'd been born and raised in London, and I learned that her father made his money with a chain of stores selling cheap tools imported from China and India. She was never a scholar, but was interested in fashion and, after leaving school, worked in better stores selling clothes and women's accessories. She liked holidays overseas and had been to Majorca, Malta and Cyprus. These trips had been the packaged all-inclusive type advertised in the windows of travel agents. She made it clear she always went with a boyfriend in tow.

She was working in a department store on Oxford Road when a woman came in to buy a rug, 'not the kind you put on the floor, silly, but the woolly kind you put on a bed on cold nights or keep in your car.' It was a slow day, with time to chat, and the customer was friendly.

'Ever so nice she was, told me she was driving to Africa and wanted to make sure she would be warm enough. Really chatty with me, asked me if I liked to travel - 'course I do and I told her so - and blow me down if she didn't ask me if Africa interested me, and took my phone number. I was really excited, and called my Dad to ask if he would lend me the three thousand quid it would cost to go along. He's ever so generous - goes off a lot himself - I'm his pet. Said he would come along, too, but was only joking. Phoned Sarah to check her out, and also phoned the bloke who fitted out her Land Rover - he and my dad got on well.'

Once funds were assured for the trip, and with her father's blessing, Angela told Sarah she would really like to join the expedition. She was introduced to Gert du Plessis, who had already signed on; the next day Sarah called her and said it was a go.

'But she hardly knew you.' I said. 'That seems odd to me.'

'Woman's intuition, innit. And she wanted to keep the crew balanced like.

'Gert was all right, dead helpful with organizing my kit. Bit hard to understand him, but I got used to it. Came with me to meet my dad and talk about tools. Dad told him to go to one of his shops, pick out anything he needed and charge it to him...'

A second man joined them, so they were four when they went on a shakedown camping trip to Scotland.

He was really nice,' she said. 'His name was Adam, and I could tell he was gay right away. Real smart dresser and up a bit, has an art gallery in Chelsea full of creepy stuff. Very skinny. Nice bloke - we got on well. He told me he had broken up with his lover, they'd been together a couple of years, but he was kicked out of the flat with nothing. Said his lover was a big bloke with a nasty streak. I cheered him up no end telling him he'd meet a new guy on the trip.'

She was on her fourth glass of Domestica, now totally uninhibited and talking loudly. I noticed how other men looked at her and didn't miss her way of making eye contact.

'Anyway, this Adam bloke dropped out at the last minute. Turned out he'd got back together with his ex. Sarah was really brassed off. I'd never seen her mad before. I told her I was not that surprised, as it seemed a bit weird for someone like him to go. She told me and Gert that the trip was going to cost more because we could not get anyone else at such short notice and would have to split the cost three ways instead of four. We said okay, except Gert wasn't happy - I think he was a bit short. At the same meeting Sarah ripped into me about packing and told me I could have only one small bit of luggage. I was bummed 'cos I'd bought lovely things.'

'How long were you going for and where did you plan to end up?' I interrupted.

'I wanted to be back for Christmas, and got a special ticket so's I could get a plane home from pretty well anywhere in Africa. There was no set plan; it depended on weather and politics. Gert was going back to South Africa, but I don't think he cared when he got there. Sarah never told me her long-term plans; she was secretive about stuff like that. I never saw her writing home. I sent loads of postcards.'

By the time we were ready to leave the restaurant, she had covered every last detail of her experiences, but she was hazy on geography and got events out of sequence.

'Nice for Gert,' I said. 'Trip like that with two attractive woman.'

'Gert!' she laughed. 'He's actually a scary guy. When we were in Rome he almost killed a crook who tried to break into the Rover. The police told us to get out of town or he would be charged. He and I gave it a go early on, but he got all possessive about me and punched an Austrian in a bar. After that I broke it off and told him he wasn't my type. He got over it and we both fooled around with other people along the way. Everybody on holiday wants to have a good time. Sarah called us cats, but I don't think it bothered her. She met a couple of guys but older like, and they just sat in cafés. Gert wasn't her type either. She's refined and he's rough. I could see he fancied her, though, and I protected her a bit - funny. Woman stuff you wouldn't understand, but she and I became sort of friends.'

We finished our dinner and lingered over coffee. It was dark outside, and the traffic in the High Street was quieter. She stretched. 'Let's go to my place and I'll show you my photos.'

Her place was a mews flat near Cromwell Road that was in need of a day of housework. To be fair, she had not been expecting a visitor. She settled me in the tiny living room and went to get into something more comfortable. She reappeared in a knee-length tee shirt.

She poured me a drink from a surprisingly well-stocked cupboard and produced four photograph albums.

The first picture was of the three of them taken by 'a nerdy kid at the ferry terminal', and from the sequence in the album they had driven through France, Italy, Greece, Turkey, Syria, Jordan and Egypt. She skimmed over the pictures of people she had met and only showed me the ones she thought I might be interested in. There were some of Sarah Oakes, including beach photos. There were lots of Angela, topless, deeply tanned, and in the company of many different men. Gert always seemed to be in the same pair of shorts, a tough-looking man.

The Rover was shown in locations that ranged from truck stops in France to the Hagia Sophia in Istanbul and the Krak des Chevaliers in Syria. In Egypt, they travelled in company with a second party in an impressive Pinzgauer that dwarfed the Rover in a picture of Mount Sinai.

'That was a big motor caravan,' she said. 'Much bigger than the Land Rover. Gert got talking to the people and it was a group just like us - one man and two women. The man was a rich Swiss guy called Werner, and the two women came from Eastern Europe. One was called Bridget and I can never remember the other's name. That's them there. Bit of a mobile sex party, if you ask me. He was a real sleaze. We climbed that mountain with them. These are the pictures I took from the top. I thought I would never get all the way up, and

I was quite chuffed with myself.'

The photos were the best she had taken. In one, the Sinai Peninsula was spread out below them like a map, with the Red Sea in semi-darkness and the group of them silhouetted against the amber sky, waiting for the sun. There was a beautiful picture of Sarah, with a glow on her face and a halo of hair ruffled by the breeze. Gert was shown with his arms around the two women from the Pinzgauer.

'That's stunning,' I said, indicating the picture of Sarah.

'You fancy her, don't you?' she said, peeling out the picture and turning back a few pages. 'Here's another nice one.' The shot was a close-up of a topless Sarah on a Greek beach. She gave both to me.

It was after one before she finished showing me the pictures and relating her experiences. She was sitting on the floor at my feet; we both had drunk too much. 'Let's go to bed,' she said.

The bed took up half the room. She lit a candle and turned off the electric lights. An army of stuffed animals watched the proceedings. There were no surprises. I had expected the ring in her navel and the tattoo at the base of her spine. The tan lines were there but faded.

I went to the bathroom to dispose of her condom and returned to find her sitting up cross-legged on the bed. The ring was hidden in the folds of her tummy. Her breasts hung conical and pink. She was lighting a cigarette, which surprised me, as she had not smoked all evening. 'Only one,' she said. 'It's the only time I smoke.'

'You were obviously having a good time. Why did you leave the trip?'

She looked at me wryly, took a good pull on the cigarette and blew the smoke in a perfect circle. 'I'd suspected something for a couple of weeks; I'm usually regular. Sarah said it was best to check. In Cairo I picked up a kit, and sure enough, I was preggers. Damn stupid. I'd lost my pills in Italy, left my toilet bag in a shower and someone nicked it. I thought I was being pretty careful, but there are times things happen like... I really expected Sarah to be mad, but she was nice and helped me get a flight home. We both got a bit teary at the airport, she hugged me and told me I was a right pain, but she'd miss me. "Hurry back or you'll miss the best part of the trip," she said.'

'But you never went back...'

'No. Another stupid thing. She'd given me a Yahoo address on a bit of paper at the airport. She'd check it when she could, she said. That way we could figure out where to meet again.'

'You have her e-mail address?'

'No. I told you, I was stupid - I lost it.'

'Things were confused when I left; I hadn't a clue which way they went. There was this problem with the Sudan; all the borders with Egypt were closed. We looked at a map and talked about Libya, but there were problems there. We were thinking of getting a boat somewhere...'

'Eritrea,' I suggested. She shrugged.

'I didn't hear anything from them,' she said. 'Sarah probably lost my address, too. I worry a bit about her. I don't trust Gert, and that Swiss guy Werner was creepy.

'The trip was brilliant, but the way it ended for me was a right shock. I'm off clubbing and the old crowd's moved on some.

'You probably won't believe me but I've been pretty good lately. You're the only man since I got back.' She gave me an affectionate pinch. 'We drank a bit too much. I'm not saying I didn't like it, mind.'

She ground the stub of her cigarette into the candleholder.

'My mum died fifteen years ago. Sarah encouraged me to think a bit about the future. More grounded, like. I want to be strong and successful like her. I've been talking with my dad about starting my own business...' *

We went to sleep after that. She slept with her back against me. I wakened after a few hours, took a shower, observed by a dusty plush elephant, and left. The dawn was not nearly as pretty as the one in her pictures.

Angela Barnes, with backing from her dad, has opened 'TwentySomething' a boutique in Islington.

CHAPTER 11

Myford ML7 Lathe.

I drove into the farmyard to find Jean putting the tabby and his box out in the sun. He was awake but not active. 'How is he?' I asked apprehensively.

'I think he's going to be all right,' she said. 'He slept for two days and I feared he would never wake up. Then yesterday Bill was opening a beer in the kitchen and we heard this meow and he was looking over the edge of the box. So I picked him up gently and put him in the litter, he had a little poop and there was no blood in it. Now he's eating a bit and asking for beer every time he smells it, so I think he will recover. He's just very sore. He's a lovely cat.'

There was a message on the answering machine from the archaeologist, Tony Morganter, saying that I should call him back. I called and explained my need to track down his Land Rover.

'Look,' he said. 'It's a long story, but I think I can help you. You say you're in Ringwood - that's near Bournemouth, isn't it? I'm not too far from you in Salisbury. I've got a group of students doing some industrial archaeology on a site here. I'm at the Red Lion Hotel. Can you take a run up and I'll fill you in over a pint?'

'Terrific,' I said. 'How about later this afternoon?'

We met at his hotel and sat in the lounge, away from the tour groups returning from Stonehenge. He was a tall, wiry, balding man, over sixty, with thick glasses and a precise manner of speaking.

After some small talk about traffic and the weather, I asked him about his work, and I learned that his field was historical engineering. He had written several books and published scores of papers about ancient inventions and their impact on the economies of early civilizations.

I told him whom I was working for and the reason I wanted to find his old Land Rover. 'I've traced it as far as Egypt, and my leads are drying up,' I said. 'It's a long shot, but I'm very interested to find out whether Sarah Oakes told you what her plans were for the vehicle after she purchased it, and if you have had any news of her since.'

He leaned forward in his chair, peering at me over his glasses as he sized me up.

'Well,' he said, 'I think I can fill you in somewhat. Let me tell you the whole story.'

He purchased the Land Rover in 1989 because he was looking for a cheap, no-nonsense vehicle that he could use during a sabbatical. He and his first wife had driven it to the Balkans to study early methods of obtaining water for irrigation; they were research partners and collaborated on papers. The Land Rover had done them very well that summer, and they'd hung onto it and used it for two or three later trips to the same area on summer holidays. It was kept in a large workshop behind his house in Abingdon.

In 1994, his wife was killed in a traffic accident while visiting her sister in France. He remarried in 1997, but his new bride was not interested in travelling anywhere by Land Rover. 'I suppose I hung onto it for sentimental reasons more than anything,' he said. 'We'd had such wonderful times with it.'

He advertised the Land Rover for sale in *Exchange and Mart*, but he wanted it to go to a good home. This eliminated as purchasers a number of young men who came to look at it. He liked the sound of Sarah on the telephone, and was impressed with her when she came to see the vehicle.

'I was honest with her. I told her it had been standing for a long time. On its last run, it made Genoa to Calais in two days.' He grinned. 'Pretty good time, eh? I was frank with her, saying that it dripped oil and the exhaust leaked a bit. I showed her the spare engine that I had for it. It needed an MOT, which I offered to get for her. I told her its name was *Geraldine*, which was the name Molly had given it. She had named it after a character in an American comic strip.

'Sarah agreed to buy it, saying it was exactly what she was looking for. She didn't dicker over the price.'

'May I ask what she paid?'

The question was ignored.

'We arranged that she would come to Abingdon to collect it the following weekend. I got the old girl started and drove her to the local garage for the MOT inspection. The only major problem was some oil in the rear brakes, and the garage gave me a quote of over three hundred quid. They obviously didn't want the job, so I decided to do it myself. My hobby is model engineering, and I have a good workshop with a Myford lathe. These small jobs always turn out to be more complicated than you think, and I didn't get finished in time.' I nodded in agreement. 'I let Sarah know I was behind schedule, and she surprised me by offering to come and help.

'I collected her at the station. She produced a pair of overalls, read the owner's manual and really got down to work on the axle - she was very organized about it. We took a cold chisel and split the distance pieces on the stub shafts. She hammered the new ones on using a short piece of pipe I cut off on the Myford.

'As we worked we shared stories. She told me her parents had driven a Land Rover from Cape Town to London in the sixties. I reminisced about adventures Molly and I had had in communist Bulgaria. My nostalgia must have been obvious. She told me she was alone, separated and with no new man on the horizon. She needed some change in her life, and had the idea of repeating what her parents had done.

'I told her that it was a gutsy thing for a girl to do,' he said.

"More crazy than gutsy," was her response.'

By five they had the entire axle back together again, but his wife, unhappy that he was spending Saturday having fun in the garage with a young Amazon, interrupted their work. He found Sarah a bed and breakfast for the night.

'On Sunday morning, we filled up the brake fluid reservoir and spent a frustrating hour trying to bleed the brakes,' he related. 'No matter what we did, the brake pedal refused to produce any pressure. We found that the adjustment cams in the rear brakes could be turned a full circle without meeting any resistance, so we took the drums off again.

'It was obvious that my wife was not going to make us lunch. I suggested she join us at the local pub, but got a pretty sharp refusal. Sarah and I went to *The Nag's Head*, where we ran into some of my students. I showed her off, in a very nice-fitting set of coveralls, with a grease smear across her forehead and dirty fingernails. My stock's risen considerably at the college.' He laughed.

They returned from the pub in excellent spirits, and found that the brake shoes had the pins in the wrong position and did not line up with the cams. They fixed this, using the Myford to make new pins, and by six in the evening had the brakes working perfectly.

'She spent a second night in the bed and breakfast, and on the Monday morning *Geraldine* sailed through the MOT. Mind you, the mechanic ignored the gearbox oil leak. Sarah had insurance organized. She gave me a cheque for the balance and dropped me off at the college. I was sad to see *Geraldine* go, but I couldn't have been happier. I sometimes think I detect a hint of her shampoo in the garage, but it's probably my imagination.'

After she left, he realized that he had not asked her if she wanted the spare engine.

'And you never heard from her again?' I asked, puzzled. He could hardly have invited me so far to share so little information.

'Not for some time, but yes, I did hear from her again. I went to Eritrea in Africa to help her fix something else.'

CHAPTER 12

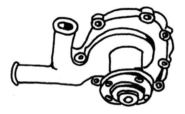

The pump was a solid cast iron housing, with a steel shaft
and bearings held in place with a grub screw.

The call from Nmeba in Eritrea came on an evening in September. It was the start of a new term, and he was meeting with one of his graduate students to discuss the framework of a thesis.

'Tony, it's me, Sarah Oakes, the woman who purchased your Land Rover,' she said. 'You remember me? I'm calling from a place called Nmeba in Eritrea.'

He had only a hazy idea where Eritrea was, and it took him a second or two to connect the woman's voice with the old Land Rover, the grease smear and the brake work.

'I can't talk too long,' she said. 'I'm at a phone place where I have to pay cash for the call, and it's quite expensive. Do you still have the spare engine for the Land Rover?'

He detected strain in her voice. 'It's still in the same place under the workbench,' he said. 'I was wondering if you would ever come to get it.'

'That's great,' she said. 'Tell you why. I've broken my water pump. I've looked everywhere but nobody here has one. Mine has eight holes in the casting and I can find them with nine but not eight. Do you think you could take the one off the old engine and send it to me?'

'Of course,' he said. 'Or I'll find you one somewhere else. Do you want it sent by post?'

'No,' she said. 'That will take too long. Do you mind trying to find a courier who can get it to Asmara? That's the capital, and I can go there by bus to fetch it. I can arrange to send you the money from my account in London.'

They agreed that she would call him the next day at the same time.

He went home and pulled the old engine out from underneath the workbench.

He counted the studs and bolts on the water pump. There were eight. Laying his spanners on the bench in a row, he first took off the fan and pulley, which were mounted on the pump. He removed the fastenings that held the pump to the timing cover, carefully putting them in a jar as he worked. He then pried the pump off the engine. He wiped up a little pool of green coolant that had spilled on the clean painted concrete.

The pump was a solid cast iron housing, with a steel shaft and bearings held in place with a grub screw. The shaft had a small amount of play, and it rumbled somewhat when he spun it in the lathe. It needed a new bearing.

Back in his study, he pulled down a well-thumbed Phillips Atlas and found Asmara near the horn of Africa. In this old atlas it was located in Ethiopia. He remembered hearing that Eritrea was a new country formed by a breakaway part of Ethiopia, and that there had been a war recently between the two.

The next morning he let his secretary know he would not be in, and went to a garage that specialized in Land Rovers. They looked at the pump, pronounced it 'knackered' and ordered in a new one.

At home he spent a frustrating hour seeking an express courier service to move a parcel from Oxford to Asmara. He was surprised to find out just how difficult this was. Few of the companies he spoke to knew where Eritrea was. Those that were capable of delivering the parcel quoted him a rate of over two hundred pounds. One helpful man cautioned him that getting commercial goods cleared through customs in places like Asmara could take weeks and would be expensive.

In the afternoon, he returned to the garage for the pump. Being a careful man, he checked the new pump against the old, and found that there were nine holes in the new one. This caused a lot of discussion between mechanics and parts people, and a call to someone called 'Old Jack'. Old Jack told them that they must have a Series IIA pump, but the type they needed was the Series II. They then called suppliers and were told that the one they wanted was no longer made, but they could repair it by using parts from the new one they had ordered.

By the time they had dismantled the new pump and assembled the parts into the old casting, he had spent ninety pounds. He went home and had a distressing argument with his wife.

While he had been out, her afternoon had been interrupted several times by courier companies with quotations on shipments to Eritrea. She felt it was not her mission to take messages for him when he was doing something for the crazy woman who had bought the Land Rover. Furthermore, he was devious, taking calls from this person at work. He stood stoically and heard her out, as he usually did. Then he went to his workshop and painted the water pump dark green using a quick drying paint. He noticed his hands were shaking.

He was back in his office by four and called a travel agent.

Sarah called at six. 'I'm in Asmara, treating myself to a hotel. Did you find the pump?'

Tony told her briefly about his day with the pump.

'I'm putting you to an awful lot of trouble.'

He then told her about the problems with couriers. 'It could take a week,' he said. 'How about I bring it out myself on Saturday?'

There was a silence in Asmara. Then, 'What was that you said?' she asked uncertainly.

'I said I'll bring it out Saturday. Flight to Cairo tomorrow night and a connection to Asmara at seven thirty on Egypt Air. Gets into Asmara at eight forty-five.'

'That's very nice of you,' she said slowly. 'But it will be awfully expensive - I just can't afford that.'

'Look,' he said. 'It will be a break for me. I wouldn't think of you paying. I hope you can meet the flight.'

'Yes...' she still sounded uncertain. 'Are you sure you want to do this?'

'I am,' he said decisively. 'I've already booked.'

He spent a frigid night with his wife, and early the next morning told her he would be away for a week. Under her baleful glare, he cushioned the pump amongst some summer clothes in his well-worn rucksack. He took a bus to the station and the fast train to London. By eleven he was filling in a visa application form in the Eritrean embassy. At a sporting goods shop, he bought some light hiking boots, a flashlight and a Swiss Army knife. Traveller's cheques came from a branch of his bank, and his ticket from

Thomas Cook on the Strand. By four he was back at the embassy to collect his passport. He caught the Heathrow express from Paddington. The water pump showed up on the security X-ray and he had to explain it to an unsmiling woman, but surprisingly the knife went undetected. At ten-thirty that night an Airbus lifted him from England.

He was flying, it occurred to him, roughly along the route that he had driven with Molly many times before. During the flight he was able to get some sleep, and a little more, with his pack on his knees, in Cairo Airport.

On the flight to Asmara, Tony Morganter was the only European. His seatmate was an Eritrean who imported reinforcing bars from Italy, a talkative type who gave him a good grounding in Eritrean history, and told him his son had been killed in the war with Ethiopia some months before. The Ethiopians had seized a large swath of Eritrean territory, and sporadic fighting was still going on. His companion was convinced the Eritreans would win the land back, but he was fearful of the cost. This man gave Tony his business card and told him to call if he needed any help in Asmara.

Walking across the tarmac from the aircraft, Tony perspired in the morning heat. There was no difficulty with customs or immigration, and the emerging crowd swept him into the chaos of the arrivals area.

Sarah was waiting against the far wall, somewhat removed from the press of bodies by the door. Thinner than he remembered, hair longer, but still with a wonderful smile. Her arms and face were a beautiful tawny brown, and she was modestly dressed in brightly coloured cotton.

She shook his hand warmly. 'Thank you so much,' she said. 'I don't know what I would have done without you. Waiting indefinitely for a parcel would have been a real pain.'

He changed some money into Nakfa, and she took him to the city in a taxi. She was carrying a heavy pack. They went to a café and ordered coffees and foccacia.

'What are your plans now that you're here?' Sarah asked.

Tony was unprepared for the question. He was a knight sallying forth to rescue a damsel in distress. The woman across the table did not look particularly damsel-like or noticeably distressed. She had expressed gratitude for his services, and had tucked the pump into her pack without even admiring the green paint. He wondered if he was making a fool of himself and wrecking what was left of his marriage.

'I don't have any plans, really,' he said. 'I assumed I could help you get *Geraldine* going and see you on your way.'

The use of the name made him harmless and disarmed her.

'Thank you,' she said. 'She's quite a distance from here and halfway up a mountain. It's a rough place. There's nowhere to stay. Are you sure you wouldn't be better off here in Asmara? There are some good hotels, and interesting tours you can take.'

He did not want her to feel obligated to him. 'Look,' he said, 'if you don't want me to come along and help get her going, I'm sure I'll have an interesting week here. But I thought we got along well the weekend you came to Oxford, and I think it would be fun to see the old girl again. Don't bother about the discomfort. I've been on pretty rough digs before.'

'Well,' she said, 'let's go and catch a bus, then.'

He had not calculated the value of the money in his pocket, but she paid for the tickets and they boarded a crowded bus that departed with black exhaust, scattering the crowd of onlookers. They left the city on a well-paved road that meandered through fields and villages. They were uncomfortably crushed by the seat in front of them, and it was noisy and difficult to talk. After a few hours, they stopped in a small town and boarded a second bus that headed off along a dirt road towards a range of high mountains.

Along the road, Tony noticed increasing numbers of military trucks carrying soldiers and weapons of various types. At a roadblock a soldier came on board, scrambling over luggage in the aisle and looking at each passenger in turn. They were not questioned, and everyone was friendly towards them.

The bus discharged them in another small town, where they found a roadside restaurant and had a meal of coarse bread, mutton, lentils and beer. It was about six in the evening.

'*Geraldine* is about twenty miles from here, up a pretty wild track,' Sarah said. 'We were on our way to visit the site of an ancient city when the pump packed it in. We took it off the engine and I tried to have it repaired here, but had no luck.' She did not elaborate on the 'we'.

At a rank of taxis, she explained with gestures where she wanted to go. The driver of the first car had difficulty understanding her, and called a friend over from another. The friend had a few words of English, and used them to good effect. 'No go,' he said. 'Army stop.'

They were invited into the second driver's dilapidated Opel, and set off at speed into a gorge in the mountains, passing irrigated vegetable plots and tiny houses. After some distance, they had to stop where a makeshift barrier had been erected across the road. A corporal in fatigues talked to the driver, and then summoned a sergeant from a tent pitched nearby. Tony and Sarah got out of the car with their packs and talked to the sergeant. The taxi driver helped with the translation.

They learned that the road to Awari was closed because an Ethiopian offensive was expected. Orders were that no vehicle traffic was to be allowed on the road. When they showed the sergeant the water pump and explained that they only wanted to go a few miles higher up the pass to repair their Land Rover, he was sympathetic but firm. He had his orders.

Sarah asked if there was anyone about who could give them permission to travel higher. He indicated that they might get permission from the local commander in town. Not in the least discouraged, she smiled at the young man and asked if he would have any objection to them proceeding to the Land Rover on foot. He raised no objection - this eventuality had not been covered in his orders. They paid the taxi driver generously, accepted the loan of an army water bottle, and set off up the unpaved road in the failing light.

CHAPTER 13

He became aware of the stupendous panorama about him as, an hour after the day faded, the moon rose, lighting bare mountains towering above and illuminating thousands of bats patrolling the cliffs.

I had long finished my beer, but Tony Morganter had hardly touched his. He spoke with great intensity about his experiences, and I could see that the events remained vivid in his mind.

'That trek up the pass was one of the most difficult things I have ever done,' he said. 'I'd not slept in a bed the night before. Less than twenty-four hours after leaving London I found myself slogging up this endless bloody hill with a woman much fitter than myself. I've never been athletic and I'm not very strong. The altitude was over six thousand feet and it was terribly hot.'

The rays of the setting sun silhouetted her long legs as she climbed up the track ahead of him. He was reminded of the images of women from a Greek frieze he had seen on the Peloponnese.

The surface was treacherous, dusty and ill maintained. After the light faded, he tripped many times, his new boots uncomfortable. Shortage of breath limited his ability to hold a conversation, and he had to stop and rest many times. At hairpin bends he would stray off the dark road and into the bushes. The pungent odour of dry scrub made him sneeze. Seeds from the bushes stuck in his socks and scratched his ankles.

He became aware of the stupendous panorama about him as, an hour after the day faded, the moon rose, lighting bare mountains towering above and illuminating thousands of bats patrolling the cliffs. As they progressed, the light gradually worked itself down to the foot of the gorge, turning the rugged landscape into a Martian crater up which he stumbled after the tall woman with the heavy pack.

Aware of his distress, she distracted him by describing how she had come to be by herself with a broken down Land Rover in the wilds of Eritrea.

After Angela returned to England, Sarah had hoped to find two additional people in Cairo to join her in the Land Rover for the remainder of the journey. The campsite in Cairo was adjacent to a hotel that was a well-known stopping place for travellers on a budget. She placed an advertisement in the lobby of this establishment but had no responses; other adventurers had their own itineraries and transportation, or were going in different directions.

The Pinzgauer became the social centre of the campground and Werner's hospitality was boundless. Every night an impromptu party lasted into the small hours. Sarah stayed away. Gert no longer used his tent, and it became obvious that Werner was sharing his companions. Sarah disliked the way Werner looked at her when their paths crossed.

'The British Embassy advised her that she should not try to get into Sudan but put her Land Rover into a container and ship it to Kenya,' Tony said. 'This would be costly, and she was determined if at all possible to drive. She found a less expensive alternative: to ship the Rover on a small freighter to Masawa in Eritrea. Gert persuaded the Pinzgauer crew to do the same.

'Like me, I don't think Sarah realized the condition of Eritrea. She had done no research, as she had never intended to cross that country. She found, as I did, that the nation was at war and had been severely bruised by ongoing hostilities with Ethiopia. There was a veneer of normality about Masawa and Asmara, but the rest of the country was in a shambles. The front extended for the entire length of the country, and there was no way to cross the southern border.

'To get to Ethiopia from Masawa, their group faced a long, hot drive down the Red Sea coast to Assab, a difficult trek through the sands of the border to Djibouti, which was neutral, and then a relatively easy drive to Ethiopia.

'Her guidebook described the ruins of Talaba, an outpost of the Aksumite civilization and one of the more remote historical sites in Eritrea. They all wanted to see something of the country, and it was easy to persuade her companions to go there.'

'I've never heard of the place,' I confessed.

'I hadn't either, but I'm hooked now,' said Tony.

'They got permits in Asmara with no difficulty, and were halfway up the pass to Talaba when the bearings in the Land Rover water pump went, and they lost all the coolant. There was a poisonous argument about this between her and Gert. The Pinzgauer towed them the remainder of the way up the pass, and they camped at Talaba that night.'

'The water pumps generally give some warning,' I said. 'That was unlucky.'

'Things were already tense between Sarah and Gert. Their relationship had deteriorated into a power struggle. Her authority rested on her ownership of *Geraldine*, but it was undermined by the fact that he was welcome in the Pinzgauer. He was reluctant to accept her leadership, and every decision she made was challenged. Reading between the lines, I think he found her attractive and was hurt that she rejected his advances. This resulted in some pretty bizarre behaviour on his part, but I won't go there.'

'Angela didn't like him much either,' I said. 'That happens all the time. You can't be too choosy about who you take on a trip like that.'

Sarah, emotionally drained, lay in her sleeping bag fighting back tears while the others partied the night after the pump broke. She had grown to loathe the sound of the air conditioner on the Pinzgauer.

At first light the next morning, she read the workshop manual and began work. She drained the remains of the coolant into a basin, detached the hoses, and struggled with the many small bolts holding the radiator in position. She had lifted it out when Gert appeared, climbing down from the Pinzgauer. They worked in silence, unbolting the fan and detaching the pump from the timing cover.

The water pump spares kit contained a new shaft, seal kit and impeller. They had no press, but Gert thought it would be possible to drive the shaft out. Using two spare spring leaves as a makeshift anvil, he struck the end of the shaft with a hammer. On the fourth blow, the pump housing shattered into three pieces.

'They're pretty brittle,' I mused, 'but they could have got away with it. They should have heated it up.'

Tony continued. 'She admitted to me that at that point she'd become irrational. She blamed Gert for the breakage, although he had been following a procedure that she had agreed to. She castigated him in front of Werner while the two other women tittered in the background, looking dishevelled and wearing nothing but tee shirts. Gert then told her she had better find another sucker to travel with her in her Land Rover; he would carry on in the Pinzgauer. "You're nothing but an argumentative bitch," he yelled. It must have been quite a scene.

'Werner then made a proposal that she dismissed outright. He suggested, smirking, that she should abandon the Land Rover and continue on her travels down Africa in the bigger truck. She would be his guest and not pay anything, so that way she would actually save money.'

'That would have really pissed her off. She obviously hated him,' I said.

'She was so offended that she would not even get into the Pinzgauer with them. Gert removed his gear from the Land Rover and the big truck left. Werner's parting words were that he would inform the police that she had broken down.

'After this, she sat in the shade looking down on the ruins for a few hours and feeling a sense of relief. No traffic passed. She told me it was eerily quiet.'

'They just left her there? What jerks. Werner could have towed her out.'

'She packed all the tools and secured the vehicle as best she could. She left a dated note inside the windscreen saying something like "*Broken down. Returning with spares. Please do not touch*". She took her papers and the remains of the water pump in her pack and went down the pass on foot. A military truck gave her a lift to the nearest town. She spent a frustrating three days trying to find a new pump or somebody who could fix the old one, but, as we know, that model was outdated, and repairing the housing seemed beyond the capability of the locals. The people she talked to felt that she would have no luck in Asmara or Masawa either.

'She was desperate when she called me in Oxford.'

'We arrived at the Land Rover about midnight and I was pretty bushed. My feet were in bad shape; I don't think I could have walked another fifty feet. I sat down on a rock and felt my pulse racing. It took fifteen minutes for me to get my breath back.

'Sarah was pleased to find that nothing had been touched. She unrolled an awning she'd added to the side, opened some cans and threw together a meal: olives, sardines, crackers and beer.'

He had no sleeping bag, but she had a rug and a plastic tarpaulin for him. He took off his outer garments, wrapped himself in the rug and fell into a dreamless sleep in the moonlight on the ground beside his old Land Rover.

CHAPTER 14

A herd of goats appeared from below.

The crowd in the bar had thinned out.

'Let's have dinner.' I said. We went through to the hotel dining room.

'What I can't understand is exactly why you went. How did you get off work so easily, and what drove you to do it? You hardly knew the woman, and it must have been a pretty costly flight.'

He grinned ruefully. 'I know. It's probably the only time in my life that I've done something completely on impulse. It was the circumstances. It had a great deal to do with my wife. I suppose the realization had sunk in that getting married again was not the smartest thing I'd ever done. We have very little in common. Nothing, in fact.'

He toyed with his water glass. 'My first wife was an American - she was an associate professor when we met. Brilliant woman.' He looked up and smiled. 'She even understood my professional fascination with pre-Roman plumbing. We travelled the classical world together and she contributed to my best work. Christy's not like that at all. She sulks when I go away to a conference or a work site. She is deeply suspicious that I will have affairs with other woman; it's ridiculous, really - I'm not like that at all. Her first husband was a colleague and he left her for an art student, so I suppose it's understandable.'

With one finger he pushed breadcrumbs into a little circle on the tablecloth. 'We've agreed to divorce. It's quite a relief, really.'

He leaned back in his chair and looked me in the eye. 'As for getting away, I'm a tenured professor, and when you get to that exalted position in academia, you can do almost anything you like within reason. And you get to write off travel so it won't cost me a penny. In fact, the trip did pay off, in a way. I've written another paper.'

'When Sarah worked with me that weekend fixing *Geraldine*, she made a hell of an impression on me. It's not that she was a scholar; although she told me she had a master's degree. It was just that she had such a lust for life. I gathered that there had been a break-up with a man and that she was upset about it - she didn't give me the details. But she was so determined to live life to the fullest. And she was very beautiful in a big way. She had hands that seemed capable of anything and she didn't have scads of makeup smeared on. She got things done in a very purposeful fashion - far faster than I could do. She knelt down on the concrete floor, fixed brakes and had fun doing it. She has a wonderful sense of humour and made me laugh.

'When the opportunity came to do something for her, I jumped at it. If nothing else, it was an escape, and I suppose I had romantic notions...'

Who didn't? I thought.

Tony slept about two hours before he was awakened by a series of explosions. These seemed to emanate from the mountains to the south, but it was hard to tell, as the echoes reverberated amongst the summits and canyons around him. The moon was still high in the sky, and he could see Sarah was sitting up in her sleeping bag near him.

She told him the explosions had started some time before, and she could hear the rattle of small arms fire, which was beyond the range of his ears. The sounds he could hear were sporadic and nasty, coming in ragged bursts of five or six. He felt a long way from Oxford. Eventually the noises stopped and he fell asleep again.

He awoke early in the morning, stiff and sore. Sarah was asleep, only the long black hair showing from the mummy-like bag. He got up quietly and looked around; it was a breathtaking scene.

They were camped in a small valley leading off from the main run of the gorge. Below them, across the road, was a level plateau about ten hectares in size that was covered with rubble and ruins of a type he had never seen. The site extended to the lip of a precipice, the valley below in deep shadow. The road he had climbed the night before emerged from a cleft half a mile away under a vertical wall of rock hundreds of meters high. It crossed over a dry creek via a small metal bridge, and curved past him to continue unseen into the heights above.

Close to the Land Rover, against the side of a large boulder, was a lean-to shed with a rusted corrugated iron roof. The ground around it was covered with small balls of animal droppings, and a tenuous path led up the canyon beyond. Rusty tin cans and broken bottles showed through the packed earth. A round glass shard - the bottom of a brown bottle - had *Meliti Italia* cast on the surface. He was in an Italian midden from the days when the pass was built. Nineteen thirty-six, he estimated.

'I really needed to wash, so I took my pack and crossed the

road to the ruins, confident that such an extensive site must have had a source of water. I was right. Out of sight of the Rover, several hundred metres away on the upper fringe of the ruins, a green patch of reeds showed me where the water was. I found a *qanat*.'

The ancient tunnel emerged from a cliff, and dripping water filled a stone trough. The surrounding soil had been ground to dust by the hooves of animals. Bottles lying about showed that the locals knew the place. A stone furrow meandering along the contours of the hill indicated the source must once have had a greater flow. He speculated that the decline in the water supply might have led to the collapse of the city. He wondered if anyone - perhaps the Italians - had ever done any work on that.

He stripped and washed, using one of the plastic bottles as a shower. Birds swooped down to drink. He applied moleskin pads to his blistered feet. Wearing clean clothes, he felt a new man. He made a cursory professional examination of the site. He could see no evidence that anyone had excavated there before.

He returned to the Land Rover and found a tousled Sarah making coffee. He told her of his discovery, and watched the stove while she bathed.

They ate a simple breakfast, and stowed the sleeping gear. A herd of goats appeared from below driven by a ragged boy of about ten. He was a cheerful character, not in the least shy, who talked to them in a language of which they understood not a word. They gave him a granola bar. He marshalled the goats with a series of whistles and headed up the path away from the road. The pungent smell of the goats lingered in the still air.

After that, they turned their attention to *Geraldine*. They unpacked the engine parts onto a tarpaulin, and Sarah duly admired the green paint on the new pump. They removed the bonnet and cleaned the rusty surface of the timing cover, smeared the mating surfaces of the pump with *Permatex* and stuck a gasket on the joint. The pump fitted perfectly, and was soon bolted in place with new hoses from the spares locker. They were reinstalling the radiator when they heard the sound of a vehicle coming down the pass.

'It was military,' Tony said. 'A drab green jeep with two men inside. It screeched to a halt on the road when they saw us. The passenger got out and walked up to the Land Rover. He was a middle-aged man, obviously senior rank, and he spoke English.

'He saw what we were doing and introduced himself. He wanted to know how we came to be there given the pass had been closed for several days. We told him the story of the water pump and he frowned, annoyed to learn that we had been allowed to walk past the road barrier the previous night.

'He made it clear that we should leave as soon as possible, as there had been a major attack on the border and the Eritrean army was falling back. He took a radio from his belt and tried to talk to someone with it, but we heard nothing but static. He waved at the mountains, blaming them for the poor transmission.

At that point they all heard the staccato chop of an approaching helicopter. The officer sprinted to the jeep and sped off down the road in the little truck. The helicopter thundered into the valley. It too was painted green. It bristled with armament. It hovered menacingly about sixty feet above the plateau and slightly below them.

'I don't know much about modern weapons,' Tony said. 'I think it was some sort of rocket they used - there was a trail of smoke. It was aimed at the speeding jeep and missed, but the effect was devastating. There was a huge explosion just ahead of the vehicle and the whole cliff face collapsed. It was like an earthquake.' He put his hands over his face. 'I'll never forget that sound. The jeep was swept over the rim of the gorge, and the road was buried under millions of tons of rock. It continued to fall for minutes. The helicopter was completely engulfed in a cloud of dust and we lost sight of it, but we could hear the engines screaming and the throb of the blades.

'I found we were clinging to each other, stupefied, as the dust blew past us. Suddenly the helicopter was right there beside us. I thought it was going to land. We could see two men, one of them holding the handles of a big gun pointed directly at us. The pilot was shouting, but of course we couldn't hear him. The man behind the gun said something to him. The pilot then waved his hand dismissively at us and followed this with a thumbs-up gesture. He took the helicopter up vertically, blowing us over into the rocks. Sarah was on her knees laughing and sobbing. I was so scared that I had pissed my pants.

'A fire blazed far down where the rocks and the truck had fallen. Flames raced up the cliff in the dry scrub as far as the road and then died back. It was impossible for anyone in the vehicle to have survived.'

'My God. Were either of you hurt?'

'I was paralysed with fear, terrified that the helicopter would return. Sarah took charge of the situation immediately. There was blood running down from a cut on her forehead. She lifted her dress, wiped the blood away from her eyes. "We have to hide the Rover from the air," she said, and ordered me to help her cover the Land Rover with a layer of brush. We worked feverishly at that.

'"Shit," she said, looking down at her colourful dress. "I can be seen for miles in this." She pulled her dress over her head and threw it under the Land Rover. We finished camouflaging before she grabbed some other clothes from her pack. She said, not unkindly, "It looks as if you should change, too."

'She was amazing. Insisted that I put antiseptic cream on my scratches but would not allow me to dress the gash on her face. I tell you this, Giles - she's one to be with in a crisis.

'Our route out was irrevocably blocked. The road had disappeared for two hundred metres and climbing over the precarious jumble of still shifting rocks would be suicidal. Damn it, Giles. If we'd finished that job just thirty minutes earlier, we would have stolen a run.

'We were in trouble and we knew it. But what could we do? We carried on with the repair work, replacing the radiator and the fan shroud, then put the water from the washbasin back in the radiator. When this was not enough, we made several trips to the *qanat* to finish topping it off. The engine sounded pretty good when we started it.

I leaned back in my chair. The mild bespectacled academic looked back at me. The story was incredible, yet he could not possibly have made it up.

'We faced a dilemma,' Tony said. 'We knew the road forked before it reached the border, and the left hand fork led to Asmara and safety. This was the route the Pinzgauer had taken some days before. But we had no idea if this road had been taken by the Ethiopians, and we were terrified that the helicopter would see us if we moved. Even travel after dark was dangerous; we didn't doubt that it was equipped to hunt by night.

'We decided to stay where we were. We felt there was a chance that the boy - the goatherd - would return, and he might know of an alternative path that we could take down the gorge. A search party might be sent out for the officer killed by the helicopter. No one would come looking for us, as nobody knew where we were. The soldier at the gorge barricade might have reported our passing, but this seemed unlikely. Even if he had, we doubted anyone would have cared.'

The hot afternoon passed slowly and he somehow managed to sleep for an hour. Sarah, restless, had unpacked and re-stowed the Land Rover, organizing everything to her satisfaction, climbing up and down the ladder from the roof and removing and replacing the camouflage.

At around four that afternoon, they heard traffic coming down the pass, and dove behind some bushes. Two lorries filled with soldiers and a small field ambulance with red crosses came into view. The trucks had Eritrean markings, and passed where Tony and Sarah were hiding without anyone spotting them. The lorries pulled up by the landslide and men scrambled about, sending another wave of rocks crashing over the edge. Tony and Sarah heard orders being shouted, and the troops climbed out of the vehicles and regrouped near the bridge.

Sarah and Tony had a quick discussion at that point and decided to make themselves known to the troops. They felt they had little to fear from them. They went out onto the roadway holding their hands above their heads.

They were met at the bridge by a sergeant with a semi-automatic rifle in the crook of his arm. The troops squatted in the shade of the lorries. A young corporal who spoke good English with an American accent translated for the sergeant.

The troops were in poor condition, some with bandaged wounds and tattered clothes. They were mostly men but about one-third of them were women. They were the survivors, the corporal said, and the Ethiopians would be after them very soon. He had been at the university in Rochester in the United States, but had come home to fight in the war.

The sergeant indicated that they would escape by a path over the mountains. It was very difficult, he said, and he would not take civilians with him. He had two wounded in the ambulance, and would try to call in a helicopter to evacuate them once he could make radio contact with his base.

It turned out that one of the wounded in the ambulance was dead. Soldiers were ordered to move the body out. The remaining casualty was a young woman who had been wounded in the pelvis. She was conscious and sobbing with pain. There was blood on the stretcher. Someone gave her an injection and she became quiet.

The troops were moved back up the road to where *Geraldine* was hidden. They surrounded the Land Rover; curious to know whom these tourists were in the middle of their war. The ambulance was driven up and parked nearby. Tony noted it was a fairly new Land Rover model.

The lorries they destroyed by the simple expedient of lobbing grenades into the cabs until they caught fire and burned. The ambulance was immobilized by smashing the radiator with an emergency hatchet. To Tony it all seemed a senseless waste.

'They left us there,' he said quietly. 'The sergeant knew I would never make it over the mountains - I was very lame and limping with my blistered feet. They said that once they had radio contact, they would call for a helicopter to come in the morning for the wounded girl and fly us out. They gave us a radio to communicate with the helicopter. I think they'd written the girl off. They went up the mountain in single file following the path the goatherd had taken, and we never saw them again.'

CHAPTER 15

"I sat for thirty seconds sweating, staring at that high khaki-painted grille only six feet in front my face."

As evening fell, they set about doing what they could for the wounded girl. The ambulance was well equipped, but they had no more than basic first-aid training. Sarah did most of the work and Tony helped, fighting waves of nausea.

They found a second stretcher and assembled it on the floor. They opened two packages with Cyrillic labels, which contained sterile paper sheets. They spread these on the stretcher. Then, using a set of surgical scissors and fighting the tough cloth, they cut the woman's uniform completely from her body. There were two wounds: a neat flesh wound where a bullet had passed through her shoulder, and a nasty fist-sized hole in her hip with shattered bone visible.

There were plastic jerry cans of water in the ambulance. They filled a bowl with water and added a disinfectant that smelled like *Dettol*. They washed her carefully, he lifting her and Sarah washing her with the solution. She was very young, with tiny breasts, puppy fat and little pubic hair. The cheap pressed aluminium dog tag around her neck looked new.

'She couldn't have been sixteen,' he said soberly. 'Still a child.'

They moved her onto the second stretcher and dressed her wounds using sterile bandages from Sarah's supply.

When they finished the girl lay inert, with only a faint pulse in her neck and her body warmth to reassure them that she was still alive. They threw the remains of her clothing onto the filthy stretcher, took it outside, and used the rest of the disinfectant to wash the floor of the ambulance. It was now dark outside. There was nothing more they could do for her.

They heated a big pot of water and washed themselves. Neither of them felt like talking. The events of the day had been so far beyond the realm of normal experience that there was nothing to say. It was futile to speculate about what the morning would bring. They did not eat. At about nine, Sarah checked the girl and found her condition unchanged.

Sleep did not come easily to Tony that night. He lay awake with Sarah between him and the solid bulk of the Land Rover. The sky was overcast and the moon lightened the clouds, but couldn't break through them. Far overhead, an occasional jetliner moaned across the heavens. He wondered what route it was on. He pictured the passengers sleeping in the darkened cabins and the relaxed crews watching their instruments while Africa unrolled in the dark beneath them.

There were no explosions in the night.

'Next morning, I was first up and found the girl conscious and quiet, with dark fearful eyes appraising me. I smiled to reassure her, and brought her water in a tin cup which she drank while I supported her. She said nothing, lying back and closing her eyes after she had drunk. I sat with her until Sarah woke up, waving away the flies that settled on her face.'

Sarah made coffee, and they ate some biscuits. Tony washed himself at the *qanat*, and, when he returned, Sarah went and did the same. They took two aluminium chairs out of the Land Rover and sat listening for the sound of a helicopter, discussing what they would do if it were the hostile one. The girl lay in the back of the ambulance, moving occasionally and making little groans. No helicopter came.

As the day wore on it became warm and humid, and clouds obscured the sun. The girl had a fever now and was perspiring. Sarah gave her some Tylenol but had nothing else for her. She would not eat. Sarah was able to learn that her name was Mara and that she spoke no English or French. They took a small plastic fan off the dashboard of the ambulance and removed the battery from the engine compartment. The hot air blowing over Mara kept the flies away.

By evening they were worried. It was clear that if help did not come soon, the girl would die. They were almost out of bottled water, and did not think the water in the ambulance or the water from the *qanat* was safe to drink. There were two courses of action open to them.

'The first option was for one of us to cross the landslide, walk down the road and summon help by helicopter. Sarah was the obvious person to attempt to walk out, but the thought of her sliding over the cliff made me argue vehemently against the idea.'

They decided to pursue the second option. The next morning they would move the girl into the Land Rover and drive up the pass, trusting that the Ethiopians had pulled back and they would be able to get down the Asmara road. With this in mind, they folded up the rear seat and cleared out the cargo area, transferring as much as possible to the storage bins on the roof rack. This still left a lot of gear in the back, but they tied much of it down with bungee cords, leaving a clear space in the middle for the stretcher.

'We spent a troubled night. It rained constantly on the awning. Neither of us could sleep - we were too worried about the next day. The girl was unconscious again, and Sarah checked her several times during the night.'

Towards morning Tony had reached out and drawn Sarah to him. She did not resist and lay with her back against him and his arm around her until the grey dawn came.

'At first light I made coffee. The battery from the ambulance had run down and the fan was silent. We moved the unconscious girl on her stretcher into the back of the Rover. The handles of the stretcher prevented the rear door from closing, so I hacked them off using the saw on the Swiss knife.

'The rain stopped as we were about to leave, and the valley gleamed in the sun. You could see steam rising from the cliffs as they warmed. Sarah rode in the back to steady the stretcher. I felt tense about the responsibility of driving, but once I settled behind the wheel I knew it was going to be all right. I started the engine, let in the clutch and squeezed between the ambulance and the shed with inches to spare. She rocked like crazy when I crossed through the water in the ditch, and I had to use low range to get up to the road. Strange, really - suddenly *Geraldine* felt just right - I knew what I was doing. I had a wave of optimism. The tone of the engine was just as it used to be - it was as if Molly were still beside me. The big wire-spoked wheel had a reassuring grip. I knew we could save that woman no matter what. I accelerated up the hill and shifted into third - '

He paused in recollection.

'As the grade increased, I double declutched, shifted from third to second and swung round the first bend. Bloody hell! I nearly collided head on with a big Russian made truck that was inching down the slope with chains on the wheels. I pumped the brake nearly through the floor and *Geraldine* slewed like crazy - we almost went over the cliff before she shuddered to a stop. I sat for thirty seconds sweating, staring at that high khaki-painted grille only six feet in front my face. We were completely surrounded by Ethiopian soldiers.'

CHAPTER 16

A blasted tank lay on its side in a ditch with weeds growing from the turret.

'I was ordered out of the driver's seat at gunpoint, and made to stand with my hands grasping the roof gutter. They opened the rear door, ordered Sarah out and pulled the covering off the girl. An officer climbed in and examined her dog tag. He came out and a discussion took place amongst the men. There was some laughter, apparently prompted by jokes. Sarah ignored the guns and covered the girl with the sheet again.

'We were pushed away from the Land Rover, prodded by guns. One of the men got behind the wheel and, after experimenting with the gears, turned it with many reversals and drove it back down the road. They walked us back to our camp, where the Rover was again parked, and we were made to squat in the shed with a guard over us. The officer in charge talked excitedly on his radio. No one spoke any English.

'They unloaded the stretcher and laid the girl in the shade near us, spread a tarpaulin on the ground and unpacked the Land Rover. The officer examined everything, opening food containers and poking his fingers into boxes. He took our passports, compared our faces to the passport pictures and used his radio again.'

Tony and Sarah watched, helpless, as the main body of troops fanned out over the area with spades. There was no ambiguity about what they were doing. They were sowing mines.

The officer turned off the radio and the Land Rover was carelessly repacked. The stretcher was put back in. The young corporal who was guarding them was given instructions along with their passports. He motioned Tony towards the driver's seat and climbed into the passenger's seat with his submachine gun. Sarah got into the back with the stretcher. The officer in charge saluted and they drove out of the camp. The whole episode took only about half an hour, but Tony said he would remember it for the rest of his life.

'We ground up the twisting road. The greasy surface made driving difficult, and I had to use low range a few times and gun the motor. Several times *Geraldine* slid sideways - once nearly into the ditch. I caught a glimpse of Sarah's face in the rear view mirror. "Hubs," she said. "Engage the hubs." I stopped, pantomiming to the corporal that I needed to do something to the wheels. He let me out to do the work. The Rover steadied after that, and we all relaxed somewhat. Our corporal conveyed that his name was Arik. We gave him our names, which he repeated carefully. He took out a pack of cigarettes from his tunic and offered one to me. Sarah said "No!" in a commanding voice and he put the pack away again.

'Shortly after that she noticed that Mara was conscious, so she demanded that I stop, gave the girl some water and set about rearranging the back of the Rover.

'Arik got out and lit his cigarette. I followed him. The view was magnificent. We were very close to the summit of the pass, and the morning air was clear. The great gash of the gorge twisted away below us with myriad small barren side valleys. We were higher than many peaks in the foreground. Far away on the horizon was the hard blue line of the Red Sea.

'On the other side of the road, a blasted tank lay on its side in a ditch with weeds growing from the turret. It had been there a long time.

'Arik finished his cigarette and tossed his head to indicate we should proceed. I drove on as gently as possible over the top of the pass. Beyond was twenty kilometres of high barren plateau. I kept an eye on the temperature gauge, expecting trouble, but the motor ran flawlessly. We reached a place where there was a fork in the road and slowed down, as there was a concentration of trucks and pedestrians. I took the right fork as Arik indicated.

'We crossed a heavily fortified area, like a scene from World War I. A group of Eritrean soldiers who had been herded into a field sat guarded by a cordon of armed men. The road was crudely bulldozed through trenches and thickets of barbed wire, and demanded low gear. The detritus of war - piles of expended ammunition and broken equipment - lined the road. With this behind us, I drove downhill through scrubland and entered a town that seemed surrounded by a refugee camp - shacks covered with blue plastic tarps. Rows of military vehicles were drawn up in the central square. Arik asked directions of a sentry, and I was directed to a canvas field hospital. Mara and her stretcher were taken inside. We never saw her again.

'Back in the centre of the town, I drove the Land Rover into a walled enclosure behind one of the larger art-deco-style buildings with a flag outside. A small group of soldiers was waiting for us. Arik took the keys from the ignition. Despite my protestations I was separated from Sarah and hustled along a corridor, down some steep steps and into a cell.'

Tony's cell had a wrought-iron gate and a barred aperture high in the wall. There was a low cot with a coarse blanket, and a metal bucket. A plastic bottle of brownish water with no cap was on the floor near the door. He was extremely indignant. He had never been in any trouble with authority in his life.

He inverted the bucket and stood on it, but he was not tall enough to see out of the high window. He went to the door and shouted 'Sarah' at the top of his voice, but there was no reply.

He sat on the cot. Outside, he could hear the sounds of people walking and the grinding noise of trucks. At one point, two men had a conversation close outside, and he smelled tobacco smoke. He shouted up at them and a brown arm came down through the ventilator holding a lighted cigarette. He did not accept this offering, and after a few seconds it was withdrawn. There was a laugh outside and the voices moved off. Smoke drifted about for some minutes and cleared other odours from the cell. At times Tony could hear muffled voices and furniture sliding across the floors above. As the afternoon wore on, all sounds diminished and the flies circling the room settled on the walls out of his reach.

As dusk deepened, there were sounds of activity in the passageway. An armed guard appeared, accompanied by a small man dressed in a smock who was carrying a plate of food and a can of Pepsi Cola. He slid the plate of food under the gate, opened the can of cola with a flourish and handed it to Tony through the bars, then presented him with a handwritten bill. Tony ignored the bill and the food. 'Where is my wife?' he demanded. 'I am entitled to contact the British Embassy.' The two men outside did not understand him. The guard reached into his pocket and produced a dirty bank note and showed it to him. He was clearly expected to pay for the food. He found the roll of notes he had exchanged in Asmara in his pocket and gave one to the small man. The two examined the note carefully. The guard shrugged, and the small man resignedly tucked the note into a pocket. Shortly after that the single light bulb in a wire cage above his head went on.

He was hungry and the food - a sort of stew - smelled delicious. He had no eating utensils and had to hold the plate to his lips and shovel the food into his mouth with his fingers.

At seven the light went out.

Early the next morning the same guard appeared with a basin of water, a tiny bar of strongly scented soap and a thin towel. Tony would have liked to shave as he had not done so for three days, but no razor was forthcoming. He demanded a change of clothes but they did not understand him. The small man returned with some coarse bread and a tin cup of coffee, but did not ask for more money.

Tony had heard rain in the night, but now the clouds had cleared and a beam of sunlight projected a distorted image of his bars onto the dirty wall. The image moved slowly down, elongated and extinguished before it reached the floor.

Two soldiers came for him in the afternoon and he was taken upstairs. One of the men said, 'Generale', and Tony was led into a big office, where a small, elderly man in uniform was sitting behind a desk. He rose as Tony entered and shook his hand.

'Good afternoon, Dr. Morganter,' he said pleasantly. 'Please sit down.'

Tony was a reasonable man, but he felt that he had been subjected to an unreasonable and uncomfortable detention. He demanded to know why he was a prisoner. He demanded to know where Sarah was. He demanded to be put in contact with his embassy.

The small man did not answer him immediately. He got up, went to the window and watched some soldiers performing a drill in the square. Tony looked at the desk. Arrayed in a neat row were items he recognized. There was the black two-way radio, a parcel of the Russian field dressings, his binoculars and his wallet. There was also a small stack of U.S. dollars, a black box with protruding wires and a pistol with a long barrel. The general turned back from the window.

'Before you demand anything,' he said, 'I demand some answers. You appear to be an Englishman - Anthony Morganter. According to your passport, you are a university professor. You had in your possession an open return ticket that shows you left from London for Asmara on Friday of last week.

'Why, Anthony Morganter, do you appear in Ethiopian-controlled territory a few days later driving a Land Rover containing a wounded Eritrean soldier and an Eritrean communications radio? You have no permission to be in this area. You do not even have a visa for Ethiopia. You were apprehended lending support to my nation's enemies. In your truck there were over two thousand U.S. dollars in a secret box in the engine compartment. There was a global positioning device hidden behind the dashboard designed to transmit your location to a satellite. There was an Israeli military firearm hidden in the driver's door. All very suspicious. Under Ethiopian law, we could execute you as a spy and the woman with you also.

'Tell me your story, Dr. Morganter. And it better be a good one.'

CHAPTER 17

*It was surprisingly heavy and he saw that the finely chiselled
decoration was exquisite.*

Tony was stunned. He had expected to have to make an explanation of events and to be released with an apology for his detention. The fact that the Ethiopians might interpret his and Sarah's actions as serious offences had not occurred to him. He decided that the best way to absolve himself was to tell the general his whole story, concluding by saying that he had no intention of contributing anything to either side in the war and that he and Sarah had acted with humanitarian intent. He denied knowledge of the money, the position transmitter or the gun. The general heard him out patiently.

At the end of his narrative the general looked at him. 'This is a crazy story,' he said. 'What you are telling me is that you do not even know this woman well and your whole journey was made on impulse. To me this is fantastic.

'It will be a wonderful bit of publicity to have you both on trial as spies or mercenaries. You and the woman will have your faces on the front pages of all the newspapers. Ethiopia will be in the news. All people in the West know of Ethiopia is propaganda, pictures of starving refugees, stories of vast military expenditures and abuses of human rights. A trial like this would raise the profile of our cause internationally, and there are men in our government who are already rubbing their hands. They will raise one hell of a stink about British spies working with the Eritreans.

'I don't think you will be shot, Dr. Morganter. But say we take a hard line? Mr. Blair will have to get involved. Your ambassador will send someone to see you in your cells, months will go by and there will be a lot of diplomatic manoeuvring. Our case will have to be plainly stated. We did not ask for this war. All Ethiopia desires is secure borders and access to the Red Sea on reasonable terms.'

'That's crazy,' Tony said. 'No one would believe you. Do I look like a spy?'

'Beside the point,' said the general. 'There is so much ridiculous propaganda put out about this conflict that nobody believes anything anymore. The Internet is full of stupid stories. One believes what one wishes to believe.'

He shouted something to the sentry outside. Sarah was brought in. She had changed her clothes and looked tired. She did not sit down but stood behind Tony and rested a hand on his shoulder. He raised his arm and pressed her hand between his shoulder and the stubble on his cheek.

'So,' the general said, 'we will try to get to the bottom of this. Dr. Morganter has told me his story and it agrees with yours.

'This morning I took a flight over the Sharmar valley. You are correct. The road is completely closed - the crew of the helicopter that accomplished that will all get medals, I think. I saw the burned out trucks and the remains of an ambulance. There has been a fire as you described.

'You have accounted for the radio and the medical supplies. These binoculars are a toy and not the equipment of a serious spy. But you have not accounted for this money, madam, and your explanation of the name on your passport and the consular notes there are interesting. You cannot explain this position transmitter and have not accounted for this weapon, which is made in the same country that makes the cluster bombs that our enemies have dropped recently on a school, killing many children.'

'The money is mine,' she said. 'Before I came to Africa, I consulted a man who had driven in Africa many times before. And he advised me to have constructed in my Land Rover a hidden compartment with some money, so if ever I needed emergency cash I would have it. And I have told you; the name on the passport is my married name.

'I know nothing about the transmitter and cannot explain it. I was not aware of its existence. The gun is not mine and I did not know it was hidden in the door. On my journey from England, I had a companion in the Land Rover. He was formerly a paratrooper in the South African army. His name is Gerhard du Plessis. I think he hid this gun in the door without my knowledge - perhaps to use it for defence against bandits. We argued two weeks ago and he decided that he no longer wished to travel with me. He left me and went on in the company of a Swiss man and two East European women. In his anger, I think he forgot to take his gun. These people are intending to drive from Assab to Djibouti in a Pinzgauer and enter Ethiopia that way. When he comes - and if this is his gun - he will admit it, for he is an honest man. I say this even though I think he is no longer my friend.'

'So you say,' said the general. 'You have told me this tale. But what sort of man would leave his woman abandoned in the mountains on the Horn of Africa?'

'I was not his woman,' she said, 'and I did not fear the Eritreans.

In my stay in Eritrea, I was always treated kindly and with respect.'

He let that pass. 'I do not think they will find it easy to go from Assab to Djibouti,' he said. 'The whole area is a mess. The people in Djibouti are not letting these problems cross their border. In fact, I think the Eritreans will not even give them a permit to drive to Assab. So I doubt if your Mr. du Plessis will be in Ethiopia soon. If he does show up, I think he will be turned back. We don't like people who smuggle guns.'

He turned sideways and looked out of the window again. 'Your story has the ring of truth,' he said. 'You English are crazy. And you have too much money. Why would a man fly thousands of miles and spend' - he picked up the ticket - 'eight hundred and twelve pounds, to deliver a water pump? And why would a woman - who could have a nice home and children in a happy country - voluntarily buy an old Land Rover and drive through areas like this where there is so much death and misery?'

He sighed. 'I have been in this army forty years. I have served under an emperor, a socialist dictator and this new 'democracy'. As a child I learned English, as I went to school with the children of the British civil servants who were here after the Second World War. As a young man I was trained in the United States for Haile Selassie. When the Americans left, I was trained by the Russians in Ukraine and first fought in this area against extremists from Tigre and Eritrea. I have fought alongside Cubans against Somalis in the Ogaden. I have been overseas on purchasing missions buying arms - to England, even. We are a proud people - do you know we have never been a colony of any other country?

186

'I fought against the rebels when we lost Massawa and Asmara, and I like to think it was I who persuaded Mengistu to get out when he did. I was at the London conference under that American Herman Cohen and helped negotiate the partition of my country into two. I dreamed of a time when there would be no more fighting and I could enjoy a quiet retirement. *Ethiopia*, I thought, could become a peaceful democracy and set an example to other countries in Africa.

'When these current problems with the Eritreans started and they occupied Badme, I got a call from the president, even though I am Amhara who fought against him when he was a Tigrean partisan. "Old Fox," he said, "we need you back in uniform," and so I came here to fight Eritreans once again. My heart is not in it this time. So many young men - and women - killed. So many maimed. Like the girl you brought here yesterday - she will live, I'm told.

'This war is over. What you have witnessed was merely a sortie. One of the many little skirmishes we must fight over thousands of miles of border every week.

'The main action now will be at conferences, and there will be resolutions at the UN and perhaps toothless blue soldiers sitting on Ethiopian hillsides to keep the peace - just as in Lebanon or Cyprus. They may even succeed in their mission, and there may be peace. I will go back to my retirement. These young people' - he waved his hand towards the troops in the square - 'will go back to their villages and thank God they were not killed or wounded in this senseless affair.

'I have not told the people in Addis Ababa your story. They only know we have apprehended two stupid tourists. They have not seen your passports. Do not speak of soldiers in your Land Rover to anyone. This gun and the position transmitter do not exist.' He dropped them in a drawer. 'Take your money, Miss Oakes, and hide it better in future.

'Dr. Morganter, tomorrow you will fly to Addis Ababa with me on a military flight. We will leave from this office at nine in the morning. You are detained as you are in Ethiopia without a visa, and I think your embassy people will put you on a plane to England very quickly. They will realize we could have used you if we had chosen.

'Miss Oakes, I will give you a permit to drive in the military zone for three days only, and I wish you a pleasant stay in Ethiopia. Do not take any photographs until you are south of Mekele.

'You will stay in this building tonight and may have the liberty of the centre of the town. Do not attempt to make any telephone calls, and stay away from military installations and the refugee camp.'

Sarah picked up the money, then laid one note back on the table. 'The men who searched my truck could easily have taken this money and not told anyone about it. I'd appreciate it if you would please give this to them to show my thanks.' The general nodded.

'And I thank you for letting me continue on my way. Would it not be possible for Dr. Morganter to drive with me to Addis Ababa if a direct route is taken?' He shook his head. Tony tried to protest but was silenced with a look.

188

'General,' she said, 'last night I could not sleep. Yesterday, when we were in the Shamar valley, the troops that arrested us were digging holes and planting mines. There is a boy living there who keeps goats. He is about ten years old and will be killed senselessly up there by himself and so will people who come after him. Please have your men go back and remove those mines.'

The general showed them to the door and gave some orders to the sentry. Orders, they felt, that related to their confinement. Then he turned to Sarah. 'I will see what I can do,' he said impassively. *

Sarah had slept in a corner of a first-floor room that must once have been a meeting room, as it was furnished with a large and dusty oval table and a set of dilapidated chairs. The clock on the wall was missing its pendulum. The contents of the Land Rover had been dumped in a heap on the floor. A few doors down the hall was a revolting hole-in-the-floor toilet with a large, dirty washbasin. Tony found his pack, took out his last change of clean clothes and washed himself as best he could in cold water. He returned to find Sarah sitting on the edge of the table, swinging her legs like a child.

'You know,' she said, 'we have been together only four days and it seems like a month. So much has happened. I feel totally drained. I won't pack *Geraldine* tonight. I'm sorry I got you into this mess, but I'm not sorry you're here.'

He sat and waited in the big room, pretending to read her guidebook to Ethiopia and watching her out of the corner of his eye. She fetched water in a plastic basin - the same one that had contained the engine coolant - and, putting a towel on her shoulders, proceeded to wash her hair. She returned to the lavatory twice for more water. She shook her hair out vigorously, bending at the waist and tossing her head back and forth so her breasts swung and drops of water mottled the whitewashed walls. She put her damp hair up with a clean ribbon, and fetched more water to wash blue underclothes that she hung on the backs of chairs to dry.

From a plastic toilet bag came lotion that she rubbed over her face and neck. She replaced the dirty patch of sticking plaster on her forehead. She dressed in a clean blouse and a skirt from her pack and replaced the unlaced boots she had been clomping around in with a pair of canvas shoes. She was beautiful.

'Take me out to dinner,' she said.

The sentry at the foot of the stairs jumped to his feet when they appeared, and followed them at a distance as they crossed the darkening square towards the shops beyond the rows of trucks. People looked at them curiously, and children followed them.

They negotiated a crowded market and found a small restaurant, where men in uniform sat drinking beer with women in bright clothes. The proprietor greeted them in English and gave them an outdoor table on a porch overlooking the street. They requested the same beer that the soldiers were drinking and after rejecting a dish of raw minced meat, they ordered a meal of chicken, spicy sauce and vegetables. As it became dark, the waiter brought out a kerosene lantern; the power in the town was out.

Their guard sat at a table just inside the door, watching them closely. They asked the waiter to serve him a meal.

The beer was cold. There were occasional bursts of laughter from the soldiers. Wind stirred the air, relieving the heat of the day and bringing with it the smell of cooking. For the first time in five days, Tony relaxed.

A dark woman, dressed in layers of torn, dirty clothing and leading a small child, padded onto the veranda from the street. She came directly to their table and nodded without speaking. She opened her hand to show them a worn beaded necklace with a curiously wrought pendant in the shape of an elongated Maltese cross. She was obviously offering to sell it. Tony took it from her and held it close to the lamp. It was surprisingly heavy and he saw that the finely chiselled decoration was exquisite. 'It's beautiful,' he said, showing it to Sarah. 'It's funny - I don't think it's Ethiopian. More like a Tuareg piece. I've seen things like this in museums.'

The proprietor came out with their meal. He said something severely to the woman, who reached out her hand for the necklace. Sarah asked, 'Why is she selling this?'

He translated. 'She says she needs money for food,' he said.

'It's beautiful,' said Sarah. 'Where did she get it?'

He laughed. 'These country people make things like this for foreigners. They melt old coins and hammer them into such shapes.'

Tony asked, 'How much does she want for it?'

The woman, when asked, held up three fingers. 'Three hundred birr,' their host said. 'Truly this woman is a thief. I am sure you could buy it for half of that in the market.'

Tony did a quick mental calculation. 'I have no birr,' he said. 'But if you give this woman three hundred birr, I will give you thirty English pounds or some Eritrean Nafka.'

'Give me fifty dollars,' said the man. 'I do not know pounds and Eritrean is worthless.'

Tony borrowed the dollars from Sarah. The transaction was done and the woman left. They started on their meal.

'I owe you for the water pump anyway,' she said.

'What will you do now?' he asked. It was inconceivable to him that she would travel alone in this strange country.

'Go south,' she said. 'I'm going to visit someone in a place called Zomba in Malawi and there is a lot to see between here and there.'

'Would you like to meet me in Addis Ababa?' he asked hesitantly. 'I don't like the idea of you travelling alone. I might be able to get a visa there and I could come down some of the way with you.'

'No,' she said. He felt rejected. They finished their food in silence, paid for their meal and left.

The market had closed. A curfew was in effect and the streets were deserted. Walking back across the dark square, he was thankful for the guard following fifty yards behind.

They went up the stairs to the room with the table.

'Stay here,' she said. 'They won't mind.'

She went out to the lavatory, and while she was gone he made himself a bed out of tarpaulins and the fringed rug on the floor on the far side of the room. When he came back from washing himself, she had unrolled her foam pad and sleeping bag on the table, and moved his arrangement up beside her own. A stubby candle was burning in an old ashtray. She was lying in her sleeping bag with arms and shoulders exposed. He saw how much paler her skin was where it had not been in the sun. He stripped to his underwear and got under the rug.

They lay in silence for a while in the heat. It was quiet in the big room, and the candle flame was absolutely steady. Outside dogs barked.

She propped herself on her elbow. 'Thank you for offering,' she said. 'It's very kind of you. If you were just hitching along the road and I'd picked you up, I'm sure it would have worked out fine. But I know, deep inside somewhere, you want more of me and I can't give you what you want. Staying together would simply make things worse. It's not that I don't like you. You are a wonderful, interesting man. But I think it will be better for both of us if I go on alone and you go back to Oxford and sort things out.'

He lay there sadly, knowing she was right.

After a while he sat up drawing the rug around his knees. He reached over to a chair for his pants and took the Tuareg pendant from a pocket. 'I bought this for you,' he said. 'Think of me and our adventure when you wear it.'

She took it from him and threw back the edge of the unzipped sleeping bag. She sat naked and cross-legged, then, raised her hands, pulled the necklace over her head and untangled it from the hair about her shoulders. The silver metal reflected the candle flame amongst the freckles on her chest.

She put her arms around him and drew his thin body to her. Her abundance surrounded him and the words seemed to come from far above him. 'I will never forget you,' she said.

Then she released him and blew the candle out.

When Tony woke it was light. There were cocks crowing and bustle in the square. Sarah was dressed and sorting out the mess of belongings on the floor.

He helped her with the loading. She scrambled up the ladder to the roof rack and he passed her bits and pieces that she stowed efficiently in the aluminium boxes. The Land Rover looked tidy, well organized and empty when she was finished. A small boy appeared with a bucket and offered to wash it.

They came for him in an old Peugeot. She kissed him and held both his hands in hers. He got into the car and was driven to a dusty airstrip nearby. The aircraft was old and may have been a DC3. As it lumbered down the runway and took off, he saw her watching and waving, standing by the Rover on the track parallel to the runway.

The embassy people collected him from a military base near Addis Ababa. He was interviewed by the military attaché and given a room in a good hotel, The next morning he was driven to the civilian airport. He took a flight to Cairo and a the next day arrived home in England. He had been away less than a week.

They were closing the bar and dimming the lights. I was having a second late night.

'That's an incredible story,' I said. 'Did you ever hear from her again?'

'Not directly,' Morganter said. 'I didn't expect to, really.'

'What was the problem with her passport, and what was her married name? Why did she have a GPS transmitter in the Land Rover?'

'She told me she had not known about the transmitter but had an idea who had hidden it. I don't think I heard the name. And there was some diplomatic problem with the passport. About two months later, I got a draft from her bank for the water pump. I never paid her for my bus fare or for that last dinner we had.

'I hope she achieved what she set out to do. I'd like to know how she's doing if you find her. She's a very brave and resourceful woman.' **

---

* *General Akando Derina now lives in retirement in Ghwer near Addis Ababa. He remembers these events well and volunteered the information that Sarah's progress through Ethiopia was closely monitored by the army and the police to ensure she came to no harm. He describes her as one of the most interesting women he has ever met, but still harbours the suspicion that she was working for one of the British intelligence agencies at the time they met.*

** *Professor Anthony Morganter continues to pursue his passion for pre-Roman plumbing from his new rooms above the quad. You can read his paper 'New Insights into Aksumite Irrigation' in a recent edition of Minerva magazine.*

CHAPTER 18

*"Once you've seen their ugly mugs a few times,
the novelty wears off."*

I drove the thirty miles home in the early hours of Monday morning feeling dead tired but at the same time exhilarated. I was living a vicarious adventure. Mulling over the stories I had heard over the course of the last week made me realize how humdrum my life had become compared with that of Sarah Oakes. I wondered where she was. Still in Malawi, or perhaps, as Angela had implied, she had finished with Africa and taken her Land Rover off to another continent. Maybe she was now in Asia or Australia.

I was awakened by the llama peering in my window. It was well after ten. I made myself breakfast, pulled down a copy of Lonely Planet's *Africa on a Shoestring*, and learned that I did not need a visa for Malawi, Mozambique, Zimbabwe or South Africa.

Zomba is a former colonial capital of Malawi that I had last visited back in 1995 when I guided my last northbound group for *International Adventure Tours*. I remembered it as a charming university town. The president, Hastings Banda, had a palace there when he was in power. Overlooking the town is the Zomba Plateau, reached by a winding road leading up from the plains. There is a good campsite on the plateau near the charming Che Kawa Hotel. The hotel has one of the nicest little bars in Africa and a sweeping view of the Shire valley. There is good hiking amongst the peaks of the plateau. I wondered if they still carried logs out from the plantations on the heads of porters. It would be good to see Zomba again, and, as it was a small town, I thought I would have a fair chance of finding out whom Sarah had visited.

If I failed to find her in Malawi, I reasoned, I would fly on to Johannesburg and put out as many feelers as I could amongst the Land Rover fraternity in South Africa.

I called my travel agent, had her book me a flight to Lilongwe on Wednesday, and asked her to get me a hire car in Malawi for a few days. I also added on open flights to Johannesburg and Cape Town. I decided to stay Tuesday night in London and buy myself a few clothes for the trip. It was exciting to be going to Africa again.

I went over to the farmhouse to tell Jean and Bill about my plans and see how the patient was getting on. Sitting in a sunbeam on the kitchen doorstep, looking pleased with himself, was Horatio.

'Don't pick him up,' said Jean. 'I think he's got some broken ribs and it hurts him if you handle him. But he's getting better every day.'

'It's the beer,' said Bill. 'If you open a beer anywhere in the house, that cat's right there. He's got an incredible nose for it.'

Tea was made and I told them what I had learned the night before. 'What a story,' said Bill. 'You've covered a lot of ground in just a week. What makes you so sure she's in Malawi?'

'I'm not at all sure she is in Malawi,' I said. 'But at this point it's all I've got to go on. Zomba is a pretty small place, and people there are sure to have noticed her even if she just passed through. If she never got to Malawi, she's probably in Tanzania or Kenya. If she did pass through Zomba, chances are she went to South Africa. I doubt she would be in Zimbabwe - the country's almost bankrupt, and there are all the problems with "freedom fighters" on farms.

'That girl Angela said Sarah was planning to drive around the world. If that is the case, she may have shipped the Rover from Cape Town or Durban, and I may be able to find a shipping agent who remembers putting the Rover into a container.'

I told them I would be away at least two weeks, and Jean promised to water my plants and continue looking after Horatio. She reluctantly accepted that I would not be able to attend her dinner with Anna on Saturday night.

That afternoon I called Melvin Noor and was put directly through to him.

'Progress report,' I said, and filled him in on what I had found out during the last week. I concluded by telling him I was booked to fly to Malawi on Wednesday evening.

'That's excellent,' he said. 'I don't know if we have anybody in Malawi, but if you need any help in South Africa, call Janice Southy at our office there. And keep me posted.'

I called Susan Minter at the Royal Geological Society and she told me she had photocopied the Du Plessis article. I agreed to pick it up from her office on Wednesday before my flight.

That evening, as I was organizing my pack, the telephone rang.

'Mr. Jackson?' asked a very Australian voice.

'That's me,' I said.

'I'm Roy Woodly. I drive for Bill Saunderson on his Africa trips - he asked me to give you a call. Said you were looking for Sarah Oakes driving an old series Land Rover. You're in luck - I bumped into her last November in Uganda.'

'That's terrific, Roy,' I said. 'I had no idea she was going anywhere near Uganda. Did Bill tell you why I want to track her down?'

'No, he didn't,' he said.

'It's her Rover I'm after,' I explained. 'Have you got a minute to tell me about it?'

'Not right now,' he said. 'I'm only in town for a few days and I'm late for dinner with a friend.'

'Where are you?' I asked.

'Parsons Green - in London,' he said.

'How about dinner tomorrow night?' I asked. 'On me. I'm staying at the Penta in Earl's Court. I'm off to Malawi the next day, but I'd really like to hear about your meeting with Sarah before I go.'

He agreed to that, and promised to meet me at the Penta the following evening at seven.

I am not a suitcase traveller. There are times when I have travelled with suitcases, but I have never really been comfortable with them. When I was married we had a lot of suitcases. Now I am back to a rucksack. It is an old one with an internal frame. I carry a minimal amount of easy-to-wash cotton clothes, a small toilet bag and a few other necessities.

Knowing it was almost winter in southern Africa and would be cold and wet at times; I put in a black Guernsey jersey and an oiled cloth coat. I took my desert boots and no shoes - I always buy shoes in South Africa, where they are a great bargain and there's lots of choice in size fourteen. The pack still looked empty, so I stuffed it with clothes that I no longer wore. Used clothing is always appreciated in Africa.

I decided against taking my sleeping bag, as my employers were paying for hotels and I was unlikely to need it. I took my faithful old Canon camera and a pair of binoculars.

Jean took me into Bournemouth the next morning, where I collected my airline ticket. At the station she gave me a kiss on the cheek and told me to behave myself. I checked into the hotel before noon, had a sandwich in a café and picked up a brown manila envelope from the Royal Geological Society. I went to the Africa Bookstore and purchased maps. I did not think I was going to have a problem with malaria driving around in a car, but, to be on the safe side, I got a prescription for some Lariam tablets and collected them from Boots.

When I got back to the hotel, I went directly to the bar. There was no mistaking Roy Woodly - he was chatting to the barmaid with a pint in his hand. I introduced myself and was given a beer.

Fit, fair-haired, barrel-chested and small, he reminded me of a bantamweight boxer. He was about fifteen years younger than I, and had one of those pink complexions you find on fair individuals who spend a lot of time in the sun without ever getting a true tan.

'So you're off to Malawi tomorrow,' he said. 'One of my favourite countries. And you don't have to drive there in a Bedford. Be bloody nice for a change.'

I told him I had done my share of Bedford driving over the

years; this got us into a discussion about our respective careers.

Roy was one of those rare individuals who can live without having a home, being quite happy to be on the road all the time. He enjoyed working for Bill Saundersen, whom he considered an 'all right bloke'. From Fremantle in Western Australia, he went to work as a welder on oil rigs in Singapore and, from there, set off to see the world. He crossed the Bay of Bengal to Calcutta and made his way overland to Europe. He had helped one of Bill's other drivers in some way whilst in Pakistan. Impressed, this man referred him to Bill. He had signed up with World Safaris when he reached England four years before, and had been driving for Bill ever since.

Africa was his favourite route. He had developed friendships with locals throughout the continent, and maintained good relationships with people at border crossings - essential in his trade. He spoke with affection of his truck, which had been up and down the continent thirty-seven times. He avoided long-term entanglements with his female customers - the downfall of many of Bill's long-distance guides.

'Uganda's on my regular route. Visiting the mountain gorillas in the Parc National des Virunga just over the border in Congo is a high point on the itinerary. I like the parks in Congo rather than Uganda as the hike in is not so tough and the bush is not as thick. You've got better chance of seeing the buggers. I don't go on the hikes myself anymore - once you've seen their ugly mugs a few times, the novelty wears off.

'I had nine guests on that trip who signed on in Jo'burg. They spent two days over the border so I had some time to myself. When

I pulled into Kisoro campsite, there was an old 109 Land Rover parked with UK plates. Pretty well set up. Looked like they knew what they were doing.

'I did some maintenance on the Bedford, and then, late in the day, a local minibus pulled in with the Land Rover guys, two men and a woman. They were speaking French. I went over and introduced myself. The woman was called Sarah - I knew she was English the moment she opened her mouth. The two men were Belgians, medical blokes taking a break from Rwanda.'

Roy was invited for dinner with them, and learned about *Medicins Sans Frontieres* and the work in Rwanda. 'Sarah told me she was going to Zomba in Malawi, so I showed her the best route down the west side of Lake Victoria. She told me she had come down through Eritrea and Ethiopia. I was interested in the route until she told me about the war. I'm not into that kind of drama myself.'

He slept in the following morning and did not see the Land Rover leave.

His party showed up the next afternoon at about one. They loaded the Bedford and headed north towards Ruwenzori. He followed a route he knew well up secondary roads near Butugota, planning to camp at a mission where he was always welcome.

Five miles from his destination, he rounded a bend in the road and stopped.

'The bridge had been washed out completely and it must have been pretty recent. To get past, the locals had made a track through the bush to the creek and up the other side. The creek was running pretty strong and a Toyota van was lying on its side in the water with a broken windshield - obviously rolled down the hill. Sarah was parked on the opposite bank with a winch cable down to the wreck and there was a crowd of guys all shouting at her. The road was completely blocked with a lineup both ways.'

CHAPTER 19

"A path leads up from there to a kloof with fresh water pools."

Roy's crew jumped down from the Bedford to get closer to the action. Roy sat in the cab of the Bedford for a few minutes by himself, watching the activity below and picking his teeth with an acacia thorn. He then took off his boots, slid down into the creek, waded through the current and scrambled up the opposite bank to the Rover.

He was a person of wide experience in similar situations and had a natural authority to which others deferred. The two doctors had done well in patching up the cuts of the van's passengers and putting a splint on the driver's broken arm, but knew little about vehicle recovery. As often happens in such situations, too many people were giving contradictory advice. Sarah was sitting in the driver's seat, bombarded by conflicting commands.

Roy leaned in the driver's window. 'This is a right balls up,' he pronounced. 'Can I help?'

'Please do,' she said. 'Everybody's shouting at me and I've never really had to use the winch before.'

'Okay,' he said. 'What gear are you in? First? No? Just hold down the clutch and put her in reverse for a sec and pay out a bit more cable.' He watched her put the Rover in reverse and went around to the front as she did this. The cable went slack and he released the dog clutch and pulled a few more yards off the drum. He went back to the door. 'Now,' he said, 'I'll go down there and see if I can sort things out. Turn her off. When you see me gesturing towards you, restart the engine and engage the clutch slowly and gently in second gear. Don't use first. If I hold up my hand, stop immediately.'

He went down to the overturned van and assessed the situation. The driver had obviously lost control on the downward slope and locked his wheels to the right. The vehicle had rolled completely over and landed on its side with the wheels facing the opposite bank. Apart from multiple dents and broken glass, it was intact.

Roy went back up the slope and asked Sarah if she had a recovery strap, which she did. With this and a coil of rope, he fashioned a rough hammock-like truss that he slid under the vehicle on each end and attached to the axles under water. He led this contraption up over the roof and secured it to the end of the winch cable. He then signalled to Sarah to start the engine and start winding the winch in. Once the slack was taken out of the wire rope, he stopped her with a wave of his hand and persuaded his many helpers to stand well clear.

He then went back up the slope. 'When I tell you,' he ordered, 'start to pull very, very slowly. Don't rev the engine. And if I tell you to stop, stop immediately.' He went down again, stood well back from the winch line and signalled her to start.

It went easily; it was not a heavy vehicle. It slid on its side for two feet and then the submerged tyres dug in. Responding to the pull over the roof, it gradually rose to an upright position and then dropped onto four wheels. The driver's door swung open and water cascaded out into the stream. The small crowd cheered.

As somebody optimistically tried the starter, he went back up the slope. 'Well done,' he said, 'but it's not going to go anywhere under its own power. Let's pull it up the hill for them.'

He waded back into the water again and spent some time undoing his handiwork with the rope. He then hooked the recovery strap through the front suspension and signalled Sarah to take up the slack in the cable. When this was done, he appointed one of his helpers to steer the Toyota and went back to join her. 'Don't rush,' he said. 'Just take it very slowly.'

The battered Toyota inched across the stream, hesitated at the foot of the bank, then started up the slope with a jerk. The Land Rover shuddered as it took the strain and the gearbox growled, but progress was steady.

He stopped her when the Toyota was a few feet from the top, where the slope flattened out. He put some rocks behind the wheels. He then told her to put the Land Rover in low-range reverse and simply tow the other vehicle the rest of the way. She did this, and a minute later the recovery was complete. She climbed out, pleased with her achievement, and thanked him. He crossed back to the Bedford and drove it through with a flourish. A few other vans and a Japanese four-wheel drive followed him without problems.

It was hot and Roy broke out a round of drinks for his crew. The occupants of the disabled Toyota departed in other vehicles. Sarah thanked him again for his help. She and her companions had planned to go on to Ruwezori Park that night, but it was now too late. He told them about his planned camp at the mission and suggested they camp there as well.

'A few yards of winch cable were still lying in the road and Sarah started the engine to reel this in. One of the Belgians picked up the hook and kept tension on the cable as it wound. As it approached the roller above the bumper, he let go of the hook and shouted to her to stop.

'I never knew exactly what happened. Instead of the winch stopping as the hook reached the fairlead, the winch just kept on running in very low gear driven by the engine. Sarah thought afterwards that her foot might have slipped off the clutch.

'We shouted at her to stop as the cable bit deep into the drum and the fairlead - which was welded to a solid steel bracket - started to buckle under the strain. I jumped out of the way.'

The *Braydon* winch is an American device that is used for very rugged applications in forestry on a continent where equipment is used very hard. This one was fully capable of lifting ten thousand pounds. When the hook on the end of the cable jammed into the fairlead, the winch kept on running as if nothing was amiss and placed great strain on the engine and gearbox.

It was a hell of a bang,' he said, 'and then a very expensive grinding noise.'

'I'll bet it stripped the worm gear in the winch,' I speculated.

'It didn't, actually,' said Roy. 'That's what I thought at first. But it was a bloody sight worse than that. She started the engine again and it ran all right, but the moment she let out the clutch, there was a God-awful racket in the gearbox. There was no way she was able to drive it another yard.'

The mission was only about five miles away, so they put the transfer case in neutral and towed the Land Rover there. It was after dark when they arrived. News of their good deed helping the people in the Toyota had preceded them.

Roy said that he had very little time for missions in Africa, as a good many of them were run by evangelists bent on saving souls, with little consideration given to the sensitivities of the locals. The Mission at Kizoma was very different, and met with his approval. It had been established eighty years prior by Lutherans and was something of a centre for learning - providing training that was both practical and useful along with a mild dose of Christian philosophy.

'I stop there every trip - usually for two nights. The camp is tidy and secure and, best of all, you can swim. A path leads up from there to a *kloof* with fresh water pools. The water comes right off Mount Speke, no bilharzia and cool. Customers love the place.'

He was a friend of the vocational skills teachers at the mission school, and had helped them set up a course in metalworking.

'We invited the folks from the Land Rover to a *braaivleis* with us that night. I spoke with Sarah about the knackered gearbox and gave her my two bits' worth on what might be broken. She showed me she had gearbox spares, kinda surprising.'

'Well prepared,' I said. 'Fellow called Sam Loos set her up.'

The next day was a rest day for him. His guests were left to their own devices, only coming together for meals, which they cooked themselves.

An early riser, Roy emerged from the bedroll under his truck at dawn, and found Sarah saying her goodbyes to the Belgians, who planned to hitchhike back to Rwanda. No sooner had they left than she unpacked her tools, spare parts and a grubby Haynes's manual.

It was his nature to help in such situations.

'By eleven we had the seat box and the floors out, and took out a ruddy great extra fuel tank that had been fitted next to the overdrive. By noon we'd disconnected the drive shafts and drained the gearbox oil into her washbasin - some bits of mangled metal washed out. My crew helped lift out the box using a long pole as a crane.'

'Pretty hot at that time of day, so we rested a couple of hours and I went for a swim. When I got back, she'd removed the clutch withdrawal mechanism and was struggling with the cotter pin on the lay shaft. I helped with that and we took off the top of the gearbox and pulled out the selector forks. We knocked the bell housing off with a log.'

The damage was not immediately apparent as they laid the parts out in sequence. None of the gears appeared to be seriously damaged, and all the bearings spun smoothly. Closer examination showed that the smallest pinion on the lay shaft had lost some teeth. A retaining ring was also on the point of failure, and had torn segments out of the lay shaft.

They stopped for supper at that point, and started to reassemble the gearbox immediately afterwards using a new lay shaft, first gear and retaining ring from Sarah's parts kit. By seven, dusk was setting in, and they had to light Roy's pressure lamp in order to see.

They knew nothing about Land Rover gearboxes, but they were both practical people and it was not a complicated mechanism.

'We were surrounded by locals all day,' Roy remembered, 'but after dark they left and we were able to talk. She told me she was an electrical engineer and an only child whose parents had driven a Land Rover up Africa many years before. She'd been married to a guy who dumped her for someone half his age after she wanted to have a baby. She had no current boyfriend. I told her about Western Australia and how I never really finished high school, about my work in Singapore and my trek from Calcutta to London. I told her about the girls in Perth and why I did not fancy settling down for a while yet.'

They worked away, drinking cold beers from the refrigerator in the Bedford. She drank one to every three of his. They needed the liquid; sweat was streaming off them. Insects singed themselves on the lamp and fell into their hair.

'It was a bit daft,' Roy said. 'But I was determined to finish, as the next day we had to head north. I was already about a week behind schedule. It felt good doing something useful for a Pommie girl with hairy armpits. 'Man, was it hot! It was like working in a sauna. All I had on was a pair of shorts and all she wore was shorts and a cotton top - I could see there was nothing else underneath, the way it stuck to her. And both of us were covered in that EP90 oil that stinks.'

The gearbox was assembled by ten-thirty and they were ready to lift it into position. Their helpers of the afternoon had long since gone to sleep. She surprised him by suggesting that the two of them could move it by themselves. She showed that she could easily lift her end of the beam.

Luck was with them that night as the input shaft slipped through the clutch without a struggle, and all that was left to do was replace the bits they had detached. By midnight, the gearbox and drive shafts were secured. They had no spare oil so they poured the original stuff back in, straining it through the fabric of an old tee shirt. They put the seat box back in a temporary fashion and drove the truck down the road and back. The gearbox worked perfectly.

She assured him she could replace the tank and floors the next day by herself.   They gathered more beer, fresh clothes, a bucket, soap and a couple of towels. Carrying the hissing lantern, they walked up through the woods to the *kloof.* There, a waterfall drowned out the incessant sound of the insects.

He placed the pressure lamp on a rock. The transparent water of the pool was surrounded by massive white boulders that reflected the light, reminding him of the set for a stage play he had seen in London. Taking care not to pollute the pool, they took water to a sandy area on the bank, discarded their filthy clothes and washed. They poured buckets of water over each other to rinse away the suds.

'She was something,' Roy said. 'A lot of woman with a great figure. It was rather surreal, really. This hot African night with all the bugs buzzing in a cloud round the lamp, a bit of a moon, and being naked on those warm rocks with her. I meet more women than you might think in this job, but she was a keeper. I wouldn't mind running into her again.'

They swam in the pool, mindful of snakes, and then lay out on the warm rocks to dry off. Later, with a dying lamp, they made their way back to camp. He rustled up an impromptu meal.

He did not tell me anything else about that night and I didn't ask for details.

The next morning, he rallied his troops early to stow the Bedford, and as they left she jumped onto the running board and gave him a parting kiss. He had not seen or heard from her again.

'But she did say she was going to Zomba?' I asked. 'What was she going to do after that?'

'Zomba was her immediate destination,' he said. 'She was vague about what came after that. Said she might go on to South Africa and stay there for a while. She wanted to keep moving, and indicated that she might go to South America at some point and drive up to the States. The overriding impression I received was that she was cagey. I joked that I would have a hard time finding her again and she quipped back, "that's the general idea."

'She did say that travelling solo is lonely and a good sidekick hard to find.'

'I sympathize with that,' I said. 'I have similar problems.'

CHAPTER 20

As I drew closer, I saw it was a military 101 gun tractor that had been converted into a motor caravan.

The man at immigration asked the purpose of my visit. 'I'm going to meet a friend in Zomba,' I replied.

He checked my onward ticket. 'Welcome to Malawi.'

I think I was the only customer they were expecting at the Budget desk. The car was a fairly new Korean box with four wheels in the corners and air conditioning. I locked my pack in the boot and headed to Lilongwe, which is about twenty miles away on a good road. I drove around the sprawling city, checking out hotels, and settled on one near the market that had an overgrown garden where I could park the car. It cost less than a quarter of an equivalent place in England.

I snoozed for a couple of hours before heading out in the early evening to stretch my legs. I ended up in the market, wandering through the stalls of produce and livestock. I had a meal at a restaurant off Kenyatta road.

Leaving the city the next morning by way of the Blantyre road, I kept a wary eye out for livestock and children. The car buzzed quite happily along. Malawi is one of the most densely populated countries in Africa, and I was seldom out of sight of human habitation. There was little motorized traffic - mostly trucks and buses. There are relatively few private cars in the country.

By noon, I had reached the intersection where the M1 road met the M8, and turned left towards Zomba. I stopped at a store in Balaka to buy bottles of the local beer and biscuits. As I returned to the car, an old man approached me and asked if I was going to

Zomba, so I had a companion for the final leg of the journey.

His name was Benjamin Chandera and he had been staying with a daughter in Balaka, making arrangements for her and her three children to come to live with him in his village, somewhat east of Zomba on Lake Chilwa. He was a farmer in a small way, and many years ago had worked, as do many of his countrymen, in the gold mines in South Africa. This must have been during the apartheid era. He had served four 'contracts' at Free State Gedult near Welkom in that country, and bore his former employers no ill will. He had seven children: four daughters and three sons. One of his sons was living in South Africa, working as a cook for a 'big man' in the Johannesburg suburb of Inanda. The AIDS epidemic had devastated his family, as his eldest son had died and now his daughter (the one he had been visiting) had lost her husband, too, and he had travelled to Balaka for the funeral.

They had buried his son-in-law, once a fine strong man - a maintainer of roads - reduced to a mottled caricature of himself. He had noticed that his daughter did not look too well herself and had told her she'd best leave her modest house and return to her home village.

It was impossible to be unaware of the AIDS epidemic in Malawi. There were grim posters everywhere warning of the dangers of unprotected sex. This courteous old man brought home the reality of the tragedy that was sweeping the continent. We drove in silence for a while and then he asked me if I had lost any friends or relatives to the disease.

I told him that I had not. I was not an authority on the subject,

I said, and in England, where I lived, there was a problem, but it was confined to a smaller percentage of the population. There were drugs available that could check the disease but not cure it, and these drugs were very expensive.

'Money is always a problem,' he said.

He asked me what I was doing in Malawi, and I explained I was looking for a woman who had driven from the north six or seven months earlier, as I wished to meet her and purchase her car. He found it difficult to understand why I simply did not buy another car. He could not remember ever having seen a white woman in his village. We reached Zomba and he asked to be dropped at the bus station, where he could get a taxi home. I asked him how far this was and he told me about ten miles. A steady drizzle was falling so I offered to drive him home. The road took us east of the escarpment on rough unpaved roads to his village, where I left him in a welcoming crowd of family. He was appreciative of the selection from my wardrobe.

Back in Zomba, the rain had stopped and children skipped in the puddles. I parked under a tree near the war memorial. I locked the car, walked over to a tailor's shop and asked to be directed to the police station.

The officer in charge was friendly and introduced himself as Captain Kazuma. I explained I was not there to report a crime but I was looking for a British-registered Land Rover that might have arrived in his area late the previous year. I showed him Sam Loos' pictures of *Geraldine*. He could not remember such a vehicle specifically, and explained that quite a number of Land Rovers and

Toyota Land Cruisers driven by whites passed through Zomba each month. Peace in Mozambique and the change in government in South Africa had increased the numbers of tourists who were visiting the area. They came in vehicles mainly from the countries to the south.

He asked where I was staying, and when I told him I had not yet registered in a hotel, he offered me his telephone to call the Ku Chawe Inn on the plateau. I accepted this suggestion and made a reservation. He then offered to post a notice for his men to read in their duty room, and said he would contact me if any of them recalled seeing the Land Rover.

I drove around the industrialized parts of the town and stopped at garages, showing my pictures to the proprietors. None remembered seeing a Land Rover driven by a woman.

There was no official campsite in Zomba itself, but I remembered one on the plateau where I camped in my safari-driving days.

The Zomba plateau is a group of wooded peaks rising above the surrounding plain. About one third of the area on top of the plateau is planted with commercial timber species - mostly pines - and these are harvested on a rotational basis. The remainder of the plateau is left as virgin forest and is almost impenetrable. It is a ten-mile drive up from the town to the plateau and the climate there is milder, making it a popular retreat.

The little hotel had a commanding location on the rim of the plateau looking down over the plains below. I was given a cottage some distance from the main building with a wood fireplace and a supply of cut wood in case I should feel cold in the night.

I unpacked and went for a walk.

The campsite was a few hundred yards from the hotel and exactly as I remembered it - an open grassy area about a hectare in extent with a simple toilet block. It was empty except for an unusual-looking vehicle that appeared to have been parked for some time. As I drew closer, I saw it was a military 101 gun tractor that had been converted into a motor caravan. It had a South African registration. A tarpaulin was lashed to some poles to form an awning. A black man was chopping firewood and I went over to talk to him.

He was a huge man with an engaging grin. He had worked up a healthy sweat and leaned naturally on the big axe as if it were an extension of his body. The truck was not his but belonged to Mr. Bob, who was off hiking with his wife. He lived nearby and liked to do odd jobs for people at the campsite.

We discussed where I was from and where I was staying, and a bit about the government and the shortage of work in Malawi. I then showed him a picture of *Geraldine* and asked him if he recognized it as a vehicle that might have stopped at the campsite during the past year. He examined the picture carefully, holding it by the edges, and shook his head. There had been a few Land Rovers, but they had not been green and the lights were not placed in the centre like so.

Disappointed, I continued my walk. It was good to get exercise. I passed through a village with friendly children and followed a rough path along a ridge through the pines. After a mile of this, the trees gave way to brush, and I scrambled a few hundred yards up to a white trigonometrical survey beacon on the top of the hill.

The beacon, a rough conical stone pyramid with a vertical metal post in the centre, was crowned by four black fins. Hundreds of former hikers had scratched their names in the faded paint with dates going back to the 1960s. I did not see a Sarah amongst them. There were little groups of ladybugs nesting in the cracks between the stones.

The plain stretched out in the afternoon light. Zomba town looked very small with lines of roads radiating from it and the occasional bus or truck moving slowly. There were signs of habitation everywhere - fields and villages - and smoke rising vertically in the air. I could hear cocks crowing; there was the familiar smell of the veldt. I was glad to be back in Africa.

On my way down, I passed the campsite again. A fire was crackling between stones and an older white couple sat in camp chairs under the awning of the converted motor caravan, waiting for a kettle to boil. I went over and introduced myself. The man was taciturn but his wife made up for any deficiencies in his communication skills. They were retired fruit farmers from the Northern Cape on an extended holiday. They had been away from Kakamas for five months and had been as far north as Dar es Salaam. They had not seen any old Land Rovers with English registrations.

I returned to the hotel and sat with a beer on the terrace. A tour group from Germany had arrived in a small bus.

My waiter was a cheerful youth called Daniel from the north of the country. He had little to do at that early hour and wanted to talk, asking me what I was doing in Malawi. I told him about my quest for an old Land Rover, and remarked that it might not even have been in Zomba and I might be wasting my time. He was interested in what I was doing, and suggested that I should go to the Liwonda National Park, as most visitors to Malawi went there. It was only an hour north by car and they might have a record of vehicles entering the park that they could show me. It was an excellent suggestion.

I showed him my pictures and he examined them carefully, then made a sharp exclamation. 'Bwana,' he said. 'I have not seen this truck. But I have seen this woman. She was here and I remember her well, as she was so tall.

'She was in here some months ago - before the Christmas holiday, I think,' he said. 'I remember it was hot and we were very busy. She came with a man.'

The couple must have come in their own car, as they had arrived independently of anyone else. They sat on the terrace and drank a few beers, then had a meal in the hotel restaurant. He was not certain if they had stayed the night at the hotel, and did not remember seeing them the next morning. He had served them dinner in the restaurant, and he remembered that there was an argument at the end of the meal about who should pay the bill. He did not know who had actually paid as they simply left the money on the table, but there had been a generous tip.

'Are you sure it was her?' I asked. 'Very tall and strong.'

'She was tall,' he said. 'Taller than the man she was with. I do not know if she was strong, but she looked very good and had nice teeth.'

He did not remember what she'd worn, but the man had had

good clothes. They laughed a lot at dinner and ordered a bottle of wine.

'She called him "Doctor",' he said, 'but he asked her not to do that and just to call him Luke. I remember it was Luke because that is my brother's name also.'

I went back to my room, changed into long pants and a clean shirt, and returned to the main building for an early dinner.

After eating, I wandered into the reception area. I found one of those guestbooks that hostelries leave out for guests to write their names and places of origin. It had a 'remarks' column for compliments and comments on the weather. The guests came from all over the world, mainly from continental Europe, but there were many Americans, British and South Africans. The record started on January first of the current year.

I took the book over to the woman at the reception desk. 'Do you have one from last year?' I asked. 'I'd like to see if some friends stayed here.'

She went to the office behind her and returned with a similar volume. I took it into the lounge and read the entries starting with the previous October.

On December third was written, 'Sarah Oakes - London, England.' There was nothing in the banal remarks column. I felt a flush of elation - my quarry had been here six months before.

The five entries above were all on the same date. Most were couples but the one immediately above Sarah's was a 'L. Wilmot' who had given his address as 'Stellenbosch, S. Africa' and remarked laconically, 'fine'. The pen used was the same colour as Sarah's entry.

The following week was completely filled by names of guests who, from their comments, were attending a conference.

I took the book back to reception. 'These are my friends here,' I said pointing to 'L. Wilmot' and 'Sarah Oakes'. 'Do you know how long they stayed?'

She took down a heavy guest register and flopped it open on December. 'Leslie Wilmot was here for December first, second and third,' she said. 'Single in cottage eleven. He was part of a group tour run by 'Malawi Experience' - they come here once a month. I've no record of a Sarah Oakes. Maybe he smuggled her in,' she giggled. 'It happens!'

'This is them here,' I said, producing my photograph.

She looked at it briefly and did not ask which two in the picture I was referring to. 'Can't say I remember them,' she said. 'We get so many here.'

'You had a conference here about that time?' I asked

'Not here,' she said. 'That was at the university, but a lot of the people stayed here. We bussed them up and down the hill each day.'

Eleven was the same cottage I was in. I went back there and sat on the bed. I looked at the photograph of Sarah on top of Mount Sinai. *If only walls could talk*, I thought. Then I was ashamed of myself. My mission was to find a Land Rover. A ton of steel and aluminium with a two and a quarter petrol engine and no syncromesh on first and second gears. It was stupid to feel resentful of an anonymous Dr. Wilmot who had stayed in this cottage months before me and might have used the room for a tryst with a woman I had never met called Sarah Oakes.

I went to bed but sleep eluded me. A chorus of frogs in the garden did not help. At ten-thirty, I gave up, got dressed again and went to the bar. A small group of Germans was having a good time at the counter. I chose a table at the other end of the room and asked Daniel to bring me a drink.

When he returned with the beer, I asked, 'That doctor who was with my friend, the tall woman - was he a South African?'

'Oh no,' he replied. 'For sure not. He was a Chewa from this country. He spoke Chichewa just like me!'

CHAPTER 21

The rangers offered to take me out to get some pictures of the Land Rovers with game.

By the time I went for breakfast the Germans had departed. I had the dining room to myself. Daniel was not on duty.

I decided to drive up to the game reserve that day and see if I could learn anything there. When I went out to my car, I found it had been washed, and three young boys were waiting around expecting remuneration for this unnecessary service. I gave them fifty kwacha. 'You guys should be in school,' I said.

Before I drove off, I showed them the picture. 'Have you ever washed this one?' I asked.

'Land Rover,' said one. 'Hundred kwacha job.' They had never seen this particular Land Rover, and I established that between them they had probably washed most visitors' cars over the past year.

I drove back down to the town. I now had a bit more to go on. No one on the plateau had recalled seeing the Land Rover, but I had evidence that Sarah had been at the hotel at least once in the company of a black Malawian with a Ph.D. degree. Moreover, this was probably on the date she had put her name in the guest book, although she was not a registered guest at the hotel.

I thought it unlikely that she would have put her name in the book if she had in fact been smuggled into the hotel by Dr. Wilmot. I have smuggled friends into hotels to save on accommodation, but that was many years ago as a youth with little money. If Wilmot and Oakes had decided to spend a few days together at the Ku Chawe Inn, they would probably have booked in as a couple, and the few extra kwacha on the bill would not have been a major consideration to them. More likely was that she had seen the guest book while in the hotel for dinner and entered her name.

At Lilwonde I turned off the main road and took the secondary road to Lilwonda National Park. The road to the national park's entrance was dusty and potholed. I picked up a young New Zealand couple hitchhiking and saved them a long walk. The park itself had an impressive stone and thatch entrance gate. I paid the minimal daily entrance fee and asked if I might talk to someone in charge. I was directed over to the park administration a few hundred yards off, which consisted of a block of offices and a vehicle maintenance yard. In the yard was a Land Rover of about the same vintage as *Geraldine* with a battered pickup body.

There were two game rangers in the office who greeted me cheerfully. I explained I was a writer for a magazine specializing in Land Rovers and was looking for a Land Rover that might have visited the park during the last six months. I showed them my photographs.

They immediately recognized Sarah and her vehicle. We examined the record of visitors and found she had stayed three days in the park the previous October in the company of a second woman from the United States. They remembered the women well; they had stayed in a rest house maintained by the park about a mile from the entrance.

Two young foreign women by themselves had been quite an attraction for the staff, and I gathered that they had been treated well during their stay. They had been taken out on special excursions by the men in the course of their duties. Their visit was during the rainy season, the grass was high and game viewing not at its best.

The women had wanted to see elephants and had been disappointed not to see any, although they had seen lions. The staff had suggested a boat cruise on the river, possibly to see elephants, but this would involve renting a boat and driver from a commercial tour operator, and they had not done so.

The rangers had been sorry to see the women leave, and did not know their destination after they left the park.

There was nothing more to be learned about their visit. Sarah had given her London address. I copied the address of the American woman.

The rangers offered to take me out to get some pictures of the Land Rovers with game. We piled into the pickup and set off in convoy across the park in a cloud of dust. It was a wonderful opportunity. My guides had a professional ability to spot animals in the dense bush and it was a thrill to walk away from the vehicles with them, rifles at the ready, and take pictures of animals with the two vehicles in the background. Three hours later I had some wonderful material.

Back in Zomba, I went to the university and found the main office. The conference in December had been organized by the faculty of business and was called the 'International Conference on the Role of Science and Technology in Development.' A friendly woman gave me a copy of the conference programme to read, along with a list of the delegates. There were no Ph.D's with the first name of Luke on the list. Further investigation showed that none of the university faculty with doctorates used the first name 'Luke'. The mysterious diner at the Ku Chawe Inn did not seem to be associated with the university.

I drove back to the centre of town and parked by the war memorial. It was a reminder that men from this little country had joined a regiment called the Kings African Rifles and had died in the service of their colonial masters over eighty years before.

Captain Kazuma had some news for me. 'We found out a bit about that Land Rover,' he said. 'It was here last year. One of my boys says he saw it parked up at the Charuna hospital.' He gave me directions.

The hospital was on the outskirts of the town, situated on a rise against the bulk of the massif. I parked outside next to a sad-looking garden with palm trees that had not been trimmed in years.

Hospitals in Africa are generally pretty crowded affairs, and this one was no exception. Overloaded minibuses ferried people up and down the hill. It was obviously a paediatric and maternity place. Queues of women, many of them pregnant and others with children, snaked into an outpatient unit. Inside the main entrance, a single large nurse strove to keep order in a crowd of people all talking at once.

On the wall by the door was a list with a sliding panel gadget that showed which physicians were in the building and which were not. Third from the top was the name Dr. Luke Chikale, and he was 'In'.

There was no order in the arrangements with the admitting nurse; she seemed to respond to the person who shouted the loudest. I stood in the doorway a few minutes, hoping to catch her eye but to no avail. The tide of humanity swirled around me. There was an overpowering smell of disinfectant. I was about to give up and see if I could telephone the doctor from my hotel, when a small East Indian man in a white coat with a stethoscope around his neck appeared and motioned me outside.

He introduced himself as Dr. Mahood and said he was a houseman at the hospital. He wanted to know my business. I explained that I would like to see Dr. Chikale on a private matter, but I appreciated that he must be pretty busy. 'We are always busy,' Dr. Mahood said. 'Be coming with me, please.' He ploughed resolutely into the crowd, which parted in deference to his white coat. The passageways between crowded wards were relatively free of people, and he bounded up three flights of stairs two steps at a time. We came to a waiting room filled with pregnant women, all of them singing together very beautifully and in perfect harmony. 'Please wait here,' he said, and disappeared. There was no place to sit. The singing stopped. Fifty pairs of brown eyes examined me curiously.

He returned in five minutes. 'Please come in,' he said. 'Dr. Chikale will see you now.' Conversation erupted in the waiting room as we left. I think they thought me a queue jumper and were speculating as to what my condition might be.

The doctor occupied a large room at the end of the top wing with an examination table and one of those glass-fronted medicine cabinets that one sees sometimes in antique shops in Britain. He was sitting at his desk, filling in details of his last examination in a manila file. An old-fashioned fan hung motionless from the ceiling. His diploma on the wall was from Edinburgh University. He was a little older than me with a dark, handsome face and a scar on his right cheek.

He put the file down. 'Thank you, Ali,' he said to my guide's receding back. 'How can I help you, sir?'

'I'm sorry to barge in like this,' I said. 'It's awfully good of you to see me. You are obviously very busy. My name is Giles Jackson and I work for a major car company in England. I'm trying to track down a woman called Sarah Oakes, and I'm hoping you may know where she is.'

He looked at me curiously. 'I may be able to help you,' he said. 'But I'm so far behind today that I think we'd better talk after consulting hours. Are you staying in Zomba?'

'At the Ku Chawe Inn.'

'I usually finish by six,' he said. 'Can I meet you there?'

'I'd be delighted to buy you a drink,' I offered.

'Well, I'll be there before seven then,' he said. 'Barring an emergency here - in which case I'll call and let you know.'

I found my way down through the wards and out into the sunlight of the parking area.

There must have been no emergencies, because he found me on the hotel terrace well before seven. He dropped into the chair opposite me and shook my hand. Daniel did a double take when he saw him.

'Welcome to Zomba,' Luke Chikale said. 'Have you been here before?'

I told him about my days with the safari business. I said I had noticed that he was trained in Edinburgh and we talked about that for a while. He had studied there on a Rhodes scholarship. He commented on the long connection between Malawi and Scotland, one that dated back to the days of the early Presbyterian missionaries who had come to the area at the urging of David Livingstone.

'I hope you will have supper with me,' I said. 'It's getting to that time. Are you expected home for dinner?'

'I'm a widower. I have a servant who looks after my children. Thanks very much. Are you married, Mr. Jackson?'

I told him I was divorced.

While we waited for our meal, we talked about the hospital and how crowded it was. We both knew it was nothing exceptional. In Africa, medical facilities are always stretched to the limit. And as for gynaecology and paediatrics, in a country with a high birth rate like Malawi's, it is almost impossible to provide facilities faster than the population grows.

I then told him about my consulting job and my interest in the Land Rover. He had seen the vehicle when Sarah was in Zomba, but had not paid particular attention to it. They had used his car during her visit; the Rover had been parked under a tree at his house. 'This Land Rover is the only reason for enquiring after Sarah?' he asked.

The question took me by surprise. 'Yes - but what other reason might you think I have?'

'If you are being honest with me, Mr. Jackson, there is no

reason for further clarification.'

I was curious and would have liked some further clarification myself, but he had effectively closed the subject. 'Did you meet Sarah in Britain?' I asked.

'Oh no,' he said. 'I finished my degree in 1979, and she was still in school then. There's no secret in how we met. It was over the Internet. I purchased a motor generator set from her.'

CHAPTER 22

First world war memorial to troops of the
King's African Rifles. Zomba Malawi 1919.

The board set up to run the hospital consisted of several leading citizens of the town, some medical staff and a state employee. 'We have the most incredibly boring meetings,' Dr. Chikale said.

The hospital was always short of money. The average family income of the surrounding population was about one-fiftieth of the income of a family in Western Europe or America. The amounts patients could contribute themselves were a fraction of the costs of the care received.

Under these circumstances, the Zomba medical system was heavily dependent on foreign aid. Most of this money was dispensed by the central government, but private donors also contributed. The hospital was fortunate that a volunteer group in Sweden had become involved in working directly with them and had been successful in raising money for specific items of equipment.

Two years before, their most pressing need had been a motor generator set. The hospital was supplied with electricity from the national grid. Most electric power in Malawi is hydroelectric, but problems in distribution and frequent storms caused disruptions, and in a hospital with operating theatres a power disruption can be fatal. Several deaths were attributed to power failures. 'In the West we would have been sued,' he said grimly.

The hospital had been fitted with a motor generator set when it was first constructed in 1950. This machine was one of the first diesel models ever built by Electroport in London. It had given sterling service for over fifty years and had been rebored three times. However, as the hospital grew, demands on this ancient machine became too much, and it could no longer be depended on in emergencies.

The Swedish group had agreed to fund a new machine. The board members felt that the old one had given most satisfactory service, and they had high regard for Electroport Ltd., who always supplied spare parts efficiently when needed.

Luke was one of the first people to have Internet access in Malawi, and he could afford the high telephone charges associated with using the service. He used the web to keep in touch with developments in his profession. He generally used his computer late at night after his children were asleep. The images on the flickering screen kept him up to date with events in the wider world.

When funding had been approved for the new generator, he had contacted Electroport and a long exchange of e-mail messages with Sarah followed. Their early communications all concerned technical details of kilowatt-hour requirements, power resumption intervals and the thickness of concrete footings.

Gradually, into this morass of engineering detail were thrown a few seeds of personal information that grew and flourished. He learned a little about the woman behind the distant keyboard directing the messages that scrolled down his screen. He found himself creating reasons to e-mail her and told her a bit about himself. He looked forward to the evenings when, in the quiet of his living room, he would see amongst his incoming mail a message from *sarah@electroport.co.uk*. He told her of his profession, his marital status, the names of his children and his religious beliefs.

As their correspondence blossomed he described his Malawi to her, 'warts and all'. He shared hospital gossip with her, and, more to her liking, described the streaky seedeaters and olive-headed weavers that nested in the fruit trees in his garden.

She told him about the death of her mother and how she had put her inheritance into her new flat in London. She introduced him to the Docklands cat that had appeared at her door the day she moved in. She kept him abreast of her travels in America and the Orient.

He invited her to come and see him if she ever visited Malawi.

He heard about Hal Mathews' stroke, her increasing responsibilities and her frustrations with her new employers.

Suddenly the correspondence terminated. On his screen a terse message had appeared, advising him that Electroport Ltd. no longer employed Sarah Oakes and her e-mail address was no longer functional. He had fired off a message to the person who communicated this information to him demanding her address, but did not get a response.

The new generator arrived in a huge crate and was successfully installed. He converted the crate into a playhouse for his children, who derived endless enjoyment from it.

Then in April of the previous year, three months after their last correspondence, he received a long e-mail from Sarah. She had purchased a Land Rover and was going to drive it to Africa and she would very much like to meet him if she passed through Malawi.

'I was so happy, Mr. Jackson,' he said. ' I'm a pretty busy guy with my family and my job, and I don't have much of a social life.'

'She didn't tell you anything about her social life?' I asked. He looked at me as if annoyed by the question and then went on.

'I'm telling you about the generator,' he said. 'She called me two days before her arrival in Zomba. I had not heard her voice before and the very English intonation took a bit of getting used to. She told me she was travelling with an American she had met in Kasungu. We arranged to meet at noon by the war memorial - I did not want her to come to the hospital at that point, and my house is rather hard to find.'

He had goaded his housekeeper into a frenzy of cleaning, and arranged to take the day of their visit off from work.

On the morning they were to arrive, he went to the memorial early so as to be there before them.

There was no mistaking the Land Rover when it drove up and the two women alighted. They were wearing dresses, as trousers for women were still discouraged in Malawi. He did not know which woman was which, as Sarah had never described herself. He got out of his car and approached them. 'Are you Sarah Oakes?' he asked the shorter one. They got that sorted out.

'Man, she was tall,' he said. 'Of course, everyone in town wanted to have a look. While I was introducing myself, women who have been my patients kept interrupting us. I can't go anywhere in this town without women coming up to me and showing me their kids. It's part of the job and rewarding, but in that case I wished I had chosen a less public place.'

He asked them to follow him home. He had an old colonial home in the nicest suburb near the university. The Land Rover followed his car and pulled into his driveway. He showed Sarah where to park it under a banyan tree.

He would not hear of them staying anywhere else and had reorganized his family so they had a room to themselves. He did not cook himself, but his housekeeper had prepared a special lunch for them all. He introduced them to his two young children, who were not yet in school.

The next day was a Sunday. The five of them drove up onto the plateau where it was cooler and went for a long walk. He realized that he had been spending rather too much time behind his desk. They did not see many birds and nothing rare, but he identified the species they did see and described their habits.

The children were shy, keeping close to their father, but gradually becoming accustomed to the women with their paler complexions and strange speech. They played hide and seek amongst the pines in the deserted campground before the group descended to the heat of the town.

The next day the American woman left on the bus to Lilongwe to get a flight back to Baltimore.

Sarah stayed until Tuesday. He took two more days off work to show her as much as possible of the town and the surrounding country. They visited the university, the national archives and the little museum.

He lanced an infection on her shoulder where a Putsi fly larva had developed under her skin. He had his housekeeper wash all her clothes and iron the seams in case other eggs were present. It was a common pest, he explained, and did not reflect on her hygiene in any way. Her underwear on his washing line amused his neighbours.

She went with him to the hospital and followed him around the crowded wards with his staff deferring to him. She was distressed by the children's wards filled with orphans, the generally crowded conditions and the decrepit appearance of the operating theatre. She was amazed that the old X-ray machine still functioned, suggesting - tongue in cheek - that it should be donated to a science museum.

He took her to see where the generators were housed. The new model dwarfed the old. An elderly maintenance man started the new machine for her and she put her hands over her ears as the big diesel thudded into life in the concrete-block shed.

They had meals at his home served by Anna, his quiet housekeeper. The meals were not a social success in that he felt that Anna - a country girl from Machinga - resented his guest. In the informality of his home, she usually ate with him and the children. Because of the new visitor, he had asked Anna to feed herself and the children first and serve a more formal meal to him and Sarah afterwards. To escape this uncomfortable situation, he had taken Sarah to the Ku Chawe Inn on the last night of her stay.

'We had a most relaxing evening together. I seldom eat out socially, and it was fun to talk to someone who had such a wide experience of the world. She is such a striking woman - taller than me - I was proud to be seen with her. She embarrassed me by saying what a wonderful service I was doing for this country, and she made me feel appreciated for not emigrating, as many of my peers have.

'I had the maintenance man from the hospital come to my place to clean the Land Rover, and it was spotless when she loaded her belongings on the Tuesday morning. She hoped to cross Mozambique that day and stay in Zimbabwe that night. I warned her about the land mines along the road through Tete. She came as far as the hospital with me, as I had arranged to replenish her first-aid kit. We said goodbye outside the hospital amidst the usual confusion of taxis and minibuses. Then I went back upstairs to catch up with the expectant mothers.'

'Did you ever hear from them afterwards?' I asked.

'I got emails from both of them,' he said. 'Wendy, the American woman, sent some nice pictures of the children taken the day we played hide and seek on the plateau. And Sarah wrote from Pretoria in South Africa.'

'Is that where she was going?' I asked.

'Mr. Jackson, you seem like a nice fellow, but I'm sorry, I don't think I should tell you. Sarah confided quite a bit to me when she was here, and one of the things she said was that she had a fear of someone following her. You've shown up here with a nice business card and a credible story, but I consider Sarah a dear friend - I can't tell you more without her permission. Forgive me the reticence.'

'You'd be helping a lot if you told me,' I said. 'I did hear that she is finding it difficult to find fellow adventurers to share the expenses of the truck. We will give top dollar for that Land Rover - about eight thousand pounds. She might find that very useful. Look, I know my story seems a bit unlikely, but if we go over to reception and put in a call to Melvin Noor in London - he's one of the chief honchos - and you talk to him, he'll convince you I am who I say I am. Here's his card.'

He looked at the card carefully in the light of the table lamp and smiled as he handed it back to me. 'You seem to have friends in high places. You've convinced me you want to buy the vehicle, and I know Sarah could use the money. She was going on to Cape Town to see if she could find her relatives. Her parents were from there - her mother was a Muslim and her father was Jewish. You could see she was not white; she would have been classified as a coloured had she lived there under apartheid. Disgusting system.'

He was one of the darkest men I have ever met. 'You might have had a few problems yourself,' I observed.

He laughed at that and ordered another beer. 'You've got that right,' he said.

She had not told him what else she was planning to do in Cape Town, but he thought there was a possibility she had been offered a job there. 'She held her cards pretty close to her chest about future plans,' he mused. 'She said things might be pretty tough for a while, and if things didn't work out in South Africa, she might drive back up Africa - in which case she promised to visit me again. I asked her if she had a man there she was planning to live with, but she denied that and I didn't want to pry too much into her affairs. She did say - twice - that once she was settled again she would invite me to visit her, no matter where that was.

'I've been thinking about her a lot. I thought she would have contacted me again by now - especially if she has a computer. But in a way I understand why. She could see I liked her and I like to think it was reciprocal. But I told her even before she came here that I'm HIV positive, and took myself out of the running.'

I looked at him, astounded. 'But you look like one of the healthiest men in Malawi.'

'Thanks,' he said, 'and I feel fine. But it's a fact. My wife died of AIDS. The new drug cocktails might have saved her, but it was too early for that. I may never get over losing her - she was a fellow physician - my partner in every way.

'With me, if it progresses, I have friends overseas who can get me anti retrovirals, so I'll probably be all right. And my kids will get the best treatment if it develops in them. But it limits my choices as far as remarrying goes - although there are plenty of eligible woman with similar problems here. I just don't want to go through all the pain again.

'So I've become a relentless crusader. I make no secret of my condition. I fight to demystify the disease and challenge the hocus pocus that spreads through the bazaars and truck stops of Africa. Education and the conquest of stigma will defeat AIDS in the long run, but it will take time and money. I do my bit by making sure that every pregnant woman in the area is tested, and if she shows positive, she gets treatment to protect her child. I lobby against drug company patent monopolies that keep the prices of the drugs beyond the reach of most Africans. I subscribe to many web discussion groups on the subject. I'm an educated, articulate voice and people listen to me. I travel widely and lecture - I'll be at a conference in San Francisco in September. I'm an optimist, and I think that before long there will be vaccines to protect people, even if those of us who are already infected will never be completely cured.'

'At least your government has stopped hiding the whole

situation under the rug,' I observed. 'As is happening in South Africa.'

'I take some credit for that,' he said.

He left at about eleven, and I went back to the cottage and packed. *

* *Some months after this meeting, Dr. Luke Chikale made an impassioned address to the International Conference on the Alleviation of AIDS. His speech was widely reported in the media and is thought to have had significant influence in the subsequent decision by international drug cartels to reduce the price of AIDS medications in underdeveloped countries.*

CHAPTER 23

Rhodes Memorial Cape Town 1912.
Currently highly controversial.

South Africa's major airport used to be called *Jan Smuts,* and the famous statesman lived on his farm in the flight path at Irene not twenty miles away. They do not honour Boer generals in the new South Africa by keeping airports named after them. With restraint, the airport is now called *Johannesburg International.* Compared with Lilongwe, it was a madhouse. I waited half an hour to clear immigration, and then got a standby seat on an SAA flight to Cape Town.

The skies over the Karroo were clear, but as we crossed the mountains into the Western Cape it clouded up. We saw nothing more until we made a bumpy landing at Cape Town airport. A wild southeaster was blowing. I rented a Nissan and a cellular telephone, then took the N5 highway to the city, driving past thousands of ramshackle migrant homes.

This was familiar ground. I once lived in Cape Town for two years. That was many years ago when I taught drawing at the Technical High School in Bellville. I rented a little flat in Newlands, drove a Volkswagen and enjoyed a passionate relationship with Sarie van Tonder, a woman a few years older than myself who taught Afrikaans at the same school. The pupils had all been white and most of them were not very bright. Sarie told me that all the clever Afrikaners had gone north during the Great Trek. I wondered where Sarie was now.

After that first stay, I have visited the Mother City many times, my varied jobs giving me good excuses to do so. Over the years Cape Town has changed. The busy port has wound down considerably, altered by the growth of container traffic. Also changed was the historical area of the docks, where I remembered eating crayfish in the blue collar Harbour Café, which is now a tourist trap. The forests of alien pine trees that used to cover the lower slopes of the mountain in the city bowl have gone. The charming old cable cars that crept up the face of Table Mountain have been replaced by high-speed monsters filled with tourists, at a price that few citizens can afford.

The Cape Town I first knew had a very different population. Citizens were predominantly 'whites' and 'coloureds' - people of mixed descent. There was a minority of 'blacks'. The effects of the migration of large numbers of black people from the Eastern Cape were only starting to be felt with the increasing spread of 'informal settlements' out on the Cape Flats far beyond Guguletu, the traditional black area. The divisions between various sectors of the population were rigorously enforced by the apartheid regime, and stubbornly resisted by a significant section of the population of all colours.

I knew I would have no trouble finding accommodation. Few tourists go to the Mother City in winter. I decided on the Garden Hotel in Newlands. The winter weather is a lot better on the leeward side of Table Mountain.

They gave me a pleasant room with a big television and a room service menu. It was five in the afternoon, and already dusk was falling. The rain lashed at the windows. Outside, rush hour traffic crawled along Main Road. There were hundreds of taxi vans and a fair sprinkling of luxury cars. A black newspaper boy wearing a plastic rubbish bag over his shoulders darted in and out of traffic at the intersection selling copies of the Cape Argus. I sat on the big bed, with my pack unopened on the floor beside me, feeling depressed.

I find it difficult going back to places that stir old memories. I have led a mostly happy life interspersed with a few rough patches. With the passage of time, the pain of the bad patches diminishes, but the joy of the happier times remains. I remembered well the good times in the Cape Town of twenty years before.

There had been a time for me when Cape Town was full of friends. Peter Maas from the university - a bastion on resistance to the government - tirelessly protesting the system. 'Pilchard' Steyn running his fleet of fishing trawlers. Peter Bezuidenhout with his deep-sea tug. Mary Wilton with her school-feeding scheme. Fred Minaar, who did something secretive in Simonstown. I have lost touch with all of them. I could not find one of them in the telephone book. Like me, they had moved on and were part of the far-flung diaspora of restless South Africans one meets all over the world.

In the morning the sun was shining and the wind had dropped. A necklace of cloud ringed the top of Devil's Peak. Doves cooed loudly in the eucalyptus as I went for my morning walk. I treated myself to a good breakfast, and set off in quest of a Land Rover.

The logical place to start seemed to be at a Land Rover dealer; I found one in the city bowl. The gleaming new models in the showroom were polished spotless, and a black man was adding another layer of wax to an already immaculate silver Range Rover.

The price was 600,000 rand. My card got the attention of the floor salesman and I was introduced to the manager. I explained my mission.

'I'm not sure I can help you much,' he said. 'You see, we don't do work on those old Rovers any more. I've been here six years and have never seen one come in the forecourt. The number of parts we sell for them is negligible. There's lots of those old Landies around, though. They used to build them here in Brackenfell, y'know. But the *ous* in the after-market shops get all the service and spares business. I've never seen the one you are looking for - for sure.

'I know there's some guys in Maitland work on them a lot. They advertise on the Internet, even.' He swung around to his screen and punched some numbers. A maid brought me some awful instant coffee.

'Here they are,' he said. 'On *Landyline*. Van Staden's Off Road. They're on Somerset Road in Maitland. Then there's two other places you could try.'

'What's *Landyline?*' I asked.

'It's a web site for South African Land Rover owners,' he said. 'Lots of people read it around here.'

I had never heard of the site *Landyline* before. From the sound of it, I might have saved myself a lot of trouble by accessing it earlier. He noted down the address and handed it to me.

'Why don't you just post a message on the site asking if anyone knows this woman?' he asked.

'I'm a bit reluctant to that,' I said. 'Nobody likes having their name broadcast on the Internet.'

'Well,' he said, 'I'm not shy and you don't have a computer here. I'll post a message asking if anyone has seen an early 109 with an English-numbered plate anywhere around. That should get some response. People love to chat about Land Rovers.' He had good keyboard skills and entered the message in less than a minute. 'Call me up later in the day and let's see if there is any response. Or you can access the site from anywhere. Here's the address.

'You are welcome to sit here and make some calls, too,' he added hospitably.

No one at Van Staden's Off Road remembered an English 109 Land Rover. I also drew a blank at The Landy Centre. At Voetstoots 4x4, however, I scored. A woman answered the phone in Afrikaans but switched to English when I spoke.

'Frikkie's out on a test drive right now,' she said. 'But I remember a woman who was here a few months ago with a Land Rover from England. She wanted Frikkie to give it a tune-up.'

'I'd like to come and see you,' I said. 'Where are you?'

'We're on Voortrekker road in Maitland,' she said. 'Just past the police station.'

Voortrekker road is not one of the most attractive thoroughfares in the City. Cheap furniture stores, liquor outlets and used-car lots predominate. Voetstoots 4x4 was not concerned about its image with the motoring public. There was a large yard surrounded by the ubiquitous razor wire and a sign warning potential criminals that the place had a burglar alarm and that any attempt to enter the premises after business hours would be investigated by an armed response team. The yard was full of Land Rovers, partly dismantled or wrecked.

259

The bare earth was black and peppered with rusty bolts and washers. A rainbow sheen of oil glistened on the surface of muddy puddles.

Business was conducted from a grimy office with a small workshop behind. An obese woman sat on a stool in the office with a cigarette in one hand and a doughnut in the other. A copy of *Die Burger* was spread out on the counter. On the walls, fly-specked posters with pictures of vacuous women advertised tools and lubricants. An untidy mess of boxes covered the floor and shelves. The boxes were printed with the name of a UK parts vendor better known for large advertisements than for good-quality products.

I introduced myself. She did not get up. *'Frikkie!'* she yelled at the top of her voice. Specks of doughnut splattered the newspaper.

A burly man with a thick black beard, dirty hands and a soiled boiler suit appeared.

'Gooe more,' he said. *'Kan ek u help.'*

'Yes,' I said. 'I'm sorry, but my Afrikaans is pretty rusty. I'm visiting from England. I'm trying to track down a woman who came to Cape Town driving an English 109 station wagon. Your wife said she came here for a tune-up.'

'I remember that,' he said, reverting to English for me. 'She was here. It was just before Christmas. She just drove down from Jo'burg and the Landy was running pretty bad. I took it round the block and it was pretty *pap*. I told her it needed a good tune-up and maybe a valve job. It was backfiring and jerking. I was amazed it got here.'

'Did you fix it?' I asked

'No,' he said. 'It was December and I was bloody busy. All the *Gauties* were here on holiday and everybody wanted things done *now*

now. I told her I couldn't possibly get to it until January. I've my regular customers to look after.'

'Did you suggest anyone else who could help?' I asked.

'She didn't ask,' he said. The concept of good customer service had obviously escaped him.

'She never came back,' said the woman. There was a note of satisfaction in her voice.

Nor would I, I thought. 'Did she leave a telephone number?'

'No,' said the woman.

'Have you any idea where she would have taken it?' I persisted.

'No,' said the woman, putting more doughnut in her mouth.

Frikkie was more polite. '*Ag*, man,' he said. 'There's mechanics all over. But I tell you - she can't have driven it too long like that. It was pretty bad.'

He followed me out into the yard. 'If you find that lady,' he said, 'tell her I'm happy to increase my offer.'

'Was she trying to sell it?' I asked.

Ja,' he said. 'At least she asked me what I think it was worth. I told her I would give her three thousand rand. Just for parts, you see.'

I did a mental calculation. He had offered her less than three hundred pounds. 'It has to be worth quite a bit more than that,' I observed.

'Maybe,' he said, 'but with no paper and running like that I thought she might go for it.'

I left him and stopped at half a dozen other repair places in the immediate area. Nobody remembered the Land Rover. Two places suggested I talk to Frikkie.

I drove up to Rhodes Memorial for lunch. It was warm enough to sit outside. The café had changed hands and was more up-market than I remembered. The city lay spread out below, murmuring. The old power station had gone and sparkling new high-rise buildings altered the vista. A bird landed on my table and pecked at crumbs. Luke would have known what make and model it was.

The restaurant crowd was cosmopolitan with only a few obvious tourists. A young black man was talking about marine lubricants on his cellular phone at the next table.

I finished my lunch and wandered down the granite steps. A bust of Cecil Rhodes stared over the city, and the inscription spoke of his brooding presence. I wondered what he would have thought of the new South Africa.

I went back to the car and stood indecisively by the door amongst the pines. A tempting trail led upward through the trees. The engineer came down the steps and opened the door of the white BMW parked beside me. 'Having a good day?' he asked.

'I'm thinking of taking the rest of the day off,' I said.

The little rental car was nimble and quick. I wove through crowded Sea Point and along the cornice above Clifton Beach to Camps Bay. From there I followed the Atlantic past the souvenir sellers and took the Llandudno turnoff. At the foot of the hill I parked and walked along through the *melkbos* bushes and out onto the rocks of the point. The sea sucked and gurgled in the crevices and there was the pungent smell of kelp. Gulls wheeled above. A favourite sunny niche in the rocks was unchanged, but it was too cool to take off my clothes. A tanker in ballast headed down through a bank of mist towards Cape Point.

Chapman's Peak Road was closed because of a rock fall, so I left Hout Bay over the *nek* and followed Boyes Drive to Kalk Bay. The sea seemed bluer here and the fishing boats smelled, as they should. I walked out on the breakwater. There was no sign of the old *Geelstert*.

It was low tide at The Boulders and I walked out onto the sand. A young mother was playing with two toddlers at the water's edge. I picked up a perfect pansy shell and spotted the shiny heads of seals in the distance.

The little car took the long hill above Smitswinkel Bay in its stride. I remembered how punishing this had been on my ten-speed in the annual Argus races. I watched two lunatic sailboarders wearing rubber suits in the waves near Camel Rock.

At four I drove up the long driveway to Groot Constansia. Workers were out pruning the vines, and acorns crackled beneath my tyres. I bought an up-to-date map of the city in the gift shop and browsed amongst the racks of bottles in the wine store.

The rush hour slowed my progress home and it was after six when I returned to the hotel. I asked the receptionist if there was any way I could use their Internet connection to check my e-mail.

There were no messages for me on the company server. I sent a note to Zomba, thanking Dr. Chikale for his help. I then logged on to *Landyline*.

The inquiry about *Geraldine* had generated a fair amount of traffic.

CHAPTER 24

My search for Geraldine was over.

I printed the messages and arranged them in chronological order. A man in Zimbabwe had spotted an English-registered 109 station wagon parked outside a hotel in Masvingo within the last year but could not remember exactly when. It had only been there one night. He knew it was a Series II because the ventilator flaps were held on with screws. He was not sure if it was heading south or north.

A farmer in Potgietersrust had followed an English-registered 109 on the N1 south of Samsburg. It had three people in it with a woman driving, heading south. It had been going quite slowly and he had honked and waved as he passed it in his Discovery. It was in December, he remembered.

An astronomer stationed at an observatory in the Karroo had been visiting a town called Beaufort West and had seen a 109 station wagon drawn up at a petrol station there. He drove a smaller Series model himself so had been interested in the other Land Rover. A woman was filling the tank on the bigger vehicle; she told him that she had driven it from England. His wife had joined the conversation and invited the woman to stay the night with them. This offer had been declined as she was in a hurry to get to Cape Town. It was a week before Christmas, he recollected, as he had to get back to work the next day to photograph a transit.

Someone called Hans had seen the Land Rover parked outside the Breakwater Hotel on the Cape Town waterfront in early January. I sent an e-mail to Hans and asked him to call me on my cell phone.

I was having a Castle in the hotel bar when he called.

He worked at the old drydock in the port and drove a Land Rover himself. He had seen the faded green Series II several times over the course of about ten days standing in a parking area on the ocean side of the old Breakwater Prison, which had been converted to a hotel. It looked interesting, so he had walked up from work one day while the dock was filling. The Land Rover had English license plates and was completely empty except for a towel and a woman's swimsuit hanging from the driving mirror. It was an interesting Land Rover and he would have liked to talk to the people who owned it. He did not have the opportunity, as it had disappeared shortly afterwards. He assumed that whoever was using the Rover had been on holiday in Cape Town and had moved on somewhere else.

Hans was a member of a local Land Rover Enthusiasts club and they were having a meeting that evening to see a video about Mozambique. He invited me to the meeting and offered to pick me up at seven.

He came with his wife in an old three-door Range Rover and we drove to a pub in Green Point, where the club met once a month. The video was starting as we arrived, so we arranged ourselves around the monitor, clutching our drinks, while the person who had been behind the camera described his adventures north of Maputo.

They had a short question-and-answer session after that, and then settled down to talk about Land Rovers. It was a familiar environment. I have been to meetings of dozens of different car clubs over the years.

Hans introduced me, telling his friends who I worked for and that I wrote freelance for *Land Rover Aficionado.* They were interested in my work and the state of the magazine publishing business in England. They queried me on my visit to Malawi and the time I had spent as a driver for International Adventure Tours.

Hans told them about my interest in the English 109 that he had seen on the waterfront. A couple of other members remembered seeing the vehicle over the Christmas holiday with a woman driving. No one could recall seeing it after January. It had simply disappeared.

They told me that it was not all that uncommon to see Land Rovers with European registrations in Cape Town. The owners did not always wish to drive them back to Europe, and sometimes these were offered for sale. In these circumstances, the selling price might be low, as the owners were usually in a hurry to leave. There was no way to legally register such a vehicle, and they were regularly broken up for parts. I expressed the hope that this had not been the fate of the one I was seeking. The consensus was that if such a vehicle had been dismantled recently, someone in the club would have heard about it.

I was back in my hotel room at eleven, discouraged. Sarah Oakes had driven as far south as she could, stayed about a week in a hotel and then disappeared. She had probably taken *Geraldine* with her.

I went down to the bar and ordered a nightcap. The place was crowded. The average age of the patrons was about thirty, and every skin colour in the country was represented. The stereo was turned up far too loud to be enjoyable. Everybody was having a good time. I felt old and unattractive. I finished my drink and went to bed.

In the morning I mulled over something Luke had told me.

Sarah had a Jewish father and a Muslim mother. These parents had lived in South Africa up to about 1965. Under the Immorality Act that was in force at the time, their relationship would have been illegal, as sexual acts between people of different races were forbidden. Muslims had been classified as coloured and Jews had been classified as white. Even in liberal Cape Town, such an affair would have caused something of a stir at the time, had knowledge of it become public.

If a police investigation had found them in bed together, they would have been arrested and possibly served time in jail.

Under these circumstances, they had met and fallen in love. I had heard of other couples that had crossed that racial Rubicon in the apartheid years, and not all the stories had happy endings. It would have been impossible for them to legally marry and live a normal family life in South Africa at the time.

An additional complication would have been that they came from two very conservative religious communities. In Cape Town, these were socially divided, and their mutual isolation was reinforced by their opposing sympathies in the Middle East.

As had happened in other cases, they had probably emigrated and married overseas. To emigrate even today you must have skills that are needed in the country to which you apply. This suggested that one of them at least must have been a skilled professional whose application to immigrate to England would have been accepted.

A complication here was their method of leaving. They had travelled overland. They must have had passports of another country, for at that time many African states had severed contacts with the South African regime and were making it difficult for South African nationals to travel north of the Zambezi.

I did not know Sarah's father's first name, nor did I know her mother's maiden name, but it was quite possible that Sarah still had relatives in Cape Town, and she might well have contacted them during her stay. I pulled out the telephone book. There were about thirty entries for Oakes. If all other leads ran dry, I resolved I would call every single one of them. The likelihood that they would be willing to discuss, with a perfect stranger, the offspring of a relative who had emigrated with a Muslim woman more than thirty years before was, I reflected ruefully, slim.

After breakfast I sat down on my bed with a local yellow pages directory and called every shipping agent I could find in Cape Town. I found several who could arrange the container shipment of a vehicle. Destination was no problem. Once the vehicle was in a container it could be shipped to Europe, Australia or North or South America. Prepayment was required, of course. None of them could recall shipping a Land Rover in a container anywhere recently.

I also tried to find a company that stored vehicles but with little success. No one knew of any company offering such a specialized storage service.

I then tried a long shot. I pulled out the article I had collected from the Royal Geological Society. I got the telephone number of Pilanesberg Platinum Mines from directory information and asked for Gert du Plessis.

He was in his office and had a surprisingly neutral accent.

'Du Plessis,' he said.

'Morning,' I said. 'My name's Giles Jackson. I'm calling you from Cape Town, although I usually live in England. I'm trying to track down Sarah Oakes, and I wondered if you knew where she is.'

There was silence at his end of the line while he digested the question. 'Hello - are you still there?' I asked.

'I'm here' - he emphasized the 'here' - 'but I haven't a clue where she is.'

I did not want to tell him how much I knew. 'When did you last see her?' I asked.

'Last year,' he said. 'In Eritrea. She offered me a lift down Africa.'

'Doesn't sound like you got very far,' I said.

'Well, we started in London, so actually we had gone quite a ways.'

'What happened to make you split?' I asked.

'We were travelling in a convoy with another truck,' he said. 'She had an old Landy and the other truck was a Pinzgauer owned by a Swiss guy. The Land Rover broke down - water pump bearings went - and I went on to Asmara with the Swiss crowd. She was bloody stubborn and wanted to stay with her truck. How do you know her?'

'I've never met her,' I said. 'I'm interested in the Land Rover. It's quite a rare model.'

'Seemed like any other old Landy to me,' he said. 'But it was a good truck. No problems with it - the water pump thing was just unfortunate. We had quite an argument when that pump broke. She blamed me for it. She's a pretty excitable woman. All smiles and laughter one day and moody as hell the next.

'I think she was jealous 'cos I was spending quite a bit of time with the Swiss gang. They were a bit younger than us and we were having a bit of fun. Werner had two East German women with him.'

'Who fixed the pump?' I asked innocently.

'Buggered if I know,' he said. 'There was a flare-up in hostilities with the Ethiopians when we got to Asmara, and they closed the whole border area to foreigners. I think they would have hustled her out of that area pretty quick, water pump or no water pump. I did go to the British Embassy and told the people there that I was concerned about her, but there was nothing else I could do.'

'How did you get home?' I asked.

'Well,' he said, 'we knew we couldn't get over the border from Eritrea to Ethiopia, so we drove down the Red Sea coast to Asaab, which was a hell of a drive. Then Werner hired a nomad to guide us across the sand to the Djibouti border, and he paid the border guards to look the other way. We spent a few days in Djibouti - which is a real rip off of a place - and we headed up to the border and crossed into Ethiopia with no problems.

'We got as far as the first town - a real dump - and we get stopped by police. And the police call in the army, for Christ's sake. And these guys really take Werner's truck apart. They searched every square millimetre of that truck. And they find booze and some *quat* we got and a bit of *dagga* and throw us all in jail.

'We sat there for a week and it was as hot as hell. Then a guy shows up who works for the Swiss embassy and bails Werner and the two women out. And I had to plead with him to tell my embassy I was there. I wait another two weeks, and finally I'm taken on a train in handcuffs, and the train takes two days to get to Addis Ababa.

'A black guy from the South African Embassy comes to see me and tells me I could be five years in jail for smuggling drugs. I have to plead guilty in some kind of court and the embassy makes me sign an I.O.U. for a ten thousand rand fine and my direct airfare home, which was another 7,000 rand or so. The whole thing then gets hushed up and they send me home by air.'

'What happened to Werner's truck?' I asked.

'They put it on the train, too - as evidence,' he said. 'They planned to stick the whole thing on me. It wasn't even my truck.'

After this experience, he explained, he had some trouble getting his old job back and was working hard and resentfully to pay off his debts. He had no desire to see Sarah again even if she was in South Africa. 'Mind you,' he said, 'that's one hell of a woman. I got respect for her.' He did not elaborate on this enigmatic statement. *

After lunch, I went to the manager's office, borrowed the

computer again and connected myself to *Landyline*. There was only one message and it was brief. 'I think I know where an English 109 like you are looking for is parked. Please call me in Johannesburg 011 567 4591. *jansevarberg@iafrica.com.*'

A woman answered my call and said I probably needed to talk to Mr. van Rensberg.

I explained who I was and why I wanted to find the Rover.

He was a professional photographer and had been down in the Cape Peninsula on an assignment in March. His assignment was to take a picture of a Polish square-rigged training ship entering the harbour. The picture was to be used in a promotional brochure designed to persuade more cruise lines to place South Africa on their itineraries.

Sailing ships still suffer from imprecise arrival dates, and he had no way of knowing what the weather would be like on the day this one arrived. He had gone to Cape Town a week in advance to look at the harbour entrance and locate good vantage points. He would decide which point to use once he knew the time of day and the weather when he took his pictures. He used a very long lens on a Mavica. In looking for a location, he went onto the roofs of several buildings and drove to the top of Signal Hill. He finally found a location he liked at the top of Bo-Kaap. He visited this place several times and took some trial exposures.

While he was in Bo-Kaap, he had noticed a fenced yard with an abandoned Mercedes Benz and an old Land Rover parked inside. The Mercedes had no wheels and had obviously not moved for years. The Land Rover had not been there long - it was cleaner and the tyres were fully inflated. It was light green and partly covered by a tarpaulin, but he could see it had an oval GB sticker on the back. He did not remember the name of the street this was on, but said that if I looked for the best vantage point over the harbour, I could hardly miss it.

In the end, he had not used the location, as the weather had deteriorated and he had to be content with much closer images.

I thanked him and promised to e-mail him if it was the Rover I was looking for.

'Bo Kaap' means *above cape* in Dutch. It is an interesting area of Cape Town that was spared the destruction of the Group Areas Act and was not demolished at the same time as District Six. It is Cape Town's historic Malay quarter. The community rises to the south of the downtown core on the slopes of Signal Hill and is separated from the city proper by Buitenkant Street. It is a jumble of small houses and businesses with a charm that is lacking in more modern suburbs where the apartheid regime sought to relocate its inhabitants.

In the seventies, when I first lived in Cape Town, Bo Kaap had the reputation of being a pretty rough sort of place, although I never found it so. I used to have my temperamental Volkswagen repaired there by a competent mechanic who had a workshop spilling out onto Church Street hill. There is an old mosque and a greengrocer, where in January you could buy the tart wild figs that are not seen in supermarkets. There was an excellent cobbler in a little alley off Pepper Street who resoled many of my shoes, cutting the tough green leather soles in such a way as to hide the stitches completely. Sarie van Tonder used a Bo Kaap dressmaker who made her costumes for school plays.

I drove into the city and parked off Strand Street, locked the car and walked up Chiappini hill. The area was less rundown than I remembered, and some of the buildings had fresh coats of paint. As I climbed, I saw what had attracted van Rensberg to the place. With a long lens, his picture would have been an attractive combination of the downtown core and the main harbour area. There was little traffic here. Children played in the street, and an optimistic woman was hanging out her laundry, holding the clothes pegs in her mouth. Far above, wisps of cloud cascaded down the cliffs of Lion's Head.

As the road levelled off, I turned right. Almost immediately I found what I was looking for.

At some time in the past, a house had burned down or collapsed and had not been rebuilt. The space between the remaining houses in the row had been sealed off. There were sheets of corroded corrugated iron at the back of the little plot. Windblown plastic bags were impaled on the razor wire that topped the chain link fence in the front. Khaki weed and blackjacks grew through a surface of mud and broken bricks. A high gate topped with spikes blocked the entrance. The gate was secured with a galvanised chain and a new brass padlock.

Towards the back of this space, with morning glory climbing over it, was a rusty Mercedes 300D that had obviously not moved for many years.

Ten feet or so inside the gate, the Land Rover was parked. A faded blue plastic tarpaulin covered the roof rack, extended down over the windows and was secured with bungee cords, leaving the lower part of the rear door exposed. Rainwater had pooled in the depression formed by the roof rack, and the winter sunlight on the water projected kaleidoscopic patterns onto the fabric.

The pastel green paint was faded and scratched. The access ladder to the roof was twisted and torn away from its mountings on the galvanized trim. To the left of the rear door was a faded British registration plate showing the number GTA 459 and an oval GB sticker marked 'Brittany Ferries'.

My search for *Geraldine* was over.

---

* Attempts made to determine the present whereabouts of Werner Böttcher were unsuccessful. Authorities in Switzerland when supplied with the registration number of his truck were not helpful. The Swiss embassy in Addis Abba denies any such person ever entered Ethiopia.

Gert du Plessis has remarried and is living in Rustenburg, South Africa. He was in the news recently after supporting striking miners in a confrontation with the police.

CHAPTER 25

*Jameah Mosque Chiappini Street Bokaap Cape Town
c 1850.*

An old man came down the street, walking carefully and steadying himself on the iron railings as he negotiated the slippery steps. He was wearing the white cap of a devout Muslim. I said 'good afternoon' to him as he approached.

'*Dag, meester,*' he greeted me. 'I do not recognize your voice. You are not from here.'

'No, father,' I said. 'I am from very far away.'

'We don't get too many tourists up here,' he said. 'A few come on tour buses, and some visit the museum. Have you been to the museum?'

'I have not,' I replied. 'I came up here to find a car.'

'Mustafa Burger is selling a car,' he said. 'But he lives down there on Jordaan. By the doctor's office.'

'The car I am looking for is that one behind this fence,' I said. 'The Land Rover, which came from very far away. From England.'

'I saw that,' he said. 'I have a grandson in England. A dentist in Leeds. Dr. Patel. Do you know of him, perhaps?'

'I have not met him.' I replied. 'Have you been to England to see him?'

'No,' he said. 'I have eleven grandsons and four are overseas. I have been once to Mecca, but otherwise I have lived here all my life. I am eighty-four and my name is Hamar Courash.' I shook his wrinkled hand.

'I'm Giles Jackson,' I said. 'Twenty years ago I was a teacher in this city. Then I went to America. Now I live in England.'

'People travel so much today,' he remarked. 'My family also. When I was younger, to visit Johannesburg or Durban was considered an adventure. I used to work as a contractor, but I have not laid bricks for many years.'

'Tell me, Mr. Courash,' I asked, 'who owns this property with the fence where we are standing?'

'I don't know,' he said. 'Long ago a family called Paneer lived here. One night the house burned down, killing Mr. Paneer and his wife. It was never rebuilt. No one built in Bo Kaap when at any time the Nats could come and break it all down, as they did in District Six. I think a man bought it cheap long ago and stored building material here. I was here the day that truck you are looking at was put here. A Cape man came and put it here, placing a new lock on the gate. I did not recognize him, although he said good day to me. There was a woman with him, and he spoke to her in English. "It will be all right here," he said. "Here is a key for you and a key for me." The woman thanked him and they drove away in an old car together. She drove, I remember.'

'Who would know who owns the land?' I asked.

'They will know in City Hall,' he said. 'Every year they send out notices for the taxes.'

I noted the street numbers of the houses on either side and, after bidding good day to Mr. Courash, walked back down to my car. The civic centre was about ten blocks away on the other side of the downtown core. I decided to walk and put another fifty cents in the meter. My route took me down Waterkant Street and past the Van Riebeck statue to the foreshore.

In the main reception area, people stood in queues to pay taxes and register vehicles. In the property office, a pretty girl consulted a computer and frowned. 'That house burned down in 1977,' she said, 'but the land did not change hands. The same person has owned it since 1958. Here is the address of the registered owner.' She handed me a computer printout and I paid a small fee.

The registered owner was Amir Kassam; his address was on Main Road in Salt River. I returned to my car just as a traffic warden was about to give me a ticket. I drove down Victoria Street. This was the garment district and, looking in through windows, I could see lines of women working at sewing machines. A black youth waved me into a vacant parking stall. 'I'm Edward,' he said. 'Watch your car, boss?'

I wove my way through crowds of shoppers and stopped, perplexed, outside the address on my printout. The building was small with only two storeys. The ground floor was completely taken up by a butcher's shop that specialized in Halaal meat. The top floor curtains were drawn. There was no outside staircase. The building was poorly maintained. The cracked asbestos roof had been repaired in many places with black patches of asphalt.

Around me on the pavement the crowd surged. A lorry loaded with produce backed into the nearby market, honking. An old black man, led by an urchin with a snotty nose, asked me for money. I gave him a rand. He thanked me with dignity and moved off slowly in his rags. It is hard to be old and poor in Africa.

The shop had a staff of about six, and the place was busy. A small queue of women waited to be served. Animal parts were arranged in glass-fronted cabinets. In the back, vapour rose from the door of a refrigerator where great sides of meat hung from hooks. Men in smocks chopped and hewed, and a band saw screamed as it cut through bone.

I like to eat meat, but this milieu made me a little queasy. For too long I have bought my protein neatly wrapped in plastic in the supermarket. I waited my turn in the queue and eventually was asked by a young woman what I wanted. Strands of black hair escaped from her elasticized cap. She had smooth olive skin, huge black eyes and the longest eyelashes I have ever seen.

'I'm not here to buy meat,' I explained. 'I would like to talk to Amir Kassam.'

She looked at me nervously, then went to the back of the shop. She returned with a middle-aged man who looked like her father. He appraised me cautiously.

It was going to be difficult to talk in the crowded shop. I gave him my card and introduced myself. He did not shake my hand. There was blood and specks of flesh on his apron. 'I am Amir Kassam,' he said. 'How can I help you?'

There was a time, I suppose, when white men with cards were unwelcome visitors in Malay businesses. I could excuse his diffidence.

'I've just come from City Hall,' I said, showing him the computer printout. 'I understand you are the owner of this property in Bo Kaap. I'm interested in a Land Rover that is parked there.'

He did not take the paper from me but reached into his pocket, put on a pair of reading glasses and peered at it. 'That is not me,' he said. 'That was my uncle. He died a month ago, Allah be merciful. If you wish to know of my uncle's affairs, you must talk to my brother. He has an office in the Good Hope Centre. His name is Mohammed Kassam.'

I gave my car watcher some loose change and drove back to the city centre. It was four o'clock and there was no parking on the street. I found an underground car park, locked the car and emerged from a flight of littered steps into Long Street.

The Good Hope Centre is one of the older towers on the foreshore. Mohammed Kassam was listed in the foyer with an office on the twelfth floor. The security guard scrutinized my business card and pointed to the lift.

It was very quiet on the twelfth floor. Kassam's office had soft grey carpeting and a panoramic view of Table Mountain. In the reception area I explained my mission to a well-dressed woman who was watering plants. 'Mr. Kassam is in court today,' she said. 'They generally recess about now. He has no other appointments, and might see you when he comes in. Would you like to wait? I can bring you some coffee.'

I sat down in a leather armchair. There was a neat stack of current magazines on a coffee table and an Irma Stern print on the wall. The thick glass muffled the sounds of the city. Cable cars crawled up the sides of the mountain, and the topmost wedge of Platteklip gorge glistened in the late afternoon sun.

He returned at five, a dark, handsome man in an expensive suit who swept through the office with an attaché case under his arm and disappeared. The woman left her desk to talk to him and returned a few minutes later. 'Mr. Kassam has to make some calls but will see you shortly,' she said.

It was nearly six when he came out and conducted me to his office. He apologized for making me wait. The woman looked around the door to say goodnight and left. Lights were coming on in the surrounding buildings and the cable car had stopped. Kassam sat behind an antique partner desk. Portraits of famous figures in the freedom movement hung on the walls. A picture of Nelson Mandela was given pride of place. My card was lying on the blotter; Kassam picked it up and fingered it as he spoke to me.

'How can I help you, Mr. Jackson?' he asked. 'Transportation law is not really my specialty.'

'I don't think I am going to need legal advice,' I said. 'And I appreciate you seeing me without an appointment. I came because I visited your brother in his shop in Salt River today. He said you were looking after the affairs of your recently deceased uncle Amir Kassam. My company wishes to purchase a Land Rover which is parked on a Bo Kaap property registered to Mr. Kassam, and I am trying to trace the owner.'

'I know of that,' he said. 'Also on that property is my uncle's Mercedes, which he was not allowed to drive. It has been there for nearly fifteen years. My uncle was a bit eccentric. I am trying to sort out his affairs. So far I have found he had title to thirty-three properties in this city. We always knew he had money, but we never knew how much. He lived alone in a flat above that butcher's shop. His wife died in 1978 and he never remarried. He has no children and left a very simple will.

'If you have a few minutes, I can tell you about my uncle; it is an interesting story that has some bearing on the Land Rover.'

'I'm not in any hurry.' I said, marvelling how a famous logo on a business card could induce a lawyer to be so helpful - especially without much chance of reward.

'He started with very little, but he used to buy cheap properties. Every month until he died he would go by bus and on foot to collect his rents, and he knew every tenant personally. He had a handyman working for him who went from place to place and did repairs as needed. The property you are talking about he owned for a very long time, and a friend of his died when it burned down. He never replaced the building. Under apartheid, land ownership in Bo Kaap was a tenuous thing.

'He was not a family man but he was generous with his relatives. My brother, as you saw, runs the butcher shop Uncle Amir owned, and he never charged him rent. When I passed my matric, he came to our house to discuss my plans for the future. My father ran a general store and wished me to go into the business with him. Uncle Amir asked me what I wanted to do. I told him I would like to be a lawyer. He made an offer to me. He told me that I should work with father and study law through UNISA - that is the big correspondence university in Pretoria - and if I passed all my first-year courses with good marks, he would pay for me to go full-time to the University of Cape Town. So I ended up five years later with an LL.B., and he was very proud of me. He knew Mr. Harris of Harris, van der Merwe and Bigelow. And Mr. Harris took me in to article. I was the only non-white lawyer in the firm.

'When I finished my articling, I was afraid I would be dismissed and have to hang my shingle out on the Cape Flats. I had met my future wife and we wanted to marry. Mr. Harris called me to his office. "Mohammed," he said, "we are very pleased with you. I would like to offer you a place in the firm. But I have been talking to your uncle and he has agreed to another proposal. It is my idea. I am a member of Rotary International and there is a very good scholarship scheme we have. I proposed you to my fellow Rotarians six months ago. The Americans have agreed. We are sending you to the University of California for a year on a bursary to study Human Rights Legislation."

'I was ecstatic, of course. It was an incredible opportunity for a non-white South African in 1978. My fiancée was heartbroken, but I simply had to go.

'I went to thank my uncle, but he brushed my thanks aside. "We need good lawyers to fight these bastards," he said, and I knew who he meant. "You must do me one favour, though. You will pass through London on your way to America. Please stop for a few days and visit your aunt - my sister Fatima - she lives in a town called Portsmouth. I have not seen her for more than ten years." I was surprised, as no one in my family had ever mentioned an aunt in England.

'I flew to England on British Airways; we did not fly on South African Airways in those days. I stayed one night in London and the next day took a train to Portsmouth, where my aunt and her husband collected me from the station in a little Morris car. I stayed with them for three days. She was an attractive woman; he was a bit older than her and taught commerce at the university. They had a daughter called Sarah, a shy, thin, gawky girl.

'I learned their story. He was a lecturer at the university here, and she was one of his students. They fell in love, but of course under apartheid that was impossible. His mother had been English, so he was entitled to a British passport. He applied for that, and the two of them went separately to Botswana and were married there. Can you imagine? A white male Jew married to a brown Muslim girl by a black Anglican priest in Gaberone!

'He went back to Cape Town by car and she by train. He resigned his post at the university and the British consul added Fatima's name to his passport - that's how things were done then. He purchased a Land Rover and fitted it out. At noon one Wednesday morning, he picked her up outside the station on Adderly Street with just a little suitcase of possessions. They drove north and sometimes she hid in the back in case the police saw them together. They crossed the border at Messina into Rhodesia and had a five-day honeymoon in Victoria Falls. They travelled up Africa all the way to England in that Land Rover, and the baby was born seven months after they arrived in England.

'My family, of course, was most upset. They had already suggested a man whom they would have liked her to marry, and she was only twenty-two. The first they learned about it was when she disappeared, leaving just a note. It was a deep disgrace - they were conservative in those days.

'My aunt was such a good person and very kind to me. I liked her husband - he was a gentle giant. They were very much in love still, and they now lived in a country where they had friends of all races and no one, bar a few bigots, was concerned about skin colour. I left for America more determined than ever to fight the unjust and demeaning system I had been born under. So here I am today with a successful human rights practice in Cape Town and no help on transportation law.'

'So that gawky teenager showed up in Cape Town recently?' I asked.

'No longer a gawky teenager but a mature woman. The story has come full circle. I have seen very little of her, but she visited my uncle frequently and he was pleased. I last saw her at his funeral and she was sad, but glad to have known him before he died. That was three weeks ago. She is here in Cape Town taking a course at the university. She promised to see me when she has a break, and I promised her that nothing would happen to her car. Here is a telephone number where she can be reached.' He wrote it on the back of one of his cards.

'Uncle Amir sounds like quite a character,' I said. 'What did he die of?'

'Old age, basically,' he said. 'But I like to think he died of happiness. Not only did he have a new niece, but a week before he died we won a settlement on the District Six properties the Boers expropriated. He was probably worth ten million the day he died. His will is generous to his relatives, but he gave most of his money to the University of Cape Town. Funny that - he never completed high school himself.'

CHAPTER 26

Breakwater Prison built 1859.

I drove out of the underground parking, up along Orange Street, and stopped opposite the gates of the opulent Mount Nelson Hotel. I turned on the map light and keyed in the number on my cellular telephone.

A voice with a heavy Xhosa intonation answered. 'Graduate School of Business. Manfred Ngeme speaking. Good evening.'

'Good evening,' I said. 'I would like to speak to Sarah Oakes.'

'I am sorry, sir,' he said. 'I am the security officer. The offices are now closed until Monday.'

'Where is the Graduate School of Business?' I asked.

He was puzzled by the question. 'Here in the Breakwater Prison, sir.'

'By the waterfront?' I asked. Something clicked into place.

'Yes,' he said. 'On Portland Road.'

'I thought that was a hotel,' I said.

'There is also a hotel here. It shares the complex,' he said. 'The telephone number is 214061911'

I thanked him and turned the device off.

The Green Point street system was confusing, but I found Portland Road without difficulty. The entrance to the Breakwater Hotel was through a gate in a high wall. I parked in an area marked 'Hotel Guests only'.

I recalled that the old prison had been constructed in Victorian times to house the convicts who were put to work building the original breakwater for the harbour. It had also been used to house Boer prisoners on their way to camps on St. Helena Island during the Anglo-Boer war. The prison itself was a rectangular structure with towers at the corners. The hotel lobby was situated in a separate building. It was quiet and there were not many cars parked outside.

A bored-looking clerk sat behind the reception desk and brightened when he saw me. 'I'm thinking of changing hotels,' I said. 'Do you mind if I have a look around?'

'Be my guest,' he said.

'You share the building with the Graduate School of Business, don't you?' I asked.

'Only the accommodation area,' he said. 'Most of the prison is the business school.'

I wandered across to the prison building, which was well lit on the outside. There was a bronze plaque from the historical monuments commission by the main gate. Above the archway was the blue book and anchor crest of the University of Cape Town with the motto *Speis Bona*.

The guest rooms were on the first-floor side adjoining the hotel lobby. I ignored these and went directly into the centre, where I found a rectangular passage floored with grey slate. It was roofed with glass and enclosed a grassed quadrangle. There was a well-lit library and many small meeting rooms with long tables in what once must have been cells.

I had thought that, at that time on a Friday evening, the place would have been deserted, but this was not the case. In several conference rooms, groups of students were meeting and having discussions over books spread out on tables. Banks of computers were being used, and an unattended printer was pushing out a long document in fan-fold paper.

On a lower level was a series of lecture theatres, silent now but well equipped, with sliding blackboards and overhead projectors.

In the passageway outside the lecture theatres was a notice board headed: 'MBA Full-time' and a long rack of pigeonholes, each marked with a name in *Dymo* tape. On the notice board were a variety of notices posted by students selling cars, looking for rides and wanting to share accommodation. There was also posted a list of examination marks in the subject 'Commercial Law'. There were about a hundred names on the list. The highest mark granted was 96 percent and the lowest 47 percent. Halfway down the list was the name 'S Oakes' with a mark of 67 percent.

A notice reminded students that the winter break started on June 22nd and classes would resume on July 9th. An examination schedule showed that the following week would be a busy one; no fewer than ten midterm examinations of three hours each would be held. *They'll need the holiday*, I thought.

The pigeonholes were clearly designed so that students and staff could communicate by putting messages and teaching material in one another's compartments. Most of the shelves were empty, but some contained piles of documents that had not been collected. Sarah Oakes had papers in her compartment, including a brown envelope with an English stamp. Clearly mail was also distributed in this way.

I went back the hotel reception. 'It's very nice,' I said truthfully. 'How much per night?'

'It's off-season,' he said. 'Only one hundred and eighty rand.'

'I'll make up my mind tomorrow,' I said. 'Is there a restaurant?'

'Cafeteria,' he pointed with his pen, 'far corner over there.'

'Would you have some note paper and an envelope?' I asked. He gave me several sheets of paper with the hotel letterhead, along with an envelope.

The cafeteria was in a building on the ocean side of the complex overlooking the harbour. A bored woman served me a heaped plate of lamb curry and rice. I added a beer at the till. The room was nearly empty.

A group of five students was relaxing by a window. One was black. Books and portable computers were stacked on a side table. All of them were good-looking young men in their thirties, well-dressed in suits and drinking imported beer. One of them had obviously just told a funny story and a burst of laughter marked the conclusion. As I passed their table, I said, 'Excuse me. You haven't seen Sarah Oakes anywhere, have you?'

None of them had seen her that evening. 'I think her group went out to Atlantis today on a QC trip with Prof. Wilson.' one ventured.

'Does she stay here on campus?'

'No,' one said. 'Too bloody expensive for most of us. She has a place by Kloof Nek - old servants' quarters, I think.'

The curry was good. After I finished eating, I took out the writing paper and wrote:

Dear Ms. Oakes,
I am interested in discussing with you the possibility
of purchasing your Land Rover, which I have seen parked in

Bo-Kaap. Could you please give me a call about this?
I am staying in the Garden Court Hotel in room 231.
The telephone number there is 567-9087. I also
have a cellular phone; the number is 83-9087-7865.
Yours sincerely,
* Giles Jackson*

It seemed awfully bland. I thought of all the things I might have added. 'I've also discussed your life in detail with many of your friends.' 'Luke send his regards.' 'Sorry to hear about your uncle.' Or more to the point: 'I have heard so much about you and can't wait to meet you.' On the bottom of the page I wrote:

P.S. I am looking after Horatio for you.

I put the note and a business card into the envelope and sealed it. I went back down to the notice board and the pigeonholes. The Sarah Oakes compartment had been emptied. I left my message in the box and drove back to my hotel.

I did not sleep well that night and lay awake, thinking. It was far too late for the phone to ring. Sarah might not even return to the campus until Monday, when she obviously faced a string of examinations.

Three weeks had passed since I had accepted this assignment. Assuming I could buy the Land Rover - and after what the hirsute Frikkie had said, that seemed very possible - all I had to do was pay for it and get it shipped to England. Melvin Noor would be happy. I would have accomplished what he wanted in less than a month.

Along the way, I had gathered enough information to write a couple of articles for the magazine. I had an open return ticket to London and could stop off anywhere. I was to be paid well for the next two months for doing nothing. I should have been pleased with myself.

I felt uneasy and unsettled, but I couldn't explain why. I was looking forward to meeting Sarah Oakes after hearing so much about her and, if I was honest with myself, I would be sorry if I didn't have the opportunity to get to know her more. This job would be over.

Maybe the reason for my unease was inadequacy. It was seeing the five students in the cafeteria on campus that did it. They were all younger than I. They looked prosperous and intelligent, and they had the confidence and good looks that characterize so many of their countrymen. Sarah was spending a year in proximity to nearly a hundred men like this.

I rolled over and plumped the pillow. *You're here on assignment*, I reminded myself. *The work you contracted to do is almost done and in a short time, too. Go home and have a dinner with Anna - she won't break your heart.'*

I did not fall asleep until after three.

It was eight in the morning when the telephone rang. I put down my razor and picked up the handset. 'Giles Jackson,' I said.

'Mr. Jackson,' said a cultured English voice. 'I'm Sarah Oakes. What on earth are you doing with my cat?'

CHAPTER 27

"Throw in an elephant and we have a deal."

'He had an accident,' I said. 'He was hit by a motorbike outside the pub. Good morning.'

'Where is he now, is he alright?'

'He's at my place,' I said. 'I live on a farm near Poole. And the last I heard he was doing fine. I spoke to the people who are looking after him yesterday.'

'This is very confusing,' she said. 'Have we met before? And why are you in Cape Town wanting to buy my Land Rover?'

'It's quite a long story,' I said. 'We've never met before. In a nutshell I'm working as a consultant to a car company. We want to use the Land Rover in an advertising campaign.'

'I'm sorry,' she said. 'But I simply can't talk about it now. I'm part of a group working on a proposal and we have to have it submitted by Monday. My colleagues are all here waiting for me. And next week I have six exams. I will be totally tied up. Could we possibly meet for a little while this evening?'

'Of course,' I said. 'Shall I come to the campus?'

'Well, I have a car, and it's not much fun here. Any other ideas?'

I knew she lived in the City Bowl. 'How about at the Mount Nelson?' I asked. 'There's a pub there.'*

'That would be nice,' she said. 'I'll see you there about nine.'

Outside, the wind had subsided and a weak sun illuminated the mountain. I needed some exercise. I put on a pair of cargo pants, my Guernsey fisherman's jersey, thick socks and hiking boots. An hour later I was walking briskly counter clockwise around the contour path. The roofs of Groote Schuur poked out of the trees below. No one else was about. At 10.15 I reached Kings Blockhouse and started up the steep trail that leads up Devil's Peak. I was soon hot and out of breath.

The city fell away as I climbed. Near the top the trail petered out, but I remembered to work around to the left and by one, after a final scramble, I was next to the beacon on the top of the Peak, with my pants soaking wet from pushing through the scrub. I rested for fifteen minutes and took the well-worn path down to the saddle before starting to climb the imposing bulk of Table Mountain itself. I found the corkscrew-like cave and pulled myself up the rocks well to the right of the waterfall.

I reached the cairn marking the summit at 2.50. Below me the city lay; a pall of smoke drifted over the townships on the flats. To the west was the deep blue of the Atlantic, and to the south I could see the Indian Ocean pushing into False Bay. The folded mountains ringing the Colonial Cape stood out clearly against the plain: the Franschoekberg to the east near Grabouw, the Hex River Peaks and the mass of the Helderberg towards Stellenbosch.

There were few people wandering around on the plateau as I traversed to the upper cable station. I ordered coffee and scones in the tearoom. A pleasant lethargy set in, but I was conscious of the short day and headed back to the junction of paths at the top of Platteklip gorge. Here I faced a decision. It would be easy to descend the gorge to the road. I opted instead for the longer route and set off at a brisk pace eastwards along the undulating rocky path to the top of Skeleton Gorge, keeping an eye on a gathering bank of clouds.

Here I fell in with an older couple who lived in the suburb of Rondebosch, and I descended the wooded gorge to the Botanical Gardens with them as rain started to fall. My new friends offered me a lift back the hotel, and by seven I was soaking weary limbs in a hot bath - excited yet apprehensive about my imminent meeting with Sarah Oakes.

A young man in a pith helmet waved me into the palm-fringed driveway of the Mount Nelson. He held an umbrella over me while I locked the car, and escorted me to the entrance. The mountain was floodlit and hung like a ghostly wave over the city. The Nelson bar was exactly as I remembered, with a bust of the admiral on a pedestal and antique prints of his engagements on the walls. I ordered a *Grolsch*, chose a padded nook under a picture of Trafalgar and sat facing the entrance watching the minutes tick by on an ornate grandfather clock. *'Get a grip on yourself, Giles'* I thought. *'This is a business meeting not a date.'*

The barman polished glasses; he had no other customers.

As the clock struck nine, a woman came through the entrance followed by the doorman; she was laughing as she slipped out of a green oilskin parka, handed it to him and wiped wet hair from her face. I rose as she entered the bar. 'You must be Giles Jackson,' she said, holding out her hand.

A firm handshake with an unexpectedly big hand, taller than anticipated, hair longer than in the pictures and held back by a malachite Alice band. A close-fitting grey knit dress with, I could not help but notice, the top two buttons undone. I took in her tawny skin, dark brown eyes, slightly upturned nose and very white teeth. She moved in a fluid way, rather like a dancer, although she was not slim. I liked her perfume.

The barman came to take her order. 'I'll have one of those,' she said, pointing at my bottle. I signalled that I'd have a second. We looked each other over. I was reminded of a blind date. Women I have arranged to meet in bars have nearly always been a waste of time. This one was not. She was attractive, wore very little makeup and no jewellery. There was an air of confidence, and a warm spirit behind the brown eyes. I had imagined this meeting for some time and was not disappointed.

She slid my beer across to me. 'Cheers, welcome to Cape Town. Have you been here before?'

'Many times,' I said. She asked about Horatio and I explained how I had been trying to track her down when the motorbike hit him and how I had taken him to a vet.

'I'll repay you for that,' she interrupted.

'He's with my friend Jean and in good hands,' I said. 'Don't worry about the vet. I'm sorry to hear your uncle just died.'

A shadow crossed her face. 'Thank you, how do you know about that?'

'I met his nephew,' I told her and explained what I had been doing since I'd arrived in Cape Town and how I tracked first the Land Rover and then her.

'I talked to cousin Mohammed at the funeral,' she said. 'It was he who called me and told me that Uncle Amir had died. He seemed very nice. Uncle died in his sleep. I had not seen him for a couple of weeks. He was a good man.' She sighed and took a sip of her beer. 'I'm not sure what the family thinks of me. To the older people I'm a reminder of something unfortunate that happened a long time ago. I think the younger ones suspect I'm a gold-digging hussy after the family silver.'

'Your cousin told me your uncle was a good man,' I said. 'And he was very complimentary about you. I think he knows the silver's safe.'

'Apparently he was very well off,' she mused. 'He was my mother's brother and my closest living relative.'

'Is that why you came to Cape Town?'

'It was a factor. I've lived all my life in England, but my parents came from here. My father never communicated with his family, but my mother sent regular letters to Uncle Amir and he wrote back. When I was a child, I loved to see his letters come, because of the pretty stamps with pictures of birds and animals on them. Where do you come from? You have a colonial accent.'

'Just north of here,' I said. 'From near Bulawayo in what is now Zimbabwe. I left a long time ago. I lived here and taught in a high school for a couple of years in the late seventies. I spent some time in America after that; I'm based in England now. I write travel and motoring stuff for monthly magazines.'

'Are you married?'

'I was once; are you?'

She ignored my question and asked the barman for some snacks. He brought nuts and potato chips. I ordered two more beers.

She talked about the university and explained that many of the courses she was taking involved working in small groups with others in her class. The groups liaised with businesses in the community, focusing on aspects of their operations. The group she had worked with that day was preparing a report for a foundry on the effects of training an unskilled workforce to accept responsibility for quality control. The report was complicated and late - it should have been completed the week before.

'The pressure on us is relentless,' she said. 'I often think the faculty here overloads us with assignments to see if they can break us down. I've never worked so hard at anything in my life. Of course, a full-time, one-year MBA course crams two years into just twelve months. The pace is brutal; many times I've asked myself why I'm here at all.'

'Why are you here?'

'I'm an engineer,' she said. 'I enjoy working as an engineer, but I've come to realize that it can be a dead-end job. I want to get into management, and an MBA is more or less a prerequisite in any bigger company today. My personal life has been a bit rough for the last couple of years, and I needed to get away from London. Last summer I lost my job and I felt it was time to do something different. It's a lot less expensive getting a degree here than it is in Europe or the United States, and this is a very good school. It was a combination of factors that made me apply here.'

'And you drove down Africa to get here?'

'Yes,' she said. 'That was a bit crazy, but the experience was priceless, and it was fun most of the time. I met the most interesting people too. I wanted to do it because my parents drove up Africa the year before I was born.'

She went on to tell me that her mother had died of a brain tumour two years before. Sarah had spent a lot of time with her in her final months, and one of the things she had kept in the cupboard by her hospital bed was a series of photograph albums. Mostly the pictures had been of Sarah's early family life. The earliest album held photographs of her parents' honeymoon in Africa on their way to England in the sixties. Faded black and white pictures. A happy week in the fabled Victoria Falls Hotel. Adventures in the Congo, Nigeria and the Sahara.

'My mother was not an intellectual person,' she said. 'She lived for my father and was never really happy after he died. She always wanted me to marry, but at the same time she wanted me to have fun. If anyone inspired the trip it was she - she always remembered travelling in Africa with my father as the happiest time in her life.'

'What are you planning to do when you have your MBA?' I asked.

'That's what everybody keeps asking me,' she said. 'To tell the truth, I've not decided. I had a vague plan to ship *Geraldine* - the Land Rover - to Argentina and explore South America. Now I'm not so sure. I'll be thirty-eight this year and I should probably start looking for a good job again. And I've found it hard to find compatible people to share the overland travel.'

'Would you stay here?' I asked.

'I've thought about it,' she said. 'There are some hoops I would have to jump through to immigrate, and I'd probably have to learn an African language to get ahead. But I don't think I will. This is an inspiring country in many ways, but I worry about the level of crime and violence. It's not bad here in Cape Town, but most of the top jobs are in Gauteng. I've heard many horror stories - I don't think I could live like that. Lately, I've been very homesick for London. I miss my flat and my cat. I like to be able to walk around at night without feeling in danger. I want to take a drive out into the country and have a pub lunch. Lots of little things seem important when I'm so far from home.'

She sorted the cashews from the peanuts and ate a few.

'Tell me about my Land Rover,' she said. 'You have come an awfully long way to find it. I'm quite surprised you found me. Very few people know I'm here.'

'I wondered about that,' I said.

'There are a few reasons why I did not advertise where I was going,' she mused. 'I did not want a particular person to know where I was, and I needed to make a clean break. But my other reason was just plain insecurity. I did not want to tell people that I had signed up for an MBA course and then have to tell them I was no good at it and got kicked off. I did come pretty close to giving up after the first month. I wobbled. It's very tough being on a course with so many really brilliant people.'

I got back to business. 'You may know that the Land Rover Company was sold recently. Ford - the new owners - want to introduce a new model similar in many ways to yours but using more modern methods and parts. They found out from a museum in England that the Land Rover you purchased in Oxford was the oldest of that particular style and that it's in pretty good condition. They want to use it in a publicity drive for the new model in America. There is a motor show in Detroit next year and they want your *Geraldine* there to impress buyers. My boss, Melvin Noor, tried to track you down but found you had left England. He hired me to locate you and offer to buy it from you.'

'Melvin Noor,' she mused. 'The name sounds familiar. How much are you guys offering?'

'Well, I know roughly what you paid,' I said. 'And I know you spent quite a bit more getting it prepared for your trip. I think we would cover all that. How much would you like?'

She laughed. It had a lovely ringing quality. 'Mr. *Ford*,' she said, 'I got the top mark in my recent negotiation course. I will not be the first to name a price. How much are you offering?'

'I thought about six thousand pounds,' I said. 'With all the gear, of course.'

She considered for a few seconds. 'That's a lot better than what I was offered by a mechanic here. But still not enough. If it's rare enough for you track me down here, I want eight. And I have bad news for you; it has something major wrong with it. On the last few days on the road, it was losing power and backfiring. That's when I decided to buy a little car here. It was so bad I had to put it into low range just to climb the hill to that yard where I'm storing it. You may get a lemon for your *eight* thousand pounds.' She stressed the eight.

'I appreciate you telling me that,' I said. 'But let's make it seven. You haven't got a hope of anyone else giving you that much. I don't think the engine matters. The factory will give it a good going-over when they get their hands on it. I'll probably just drive it as far as the container dock.'

'I suppose I'd better take your money,' she said sadly. 'It will be a bit of a wrench to see *Geraldine* go. I had a wonderful time with her. She was a bit temperamental, but she hardly ever let me down. Did you know I drove over thirteen thousand miles? Most of it on the most atrocious roads. Clear across Europe and the Middle East. Right down East Africa. Mountains with gorillas, and lakes pink with flamingos. Kilimanjaro and Zambia. Everywhere I went, she made friends. If she had not become sick like this, I would have taken her to Zimbabwe on my holidays next week. I missed Victoria Falls on my way down; I was in such a hurry. I wanted to go to another game reserve. I drove the whole length of Africa and never saw an elephant. Not a single damn elephant. It's a shame to have come so far and never seen the wild parts of South Africa.'

'What are you going to do with your holiday now?' I asked.

'I don't really know,' she said. 'I'm a bit stuck. The Mazda I bought is truly a basket case - it uses about a litre of oil with every tank of petrol, so I can't take it very far. One of the guys on the course wants me to go with him to Durban, but I'm not all that keen on him. He thinks he's God's gift to women. I'm probably going to sleep for a few days, then I might take the Mazda along the Garden Route for a week - it can probably handle that if I take it easy. Or I might still go up to the Falls for a day or two by air. It's a magical place.

She yawned and stretched. 'Excuse me,' she said, and asked the bartender where the women's washroom was. I watched her cross the room, the Sarah I had constructed in my mind totally eclipsed. She was everything I heard about her and more. For the first time in years I was in the company of a woman who entranced me. Ruefully I recognized that she saw me as simply a convenient way of disposing of *Geraldine,* and that after I concluded the purchase, I would probably never see her again.

She came back, settled herself into the corner, kicked her shoes off and stretched her long legs out on the padded bench. She ran both hands through her hair, pushing it back and adjusting the headband. I noticed the white scar on her forehead - a legacy of the adventure in Ethiopia? She looked at her watch. 'Giles, I'm beat and have stuff I have to do tonight. Why don't I give you my email address, you talk to your boss in London, and I'm sure we can tie this up - we're pretty close.'

It was late. I recognised that I was running on adrenalin and I did not want her to leave. My day had also been exhausting. My legs were stiff and I felt a bit light-headed. Perhaps it was the beer but it was more likely her proximity. A crazy idea thrust itself into my mind.

'I'll make a deal with you,' I said. 'And I know it's going to sound a bit weird because we don't even know each other. I'll give you your eight thousand pounds. It's certainly not a condition of sale, but I'd like to propose something. I'll get her running and you join me on a last safari in *Geraldine.* We can go up through Namibia and the Caprivi Strip to Victoria Falls. It's incredible country and I know it well. It will take two weeks to visit the game reserves, camping most of the time. It's pretty remote. It won't cost much.'

She looked up at me, astonished and obviously totally unaware of my feelings for her. She closed her eyes for a few seconds and opened them again. She laughed, swung her feet down and stretched her hand across the table.

'Throw in an elephant, Mr. Ford,' she said, 'and we have a deal.'

---

* *The cozy nautically themed bar at the Mount Nelson Hotel, where this meeting took place, has since been replaced by something called 'The Planet Bar.' This establishment is seldom frequented by students or down at heel adventurers.*

CHAPTER 28

Victoria Falls.

We discussed how I would pay her for the Land Rover. Because the carnet was in her name, it seemed easiest to make the actual transfer of ownership take place at the end of the holiday when *Geraldine* was shipped to England. Sarah wanted to be paid beforehand, however, and I told her I could arrange to have the funds deposited in her English bank account. She wrote down the account number and the branch for me.

She went to the reception desk, came back with some notepaper and made out a simple bill of sale on the spot. 'This is *voetstoots*,' she said. 'Do you know what that means?'

'As is where is.' I said. 'In this country, it's a legally binding term.'

'You are going to be totally on your own organizing this safari. I won't have any time off at all until next Saturday. When will we leave?'

'Saturday morning. We have a long way to go. I'll get everything that we'll need. You have your own tent and sleeping bag, I would think. We can pick up food along the way.'

'I have a tent,' she said. 'But I usually sleep in the back. There's a board that extends over the passenger seat. You probably don't have a tent here, so you can use mine. It's stowed in the Rover. Here are the keys. The big brass one is the key for the gate. What happens if you can't get her running?'

'I'll get her running,' I said confidently.

'I have only one stipulation to make,' she said.

Here it comes, I thought. *I'm going to have to promise to keep my distance.*

'There's a full moon on July 5th. I want to be at the Falls that night...'

'I think that's doable if I plan it right and I can understand why you want to be at the Falls on a full moon; I've heard it's an absolutely spectacular sight.'

She smiled. 'I don't have a telephone at home. Here's my cell phone number. Don't call during the day - I keep it turned off while I'm on campus. I'll call you for progress reports during the week.'

We left together. Her car was small with rusty patches. I followed her down the avenue and we went in opposite directions on Annandale Street. I drove home along de Waal Drive, singing to myself.

CHAPTER 29

Lauber's men working on Geraldine.

The next day was Sunday. I woke up feeling stiff from my exertions of the day before. The sun was shining, and my anxious mood of the past few days no longer weighed me down.

I drove up into Bo Kaap, parked outside the fenced yard, opened the gate and walked around my new purchase. I untied the bungee cords, climbed up on the roof and lifted the edge of the tarpaulin. A pool of water cascaded down over the bonnet.

The headlamps were missing completely. The plastic tail lamp lenses were cracked and the red plastic had faded to pale amber. There was a deep scratch in the bodywork near the petrol filler, a wing mirror was missing its glass, and the offside windscreen had a crazed impact crater near the centre. The tyres had plenty of tread left on them, though the spare looked a bit iffy.

The interior smelled musty and damp; a garden of moss flourished in the window runners. A hole in the fabric of the driver's seat had been repaired with gaffer tape. The driver's floor mat had worn away under the accelerator pedal, and the clutch pedal rubber was missing. The red knob on the transfer lever had been tightened down too far and cracked. The brass balls on the door hinge pins were completely worn out. There was a four-inch tear in the headliner.

Under the bonnet, everything looked to be complete, although it was dirty and plastered with mud. The engine oil was full and clean. The coolant was within half an inch of the filler neck. Oil splattered on the inside of a front tyre suggested a leaking hub seal.

The steering wheel had three inches of free play. The rubber strap holding the muffler had parted and had been replaced with a piece of fencing wire.

I put the key in the ignition. The red light came on, but the battery was almost completely discharged and would not turn the engine.

Two spare leaves for the parabolic springs and a Hi Lift jack were bolted to a bracket spanning the winch drum. The winch cable was badly wound, and kinked. The roller fairlead was bent and the bull bar was slightly twisted. The sand ladders did not appear to have been used. The bolts holding the roller awning to the gutter had rattled loose, elongating the mounting holes.

Considering the truck was nearly fifty years old and had recently been driven over thirteen thousand miles, it was in remarkably good condition.

In the stowage area in the back was a large plastic clamshell tool kit, totally complete. There was a twelve-volt refrigerator left with the door ajar. The first aid kit was strapped under the rear seat. A fifteen-gallon plastic jerry can marked 'Water' was secured in a vertical position.

Two watertight aluminium boxes on the roof rack held an assortment of camping gear, pots, a blackened kettle, a propane stove, a mosquito net and a folded tent. A mantle lamp was missing its glass cover. There was also a plastic box of laundry soap, a drawstring bag full of clothes pegs, a good assortment of spare parts and a stack of well-thumbed Michelin maps. A big axe was padlocked to the roof rack.

'Good morning,' said a voice below. I had not seen Hamar Courash enter the yard. 'You have unlocked the gate, so you must have found the owner of the truck.'

'Good morning, Mr. Courash,' I said. 'I did, and she has agreed to sell it to me. I am inspecting my new purchase.'

'Truly this is an old one,' he said. 'The paint is falling off, but it has not rusted. That is strange.' The Cape weather was notorious for rusting vehicles.

'It is made of aluminium, not steel,' I said. 'The people who started making these used aluminium from aeroplanes. So the outside does not rust.' I locked the boxes and climbed down to the ground next to him.

'You are up early,' I noted. 'Are you not cold?' There was a chill to the morning air, and even I was feeling it.

'I am always up early,' he replied. 'I do not sleep as much as my wife, and I like to walk when the sun is shining.'

'Tell me,' I said, 'do you know of a mechanic who could help me with some repairs to this truck? I am not sure how much is required, but it must be done in a few days. When I lived here before there was a man on Church Street hill who was good. Is he still there?'

'I know who you mean,' he said. 'He moved long ago out to the flats. His son now runs the business. But there are others. Will you be here long?'

'I will be away for about an hour,' I said. 'But then I will be back.'

I unfolded the tool kit and, using the spanners to disconnect the heavy battery, lifted it out. I placed it on the floor on the passenger's side of the rental car. Using some wire from *Geraldine's* spares kit; I connected the battery to the battery of the rental car and started the engine. I then put everything away in the Land Rover, closed and locked the gate and went for a drive up the N1 towards Stellenbosch. After half an hour at a good speed, I turned back and retraced my route.

Back in Bo Kaap, I put the recharged battery back in the Land Rover. I filled the carburettor with the hand lever on the fuel pump, and tried the starter again. After a few splutters, the engine started and ran roughly for thirty seconds. It then backfired and stopped. I tried again with the same result. *Electrical problem*, I thought, and took the cap off the distributor. The points were dirty and worn.

There was a new set of points in the spares kit. With a small screwdriver, I loosened the old set and lifted them out. The problem with the distributor became immediately apparent. The small pigtail wire connecting the points to the coil fell off when I moved it.

There was no spare pigtail in the spares kit so I improvised by cutting the insulation off, shortening the wire and clamping it under the input terminal. Not having a feeler gauge, I set the contact gap by eye, replaced the distributor cap and tried the engine again. It started and ran smoothly. The ammeter moved up into the charge area. I set the speed up a bit with the hand throttle and waited for the engine to warm up.

Hamar Courash appeared with a younger man whom he

introduced as Sam Lauber. 'But you no longer need a mechanic - it runs,' he said.

'I still need a mechanic,' I said. 'There is much to be done. Can you work on this Rover next week, Mr. Lauber? We need a covered garage. I also wish to work on it at the same time.'

Sam Lauber agreed to that. He had a small workshop on a back street in Salt River. He drove the Rover there after helping Mr. Courash into the passenger seat. I followed in the rental car. The workshop was big enough to hold four cars. It was untidy, but reasonably well equipped. We spent some time discussing the work to be done and the costs involved, then I drove them back to Bo Kaap and arranged to return to Lauber's workshop the following day to give him a go-ahead on the work.

On Monday morning I called Melvin Noor.

'I'm in Cape Town,' I said. 'I've located the truck. It needs a bit of work but it's in pretty good shape. It's not being used at present. I've agreed to buy it for eight thousand pounds with all the safari gear included. The transfer won't go through until the middle of next month. The same woman still owns it but it is being used for a few weeks for a trip to Botswana and Victoria Falls. I'm going along, too. After that, it's ours.'

'Great stuff,' he said. 'That was quick. How did you angle the trip to Botswana? Wish I could come.'

I ignored the question. 'I've got a suggestion to make,' I continued. 'The paint's in pretty rough shape and there are a few dents. Why don't I get it done up and painted here. It will cost a fraction of what it would in England, with the rand as low as it is. I've got some time to kill, and I'll make sure we get a really good job.'

'Excellent idea,' he said. 'Get our people there to help if you need to. Once that's done, you might as well ship it directly to Detroit. We won't need it here in England. Tell me more about this safari.'

'Sarah Oakes - the woman who owns it - is taking an MBA at the university here,' I explained. 'The first two weeks in June are the mid-year break. She wants to go to Victoria Falls, and I've offered to show her some places I know in Botswana.'

'Lucky bugger. Put it on the expense account. I gotta go. I'll put you through to Veronica.'

That efficient woman wrote down my instructions about paying for the vehicle. I also asked her to courier me some registration transfer forms, which must be signed when a British vehicle is sold.

When I arrived at his shop, Lauber already had the wheels and the brake drums off the Land Rover. All the shoes were showing signs of wear, and two of the drums looked gouged. The right front hub was coated with oil. He had found that one of the rubber bushings in the frame had worn out, and the shock absorbers were loose in their mounts. Oil was seeping from the back of the engine, and the handbrake drum had been spinning oil onto the underside of the fuel tank.

I made a list of the parts required. Almost everything needed was in the spares kit. There was nothing that could be done about the main seal on the engine, but I asked him to dismantle the handbrake.

Next, I called Chris Howard, the Land Rover dealer. I thanked him for his help and told him how I had located the Land Rover using the *Landyline* web site. 'Remember I told you we wanted this one for the Detroit motor show?' I reminded him. 'I would now like to get it painted before I ship it. Who do you send your paint work to? I'd like to get it painted this week.'

'Usually we use Vermeulen's,' he said. 'They do good work and they understand how to do the aluminium. But getting it done this week may present a problem. They may be busy.'

As it turned out, Vermeulen was busy, but the idea of painting a Land Rover that was to go into an American motor show appealed to him. He drove round to Lauber's shop in a bright blue BMW and the two of us went over the Land Rover together.

'Okay,' he said. 'I can do it. I'll postpone another job. Outside only. We take out the dents and prep it. Mask the galvanizing. Etching primer. I'll check the paint code - it's probably still listed. But you take off the roof rack and strip out all the door rubbers and window tracks. If you bring it in first thing tomorrow, I'll be finished Thursday afternoon.'

While Lauber worked away on the brakes, I started removing the rubber seals from the doors, shearing off the aluminium rivets with a small chisel. I then went to work on the sliding windows, fighting rusted screws and breaking out bits of corroded runner. Two hours later, I was finished and had all the sliding panes stacked in a heap on a workbench. I then went to work on the windscreen, removing dozens of small screws to make it possible to extract the thick glass. After Lauber had the wheels back on, I helped him bleed the brakes.

I unbolted the storage boxes from the roof rack, and we took off the rack itself with the help of two friends from the upholstery shop next door. The man from the upholstery shop agreed to repair the torn cushion, but suggested that he recover all the seats so they matched. The price quoted was very reasonable, and he produced a material sample book that had a grey vinyl close in colour to the Elephant Hide original.

It took another hour to unbolt the front bumper and remove the winch.

By six in the evening we were done, and drove the windowless Rover around for a few blocks in the rush-hour traffic. The brakes worked well, but the engine still felt underpowered, although it ran smoothly enough.

I delivered the windowless vehicle without its front bumper to Vermeulen's the next morning and left it with three young men sanding busily at the old paint.* I found a glass place to cut two new windshield lenses and sell me twenty meters of fuzzy window track. A welder was located to fabricate a new winch fairlead. Chris Howard ordered new door seals from Johannesburg.

Cape Union Mart sold me a warm sleeping bag and a foam pad to put under it. I spent some time looking for good maps, but there were none available better then Sarah's. I purchased the Cape Town Opera discs of *Aida* and *Madame Butterfly*.

On Friday morning, I collected a rejuvenated *Geraldine* from

Vermeulen's. They had done a superb job, even taking off the sunshield to paint the roof. The colours were just right – bronze green and limestone. The wheels had been sandblasted and painted. There was not a scratch or dent on her. Only the faded lenses on the taillights betrayed her age.

I spent the day working with Sam Lauber to put everything back together again. *Geraldine* looked magnificent. The newly recovered seats made the door panels look shabby, so the people next door recovered those, too. We got the roof rack back on and reassembled the winch. We found that the linkage between the accelerator pedal and the *Solex* carburettor had slipped out of adjustment, which explained the lack of power. At six I gave her a trial run out to the airport, with Lauber following in the rented car. She ran quietly and well. We returned the rental car, and I drove Lauber back to his shop, where I settled his bill.

The whole restoration had cost less than two thousand pounds.

I plugged in the refrigerator and went to a supermarket and a bottle store for some basic supplies, then stopped at a garage to fill the tanks. An older man got out of his Jaguar to look. 'A sixties model, isn't she?' he said. 'I drove one for years. Best darned vehicle I ever had. They go on forever, don't they?

It was well after seven when I got back to the hotel. There were two telephone messages for me at reception. The first was from the British Consulate in Cape Town, asking me if I could advise them of the present whereabouts of Ms. Sarah Oakes. The second asked me to call Melvin Noor. *Both offices will be closed for the weekend*, I thought, and made a mental note to call from Namibia on Monday.

There was also an e-mail from Melvin's secretary.

> Mr. Jackson, I'm not sure if you have left on your safari yet, but Mr. Noor had a discussion yesterday with the Liability Insurance people and was advised that you should not be using a company-owned vehicle for personal use, especially in wilderness conditions and with a passenger who is not an employee of the company. Immediately terminate this journey and call me after you get this message. Veronica Parsons. Secretary to Mr. Melvin Noor, VP.

Sorry Melvin, I thought. *You've just missed me.*

---

* *The afternoon Geraldine was receiving a new coat of paint happened to coincide with a meeting, in London, England, of the Select Committee for Establishing Minimum Consumption Standards in Passenger Vehicles. Mr. Melvin Noor chaired the proceedings.*

CHAPTER 30

'I feel like I've been kidnapped, Mr. Ford.'

On Saturday the weather was vile. I awoke at six to the sound of rain lashing the hotel windows. The mountain was invisible. I was the only guest in the breakfast room. I checked out and loaded my kit into the Land Rover; it was incongruous to be heading out on safari in such miserable conditions.

There was little traffic. A bedraggled boy at an intersection sold me the *Cape Times*. The heater did a miserable job, clearing moisture only from the lower third of the windshield. The screen wipers struggled.

Sarah appeared immediately when I pulled up outside her house. She was astonished when she saw the vehicle and circled *Geraldine* appreciatively before dumping a sensibly sized rucksack on the back seat along with a sleeping bag, a Tilley hat, a red tartan rug and a camera case. '*Geraldine* looks incredible,' she said. 'We should start calling her *Cinderella*.

I was at an end-of-term party until one this morning. I'm feeling rather fragile. Isn't this weather awful?'

She was wearing a waxed *Kakadu Traders* jacket, faded blue jeans and a ribbed military khaki jersey. Her boots were scuffed and the Tilley hat thrown on the back seat had lost its shape. Her hair was drawn back in a thick ponytail and secured with a band. She was tall in the passenger seat and her knees came close to the parcel shelf. 'Let's go,' she said.

We drove through the sodden, virtually deserted city centre. Water was backed up in storm drains, and the few people we saw were hunched against the wind and struggling with their umbrellas. Lanes between the shacks in the townships were rivers of mud. An electrified fence surrounded a steaming oil refinery. Skeins of high-tension lines converged on the nuclear power station. Out on the national road, *Geraldine* accelerated slowly to a steady sixty miles an hour across the flats. She seemed to be pulling well. As the engine warmed, the heater did a better job and the windscreen dried.

'She's going beautifully,' Sarah said. 'And you've fixed the heater. I could never get it to work.'

'How did the exams go?' I asked.

'Well, I think,' she said. 'The statistics one was a bitch but I probably did all right. I have a sense of great relief. They say if you make it through the first half of the year, you will almost certainly complete the second. And I have an interesting thesis to start when I get back.'

Sarah had not had any breakfast, so we stopped in Malmesbury for some coffee and scones. She drove after that, as far as Citrusdal. The heavy rain gave way to scattered showers, and occasionally a weak sun broke through. Off to the right of us there was snow on the Cederberg. At Clanwilliam we stopped and purchased a supply of food. Fruit with bread, cheese and tomatoes did for lunch. I was driving as we crossed the Olifants River, and Sarah had fallen asleep in the passenger seat, leaning against the door with her boots off and her legs curled up. Her feet were surprisingly small.

It had been many years since I had driven any distance in a classic Land Rover. I had forgotten how cramped the driving position was for my seventy-seven-inch frame. Water dripped onto my knee from a seam in the roof, and the green knob on the overdrive shook. *Geraldine's* familiarity, however, redeemed her faults. Driving her was like a reunion with an old mistress. The reasons we had parted were patent, but the affection remained. The knobbly black banjo steering wheel felt wonderful, and communicated with the road as no power-assisted steering could. The speedometer, never steady, fluttered seductively around the true speed. The ammeter twitched as the regulator cut in and out. The coachwork tilted on the tighter curves and swayed when the wind gusted.

Laurens van der Post once wrote of the musical sound made when his Land Rovers travelled fast. *Geraldine* sang as she worked her way north. Harmony prevailed. The wind whistled past seams in the doors. Something rattled in the firewall and the heater fan whirred. The red knob of the range shift lever vibrated against my shin. The transfer case chimed in with a high-pitched whine on the long downgrades. There was a slight rumble from the rear differential. The wiper blades beat irregular time when needed and the tyres hummed on the road surface. The transmission made a satisfying clunk into third on the occasions when a lower gear was needed. On steeper hills, the bass voice of the air cleaner became a growl.

All afternoon I drove up the N7 in gradually improving weather. There was little traffic across the Bokkeveld. Fast cars passed me. Occasionally I overtook heavy lorries, their drivers invariably pulling onto the verge of the two-lane road to let me pass.

The clouds cleared as the sun gradually worked round to the left and shadows lengthened. The little towns with the tall church steeples became farther apart. At Bitterfontein, I stopped for petrol. A locomotive in the rail yard opposite the service station was shunting wagons loaded with copper ingots, but even this racket failed to wake the woman wrapped in the red plaid rug.

An hour later, as the sun was setting, we crossed a rise where the landscape ahead lay bathed in an eerie pink neon glow. I pulled over onto the shoulder and cut the engine. The road stretched north and vanished into the purple haze. Pinprick lights marked an oncoming truck miles away. There was not a tree in sight. Jagged *koppies,* cast at random on the rocky plain, projected elongated shadows like a zebra hide. Sociable weaverbirds swirled around a giant nest on a telephone pole chirping plaintively.

This stop awakened my companion. We both got out and stretched. It was too cool to linger. Sarah apologized for sleeping so long, and took the wheel again. I sat in the passenger seat shearing slices off a stick of *biltong* with my clasp knife. We did not talk. It was a companionable silence. Two weeks stretched ahead. There would be lots of time to get to know each other better.

At seven we rolled into Springbok, the largest town in Namaqualand. We had a meal of *boerewors* and mashed potatoes in the only restaurant open. The walls were decorated with portraits of local mining pioneers and other notables. There were souvenirs for spring tourists, and cabinets filled with samples of local minerals and semi-precious stones.

Fifty miles north of Okiep, I turned off the highway through a broken gate and bumped across the stony *veldt.* The headlights illuminated a rusty windmill with a twisted vane. I pulled up next to a circular concrete reservoir. We were both tired, and the temperature was dropping steadily. The sky was cloudless and there was no need for a tent. I spread the tarpaulin on the ground, unrolled my new foam pad and wriggled into the sleeping bag. Sarah moved around in the back of the truck, making herself comfortable and then put out her light. 'Thanks for inviting me,' she said through the side window. 'Good night, Giles.'

It was very quiet. The cooling engine made little clicks and gurgles. Nothing moved on the highway. The clear sky of my childhood arched over me, the Milky Way a jewelled band and every major star a friend. The half moon was rising fast, and departing Venus kissed the western horizon. A satellite picked a leisurely course across the field of the Southern Cross. A Bessemer trail recorded the fall of a meteorite near Beta Centauri.

'Are you awake?' An audible whisper.

'Yes. I'm watching satellites and shooting stars.'

'I'm sorry I wasn't much help driving today. I don't think I've had more than four hours sleep a night for the last week. Now I'm all wound up.'

'Have some of that red wine,' I said. We had brought a box of *Swartland Cellars*. 'Just don't ask me to get up and pour. It's freezing out here.'

'It's not much better in here.' The light went on and the truck rocked a little as she moved about. 'Would you like some?' She passed out a mug. I tapped the tin rim against my teeth in the dark. The wine had the unmistakable smoky South African flavour.

'Where exactly are we and where are we going?' We had not had the opportunity to plan a detailed itinerary.

'If you draw an imaginary map of the country we are right up in the top left-hand corner. Not far from the Richtersveld National Park. West of us is the start of the Skeleton Coast. We must be quite close to the border of Namibia. This is a very dry area, and it's beautiful in spring when it's covered with flowers. Blazing hot here in the summer though.

'We'll cross the border tomorrow and press on north. We could stop at the Fish River Canyon - it's spectacular - but we have a lot of ground to cover, and it's out of our way. I think we should push as far as Etosha over the next two days. It will mean long hours on the road. After that it gets much more interesting. From Etosha we cross the Caprivi Strip to the Chobe area and Victoria Falls. We can come down through Zimbabwe on the way back to Cape Town. That's the general idea.'

'What's at Etosha?'

'Lots of game at this time of year. And it should be a lot warmer than here.'

'Have you ever driven this way before?'

'Only as far as Windhoek. I've never been to Etosha. And I've never been along the Caprivi. To go into that area used to be pretty difficult.'

'Will we be near where you come from in Zimbabwe?'

'Very close - if we come down through Bulawayo. I would like to stop there and see the farm where I was born. It's called *Jacksland*. I grew up there and it was a wonderful childhood. The farm is about twenty miles west of town. I'd love to show it to you.'

Some minutes passed as if she had fallen asleep.

'I feel like I've been kidnapped, Mr. Ford. I had so much on my mind when I agreed to this. I had misgivings last week. My classmates thought it was a crazy idea. I'm lying here wondering if they were right. Here I am - camped out miles from anywhere - with someone I did not even know ten days ago. You may be some kind of psycho. At your trial, the defence will point out that I met you in a bar.'

There was no easy response to this, and thus a long silence. Far away across the plain, a lone jackal complained to the moon.

'Will I see my elephant?' she asked.

'I think I can promise you an elephant,' I said.

I awoke to a white world. A hard frost covered everything. The thin grass was spiky, white and welded together. The sun was below the horizon, its rays lighting the tops of the *koppies*. As I lay watching, the daisy wheel of the windmill gradually turned amber.

Reluctantly, I slipped out of the sleeping bag and went to pee behind an outcrop of rocks. There was no sound from the Land Rover. The windows were misted with condensation and the windshield was galvanized with rime. The canvas water bag hanging on the front bumper was a solid lump.

The water in the concrete reservoir was covered with a centimetre of solid ice.

It was tempting to wriggle back into the sleeping bag, but I had resolved that I would exercise on this holiday. The nearest *koppie* seemed about a mile away and about five hundred feet high. I set off across the stony ground, passing the occasional quiver tree. There were no signs of any domesticated animals or game. I wondered why the windmill had been installed. Drilling boreholes is an expensive business.

The *koppie* had steep sides but presented no challenge. I reached the top a little out of breath and feeling the first warmth of the sun. Five miles to the north and well below me stretched a valley with a green ribbon of trees, and I realized this was the Orange River, which forms the border between Namibia and South Africa. On a flat shoulder just below the summit of my *koppie* were the ruins of a blockhouse - one of the crudely built fortifications thrown up by the British during the Boer War. In a depression in the rocks were the crushed remains of old tin cans - containers for rations issued to troops fighting that war a hundred years ago, and preserved in this arid atmosphere.*

On the way back to the camp, I saw the desiccated skeleton of a large tortoise - the shell intact and polished, and the tiny bones bleached by the sun.

Sarah was brushing her hair. She had started the stove and made coffee. Fortunately, the water in the plastic jerry can inside the Rover had not frozen. The coffee was the proper kind, not the sickening instant variety cut with chicory that was so common in southern Africa.

The cold did not encourage standing around. We were under way by eight, and by nine had crossed the border into Namibia.

---

* *The ruined structure found by Giles on his morning constitutional is probably not a British fort as there is no record of such a defensive structure being built this far north in the Cape Colony during the Boer War. There was a line of blockhouses extending east from Lambert's Bay but this is about 200 miles to the south of the location described.*

CHAPTER 31

Jackals seeking scraps, passed like swift miniature ghosts.
(Canis Mesomelas)

There were few other vehicles in the camp at Hatali and, since they were some distance off amongst the trees, it was as good as having the place to ourselves. Our campsite was well organized and comfortable. We had unrolled the awning on the truck and zipped the sides into place. The campfire crackled and sweet aromatic smoke was rising in the evening air; the old black kettle steamed. I had made tea and was looking at a map of Botswana. We had been two days at Etosha, and the next morning planned to start heading northeast.

We stopped in Windhoek for a few hours to get supplies. I had been pretty relentless about covering distance, and we had travelled almost two thousand kilometres in three days, which is good progress in an old Land Rover. We shared the driving almost equally. For the last two days we had relaxed in the vast park, content to park near waterholes and watch the game. We had seen a good variety of antelope, a leopard and a pride of lions sleeping in a grove of mopani. We had not seen any trace of elephants.

My companion had just returned from a shower, wearing a white tee shirt and green shorts. Her hair was damp and she was walking in *takkies* without socks. Her legs were long and brown. She hung wet clothes on a line strung between two trees. She had blue underwear.

'This is heavenly,' she said. 'And it's your turn to cook.'

I passed her the mug of tea. 'I was crazy to suggest this. We need two months, not two weeks. We could have gone to Cape

Cross and the Skeleton Coast. Crossed the Kaokoland. Are you sure you have to be back on the 9th? I can't see how we can go to the Okavango, to Himba country and to Victoria Falls. We don't have enough time.'

Her head was close to mine as she looked at the map. She smelled good. 'Here's where we need to make a decision,' I said. 'It's plain sailing until here, where we enter the Caprivi, but there we face the decision whether we should carry on to Katima Mulilo and approach the falls from Zambia, or go down into Botswana and take the tracks across the north side of Moremi to Chobe.'

'My life seems to be one big rush,' she said. 'I would rather take it easy. It will take us four days to drive back down from Victoria Falls to Cape Town. That means we have a week before we have to start thinking of going back. Let's skip the Himba and take the northern route. I really want to go to the Falls.'

'Going that way, our route is going to depend a lot on the annual floods,' I said. 'If the water is really high, we may not be able to cross some of the watercourses and will have to backtrack. We will then have to go right down to Nokaneng and round to Maun.' I showed her this on the map.

As the air cooled, we put on warmer clothes. The squawking birds in the trees had gone to roost. Drawing our chairs closer to the fire, we watched bats darting above us in the twilight. Jackals seeking scraps, passed like swift miniature ghosts: smoke became invisible in the dark. I threw on more wood and red sparks swirled up, mingling with stars and flickering out. My Caesar salad had been a success, and the simple barbecued steaks with baked potatoes were delicious. The Sarah Brightman album ended. Apart from the settling noises of the fire, there was silence.

'How long have you been a journalist?' she asked.

'About eight years,' I said. 'My parents were farmers and wanted me to farm too. I was crazy about cars and persuaded them to send me to a technical college. I served an apprenticeship as a fitter, but I was good at mechanical design and ended up with an engineering diploma.

'There was not much work for designers in Rhodesia in those days, so I went to Cape Town for two years and taught in a technical school. I got a job in England after that, with an aircraft manufacturer - doing drawings at first, but when they found I wrote reasonable English, I started doing technical manuals. *'How to Change the Tyres on a Trident'*. Stuff like that. When I was twenty-eight, there were loads of jobs for aerospace people in North America, and with my experience I got landed immigrant status in Canada and worked for a company in Vancouver. We subcontracted for Boeing in Seattle, and I used to commute a lot over the border.' I threw a bigger log on the fire.

'But I had this love affair with English cars. I've always owned one. Everything from Jags to Minis. I started writing articles about them about ten years ago, and found there was a ready market. I focused a bit on Land Rovers because of my African roots, I suppose.'

'And you were married in Canada?' she asked.

'For about five years.'

'What happened?'

I did not reply immediately. How does one sum up a marriage in a few words? I remembered the house in Burnaby - a suburb of Vancouver - with the sound of traffic from the Trans-Canada Highway and the distant view of Mount Baker. The holidays in Hawaii. The trips to Vegas. The station wagon. The cottage in the Gulf Islands. The skiing at Whistler. The orange *Congoleum* floor in the kitchen and the shag rug in the den. The distressed furniture from Sears.

It was hard to believe I had lived there.

Patricia closing her antique store after six months of lousy sales. Patricia in a hideous lime green real estate outfit. The obsession with diet. The blind faith in fads promoted in magazines. The regular copies of *People*, *Canadian Geographic* and *Western Living*. The evenings when she would watch comedies on TV while I messed around with cars in the garage.

Backyard parties in summer with groups of friends from work. Cutting the grass with the riding mower. Fixing bikes for children on our street. 'Mr. Jackson, you talk funny.'

The sap bubbled out of the end of a log, and a greenish flame consumed a small piece of aluminium foil amongst the ashes.

'She got pregnant the first year we were married, but miscarried at 4 months,' I said. 'We decided to wait before trying again. When we decided the time was right, nothing happened. We both had all kinds of tests, and the specialists couldn't find anything wrong with either of us. It put a hell of a strain on our relationship; then, just when we were considering adoption, she told me she no longer loved me and wanted a divorce. She lied and said there was no one else, but that simply wasn't true.

'What was true was that whatever magic had brought us together had died too. Looking back now, the split was inevitable and I accept my share of responsibility...

'So we split up. We sold the house and divided everything more or less equally. She and the other guy moved in together. That didn't work out too well. She finally married someone in Calgary who had a couple of kids. Never had any of her own.

'As the divorce went through, the 767 was coming down the pike and there was another mountain of manuals that needed doing. But I needed out. I sold the Healy and my tools and went to England. I took a completely different job driving for a long-distance safari company here in Africa. That took up about nine months a year. And I started getting published.'

'Do you have anyone now?'

I thought of Jean and her brigade of Hampshire hopefuls. 'No one in particular,' I said. 'I'm forty-five. It's a very in-between age. I know a few nice women, and I suppose if I zeroed in on one, I could make myself presentable enough to get into an exclusive relationship. But I'm a bit gun-shy. Single women my age are usually pretty well established and set in their ways. They sometimes have teenage children and complicated relationships with ex-husbands. I would have liked to have had children, but it's getting a little late now. The older you get, the more compromises have to be made.

'How about us younger women? Thirty-somethings.'

I laughed. 'In that category I have plenty of competition from thirty-something males.'

'I can't see why,' she said. 'You look like you're under forty. You can cook, fix cars and write. What more could a woman want?'

'You'd be surprised," I stood up and used a branch to re-organize the fire into a smaller pyre. 'Tell me about university life. My research indicates you are one of eleven women on a course with ninety-three men. From my observations, they are in the prime of life, natty dressers and future captains of industry. This seems to be a situation that would make many of my female acquaintances turn green with envy.'

'Well, there are some very nice ones,' she said seriously. 'Most of those are married, and some are in long-term relationships. Do you know they even have a support group for students' significant others in Cape Town? Mostly women who have to put up with their partners' long hours, erratic schedules and total preoccupation with study. Amongst the single men, there are only about three I would consider a relationship with, and none of them seem particularly interested in me. In the common herd quite a few have made passes at me, but quite frankly those ones don't do much for me. And nothing is secret in the prison. We are like a lot of bacteria under a microscope. If I were to sleep with say, Doug James, everybody from the dean down would probably know about it the next day. I'm a pretty private sort of person, and I would hate that.

'The chances of meeting and developing something with anybody outside the university are zero. There's absolutely no time. It also doesn't help that I was married before. People are quite conservative here. A separated or divorced woman is frowned upon. It seems different in England.'

How long have you been divorced?'

'We split up about two years ago.'

'Can I ask why?'

'The usual. He was having an affair.'

'And no children?'

'No - the time never seemed right. Yet we were together almost seven years.'

'Where did you meet him? University?'

'No, he's older than that. So sophisticated. He swept me off my feet. I couldn't believe he wanted me. He'd been married before. When we met, he was in the family business, but he got into politics. That was one of the things that screwed us up.'

'Do you still love him?'

'Christ. What is this? An inquisition? It's not simply a matter of love. You wouldn't understand.'

The crackling of the fire magnified the silence that followed.

'I met Hal from Electroport a few weeks ago.'

She poked at the ashes with a stick. The firelight on her impassive face gave her the complexion of an American Indian. A little zephyr of wind stirred the flames, and the wood hissed and sputtered.

'How is he?' she asked.

'I only saw him once,' I said. 'He was frail, but there was nothing wrong with his mind. I went to his house to ask if he knew where you were. He told me he had no idea where you had gone, but something about the way he talked of you led me to ask if you had been lovers. He trusted me and told me the whole story. I found it beautiful and moving. He wanted to get it off his chest - to tell someone before he died. He's dying - but you know that. I was a sponge to soak up a release of hidden emotions. I was going to say confessor, but he wasn't confessing. He is proud of you. He loves you. I have to say I admire him for letting you go. And, knowing you now, I think it must have been the hardest bloody thing in the world to do.'

She was silent after that. The sound of *Boeremusiek* drifted across the campground, and occasionally there were gusts of laughter. An accordion started playing solo, and they sang 'Jan Piereweit' and 'Sarie Marais'.

The tears came then. She wiped her eye with the back of her wrist and smudged charcoal across her cheekbone. After a while, I moved my chair next to hers and put my arm around her shoulders, pulling her against me. Her back was surprisingly muscular. She did not resist and rested her head on my shoulder. Her cheek was warm from the fire.

The flames gradually died down. I did not get up to refill her glass. An owl hooted out across the expanse of the *pan* and it grew colder. The hurricane lamp flickered. The singing faded beyond the trees.

'Christ, Giles. What a mess I've made of my life.' Then she stirred, kissed me on the cheek, took a flashlight and headed off in the direction of the ablution block. I poked the unburned ends of logs into the fire and warmed my back, sipping wine and wondering what to do next. She returned and busied herself laying out her bedroll under the awning and brushing her hair. Then she came to me and put her arms lightly around my waist.

'I don't want to make love,' she said. 'But I want to sleep with you. Would you bring your things over?' I unrolled my pad and sleeping bag next to hers. She undressed quickly and got into her bed. I closed the mosquito net flap and followed her example. Firelight flickered on the canvas walls. She slid the zipper of her sleeping bag halfway down and reached across for me. I put both arms around her and drew her to me. Her breasts felt hard and warm, and her hair tickled my nose. I slid my hand down her long back to the crease and, cupping one cheek, pressed her belly against me. She lay with her head on my arm and her hands against her sides. It was so quiet I could hear her breathe. Long minutes passed, but I could tell she was awake. Then she stirred, put her arms around me and gave me a long kiss. 'Good night, Mr. Ford,' she said, and went to sleep on my arm.

I lay awake listening to her breathing and feeling her slow pulse. There was a heady aroma about her of healthy woman, musky sleeping bag and wood smoke.

The fire subsided to a soft glow and an occasional crackle. The three-quarter moon rose and drew an image of *Geraldine's* roof rack on the canvas ceiling. A lion roared and was answered by another in the northern distance. The owl called many times before I fell asleep.

CHAPTER 32

Kwevoel. (Corythaixoides concolor)

When I awoke, the sun was well above the horizon and camp had been struck around me. 'Come on, lazy bones,' she said, handing me a coffee. 'You said we have a long way to go.' She was wearing shorts, which matched her military sweater, and the scuffed boots exaggerated the slimness of her ankles.

There was a small supermarket in Tsumeb - a mining centre, and the last town of any size we would see for a week - where we stocked up on provisions. We pushed a trolley up and down the aisles, selecting things we liked and stowing them in sturdy cardboard boxes. The girl at the checkout counter must have had San blood, as she was only five feet tall and made the two of us look like happy giants. The locals doing their shopping smiled at us. An old Boer wanted to talk as I passed parcels up to Sarah on the roof rack.

We made a detour to see the Hoba Meteorite. By eleven we were driving up the lonely stretch of road that links Grootfontein with Rundu on the Okavango River. The ribbon of tarmac cut across the plain like a knife slash. It was a crystal clear day and appreciably warmer than any we had shared before. An occasional mirage flickered on the road far ahead.

We did not talk much. As the day warmed, we opened the vents in the bulkhead and the roof. The transmission sang. Before, there had been a slight reserve, and today it was gone. I studied her. Her eyelashes were long and her eyes were very dark behind the sunglasses. There were wrinkles at the corners of her eyes. She drove with both hands on the steering wheel. She had long fingers with short nails, and a twisted copper African bangle on her wrist. The draught from the ventilator ballooned the sleeve of her shirt, showing a round brown freckled shoulder and the strap of her bra. I reached over and touched her arm and she smiled and drove on.

Every year a miracle happens in tropical Africa. In wretched Angola, where diamonds fund a futile civil war, rains fall in the highlands of the Cuando Cubango, a vast sparsely populated region of savannah woodland.

The eastern part of this great area drains down through the Luiana and Chobe rivers to the Zambezi, where the water joins the main flow of that great river and thunders over the Victoria Falls, eventually draining into the Indian Ocean. The western area has no outlet to the sea, and the water is carried down the Cuito and Okavango rivers across that peculiar pedicle of Namibia called the Caprivi Strip, dissipating into the sparsely populated reaches of Northern Botswana. In a good year the water fills innumerable *pans* and extends as far as Lake Ngami on the northern fringes of the Kalahari Desert.

This annual inundation is one of the marvels of Africa. There are summer rains here when the bush turns lush and green, but without the seasonal floods from Angola, the winters would be dry indeed. The waters from the northern mountains fan out in June, July and August over a vast region of bush called the Okavango Delta, creating a swampy oasis that is a magnet for millions of birds and hundreds of thousands of animals.

Our destination was not the heart of the delta or the Moremi

Wildlife Reserve, which it encloses. Surface travel is impossible there in the floods. Our destination was the Chobe National Park in the far northeast of Botswana. The timing of the flood was important to us, as extensive water inundation would make it impossible for us to traverse the route I planned and might force us into a long detour to the south.

When we arrived, with Sarah at the wheel, there seemed to be only one official at the Botswana border. He was interested in the English registration and was disposed to talk, as he had little else to do. There were no other vehicles crossing. A group of men was working on a broken-down transport lorry. Sarah took the little toilet bag she kept behind the passenger seat and went to make a telephone call. I could see her in a dusty booth across the compound slapping the occasional fly. She seemed to be having an argument.

'Will we be able to cross to Chobe with this?' I asked.

'I cannot answer that,' he said. 'It is for you and God to decide.'

'You drive,' she said, and was silent for half an hour after we pulled away from the customs post. I did not ask what her call had been about, and she did not volunteer any information.

When were you last here?'

'Six years or so ago,' I said. 'I used to bring groups through when I drove. We would come up from the south through Maun, and we had an arrangement with an outfitter there to have the guests take *mokoro* trips into the eastern delta. Then we would go up through Chobe to Zambia and on north. But my involvement with northern Botswana goes back a lot longer than that. When I was in high school,

I had a math teacher called Shwartsky - a keen amateur naturalist who loved to organize trips into the bush with students. He had an old *Willys* Overland Wagon - a sort of high box on wheels, but pretty capable. Bulawayo is only a few miles from the Botswana border. I was one his favourites, I suppose. I went with him on holidays all over this area. It was much wilder then. There were no safari lodges, and no veterinary control fences like there are today.

'He taught me to love the wilderness. He was a superb shot and could live off the land for weeks. He never killed anything except for food. I learned most of what I know about African animals from Shwartsky. He had a memory like an encyclopaedia and was a very good teacher.

'Once, I recall a group of us were with him one July holiday. We were out somewhere west of Chobe, where you and I will be in a few days. He was helping a man from the Transvaal museum who was doing a study of gemsbok migrations, and my friend Robin Holidell and I were helping count - which is pretty boring when you are a teenager. We were being harrassed by a *kwevoel* - that's a bird that follows hunters and makes a bit of a racket - and I shot the *kwevoel* with my .22. Shwartsky was pretty upset. He said it was a crime against God to shoot an animal needlessly. "Look what you've done, Jackson," he said, pointing at the pathetic bunch of bloody grey feathers. "What have you achieved? You had one second of primitive gratification when you squeezed that trigger. You have needlessly killed one of God's creatures. It's people like you who will ruin Africa." I felt ashamed and sick. After that I lost interest in shooting.'

Later in the afternoon we were far from the main road, travelling on a rutted track with parched dry thorn bush on our left and the riverine forest on our right. We had passed the last small village with cultivated plots two hours before, and the area was becoming pretty wild. An occasional trail branched off to the right towards the river, but in the dry scrub to our left there was no sign of the track I was looking for. There was little game about, although we saw occasional groups of impala that danced off into the bush. There was a great variety of birds. I wished I had a better map and a GPS. Given more time, I would have planned things better. In really wild country, sensible off-road travellers go with at least two vehicles. We were out on our own. We had plenty of food and water. I had great faith in *Geraldine's* reliability, but I did not want to do anything stupid. If we started finding deep sand or had to ford an appreciable depth of water, the wise course would be to turn back and take a better-established route.

We saw no other vehicles. The road was passable enough and headed purposefully southeast. Sometimes it divided into several parallel alternatives where dried mudholes showed the perils of the rainy season. There were areas of hard sand that bypassed loops in the river. At other times the track hugged the bank, winding between the boles of fan palms and sausage trees. There were extensive stands of papyrus reeds in the swamps, and occasional places where water lapped the bank a few yards away. Most of the time it was possible to drive in high-range third. Frequently the rutted trail traversed a *donga* or small valley and we drove down the sides cautiously, crossed muddy watercourses and ground up twisted slopes in low range. The driving was quite exhilarating, and we shared it.

The majority of four-wheel-drive vehicles are never driven to anything close to their true capability. On the long drive up through Namibia, the old Land Rover had shown her age, being less comfortable than her successors, underpowered and unable to keep up with modern traffic. Here, however, she was in her element. The iron four cylinder delivered just the right amount of low-end torque, and the supple parabolic suspension allowed the solid axles to flex to match the contours of the ground. We had to watch the brakes that faded from repeated immersion in the creeks, but the engine braking was usually all that was needed on the short descents.

At four in the afternoon, I found what I was looking for. The track branched, with the left-hand fork heading northeast across a sandy plain covered with burned grass and scattered acacia. I was driving at the time and followed this for a couple of miles, then I stopped. 'This must be it,' I said. 'But it's getting too late. Let's camp near the water.'

We turned back and retraced our route to the fork from where tracks fanned out seemingly at random. I followed the most obvious one, wandering down through a series of muddy depressions. After several miles of unpromising camping territory, we climbed out onto a wooded peninsula overlooking a wide lagoon. There were signs of previous visitors. Dead trees had been hacked for firewood. There was a fireplace, and a primitive toilet back amongst some bushes. A rusty barrel containing old cans was peppered with bullet holes, and some tarnished cartridges lay scattered about. There were wooden racks for game. A huge dead tree had fallen perpendicular to the shore and penetrated the fringe of papyrus reeds far enough to reach open water.

It was a beautiful place. There were few flies. There were signs of elephant, with downed trees and dried heaps of droppings, but none were recent. A hive buzzed somewhere in the treetops. Someone had nailed crude steps to the side of the fallen giant, and we scrambled up onto the trunk and walked out to the end, where it angled down under water. Withered branches whitened with fish eagle droppings poked skyward. The water was clean and clear. There were *hoopoe* holes in the sandy bank. Weaverbird nests swayed in the tops of the reeds. A sacred ibis flew off across the smooth water. There were no signs of crocodiles or hippos.

'Can we swim?' she asked.

There was no habitation nearby, so the chance of bilharzia was low. 'You would have to be quick about it,' I said. 'Splashing might bring up some crocs. I'd hate to lose my co-pilot.'

The area surrounding the camp had been well picked over for dry firewood, so we made an excursion around the surrounding woodland in the Land Rover, cutting dry branches with a bow saw and stacking them on the roof rack. I did not know what the situation was with lions, and did not want to sleep without a fire smouldering. On our return, I sawed the dry wood into faggots and Sarah split them expertly, swinging the heavy axe high over her shoulders. We got a good blaze going and set up camp.

Sunset painted the western sky vermilion, leaving a luminous glow on the water. Mars was at its closest to Earth and hung like a red ball. Venus glowed near the horizon as the air cooled.

I left the fire and walked some way back up the trail. A neon green glow-worm lit a few square inches of a crevice between two stones. A small animal ran off in the gloom. *Young warthog or a porcupine*, I thought. I moved the beam of the powerful flashlight in an arc through the surrounding bush. No eyes gleamed.

Looking back towards the campfire, it seemed an enchanted place. The pressure lamp glowed in a tree, and the amber light of the campfire flickered. The stubby nose of the muddy truck pushed out from behind the awning with its tied-back nets. Sarah still had the Tilley hat hanging behind her head and was preparing food on a board resting between the two wheel arches across the safari door. A crusty loaf of German bread was sliced and a bottle of wine glowed red on the folding table. A muted Anna Moffo sang *Madame Butterfly*.

A wave of almost painful emotion swept over me. It was a strange feeling of gut-wrenching joy that brought tears to my eyes. I would not have traded my situation with that of any other man in the world.

I went quietly back down the path, moved up behind her and put my arms around her. 'I want you to know,' I said, 'that you are with the happiest man in Africa.'

She dropped the knife and the half-sliced tomato rolled off the board. She put her arms over mine and hugged them against her. Then she twisted round to face me. 'I'm glad,' she said simply. I did not have to bend to kiss her.

We finished supper and cleaned up. I was worried about baboons, so we stowed gear and food back into the Rover. We sat some while beside the fire in companionable silence. Hippos bawled at each other across the lagoon. *Nagaapies* called in the trees. We might have been the last two humans on the continent.

There had been no thought of pitching my tent. I washed, brushed my teeth and watched as she laid out the two sleeping pads and covered them with her sleeping bag. She then spread mine on top and covered it with the plaid rug. 'Come to bed,' she said softly.

I removed my boots, turned the lamp low and took it inside. The light barely reflected off the ochre walls and the dusty flank of the truck. The night pressed against the transparent mosquito flap, but there was no one to look in.

She knelt on the bed, undid the buttons on my shirt and lifted it over my head. She undid my belt and I pushed off my pants and underwear. She raised her arms as I pulled the tee shirt over her head. She arched her back and clasped her hands behind her head as I reached behind her to undo her bra.

Her breasts were warm and heavy in my hands and the nipples salty to kiss, with unexpected fuzz. I sat cross-legged on the rug and drew her to me, lifting her hips to slide the clothes down her thighs and up over her knees. She leaned back submissively, running her fingers lightly along the arm that pinned her to me, then raised her lips to be kissed.

My hand explored downwards from the firm breasts across the softness of her belly and deep indentation of her navel. I parted the thick hair and felt the warmth of her. I ran the tips of my fingers lightly down along the moist ridge at the top of her thigh until I felt the swell of her bum.

She sighed and wriggled down lower, parting her knees. I caressed her slowly and gently backwards and forwards, timing the movement of my hand to the regular call of the nightjar across the lonely swamp outside. The nipple swelled in my other hand.

Perhaps ten minutes passed or it could have been an hour. She reached both hands up and pulled my face down to hers. 'If you go on doing that,' she whispered, 'I will leave you far behind.'

She rolled over and reached up for me. There was no resistance, just deep, tumultuous warmth that seized me and pulled us together. She left the nightjar and me far behind. She did not cry out but made a sort of low breathless moaning sound that came and went. I doubt if she felt when I was spent. I lay on her, feeling the waves recede. She held me firmly there, with arms and legs around me and her face against the sweaty stubble of my cheek.

Long minutes passed and then I felt something very like a sob. I raised myself on my elbows and saw there were tears in her eyes. I sensed this was something she did not want me to see so I reached over and turned off the lamp.

I disentangled myself and, rolling her on her side, covered her with the sleeping bag and snuggled up behind her. The sobs subsided. 'I'm sorry,' she said softly. 'It's just me. I'm really very happy.'

Much later that night she woke me up, unzipping the net and slipping out into the moonlight. I thought uneasily of hyenas, but she did not go far, peeing close to the front of the Rover and slipping back inside. She then proceeded to rouse me with a series of very provocative manoeuvres that I was happy to reciprocate. We made love again. It was earthy and companionable. There were no tears and we went to sleep very close together.

CHAPTER 33

Saddle Billed Stork. (Ephippiorhynchus Senegalensis)

She was asleep when I woke the next morning. The sun was up. Reflected light from the water was playing on the underside of the fan palm leaves. Birds chattered in the foliage.

She slept on her back. A freckled shoulder was inches from my face. Her skin was finely textured, like the shell of an ostrich egg. Her ear was pierced for earrings. A little salt had dried at the corner of her eye. The long eyelashes touched her cheek. Her breast lay against her arm and I could see tiny veins through the skin. The big brown nipple was almost completely flat. Her clenched hand seemed big for the slender wrist, which was discoloured by the copper bracelet. She was very beautiful.

A little chameleon had climbed the door flap and was feasting on insects trapped in the netting. Its movements were slow and deliberate and it rolled its eyes as it walked.

I decided to get up. I took the plastic Envirosoap container and a towel from the back seat, eased the zipper up and stepped out into the sunshine.

Dew covered everything, but steamed off as the sun reached it. I walked barefoot across the fallen leaves. As I climbed onto the log, a clawless otter slipped off the end into the water and disappeared with scarcely a ripple. The water was cold and I stayed in only long enough to soak myself, wash and rinse. A submerged tree limb made it easy to climb out. I sat out on the warm wood drying off in the sun. A naked animal. One of millions in the Okavango.

Fish scales from the otter's breakfast sparkled. There were

antelope on the opposite bank but they were too far away to identify. A saddle-billed stork was fishing perhaps eighty yards away. Dragonflies darted amongst the papyrus. A solitary hamerkop flew west with steady pumping of his wings. Busy wasps collected water, and sand martins zoomed overhead.

This was as it had been for thousands of years. Once there had been innumerable vistas like this in Africa. In three hundred years virtually all had changed. The white man had come with engineering, chemicals and ideas. Uncountable thousands of men had been traded for beads and sold into slavery. Hundreds of tons of ivory had been taken to build Victorian pianos and billiard balls. The black rhino was almost done, his horn an Oriental remedy for impotence. Roads run where only paths had been. The quiet *mokoro* is being replaced by the Evinrude and the Cessna. North of me, boys fought with AK47s. To the east, men sweated a mile underground for gold. The diamond that the successful dot-com millionaire gives his wife for Christmas costs the arms of the teenager in Sierra Leone. The *gemsbok* is impaled on the game fence so the housewife in Dortmund can buy cheap beef. The grunting diesel spreads the scourge of AIDS.

I did not hear her approach. Long years of noisy driving have dulled my hearing, and the log had not stirred. I wondered if a lion could have crept up on me as easily. She knelt behind me and put her arms around my neck. She smelled sexy. I kissed a wrist. 'You're blocking my sun,' I said. 'And I've had a bath. You have a sensual miasma about you. You'll attract the flies.'

You are my sun,' she said. 'And I'm yours. Feel my warmth on your back. I'll share my flies with you.'

'I'm sitting here *kaalgat* recharging my batteries. Last night an electrical engineer drained them completely.'

'You escaped,' she said. 'I wanted proof of Fleming's right-hand rule this morning, but you were gone. Your magnetic field brought me here. Hold this towel.'

She jumped with surprising agility, clasping her knees to her chest and made a perfect cannonball into the water. The stork squawked and flew away, and the antelope on the opposite bank bounded from view. 'You scared my friends,' I said, helping her out.

'Keep looking for them,' she said. A lot of soaping went on behind me, and then she went in again with a more graceful dive. I helped towel her off. There was a lot of her. 'You have child-bearing hips,' I said.

'Unused thus far,' she said. 'Let's have breakfast. I'm starving.'

She put on her *takkies* and a minimum of clothing.

She used the stove.

'Two eggs?'

'Three, please, with bacon and about a foot of *boerewors*.

'That is mega cholesterol. You'll die in your forties.'

'I am in my forties. And I plan to work it all off today.'

'Well, I'm going to give you some fruit, too...'

So started a golden day.

We did not drive anywhere. *Geraldine* rested under the

moporota tree. There was nowhere to go. No other spot in Africa could have done us so well. Cape Town, London and Detroit were on another planet.

We explored our Eden on foot. We had no gun and armed ourselves with stout sticks. It became obvious we were on an island. If the water were to rise a few more feet the track would flood.

The place was about three miles in circumference and completely fringed with papyrus. It teemed with game. A honeyguide tried to distract us with its rattling call. A troop of chacma baboons followed us at a safe distance. Waterbuck were everywhere, and we saw vervet monkeys amongst the knob thorn branches and in the fever trees. A mongoose stared at us before vanishing in the tall grass. Three timid red lechwe bounded from sight into the reeds. We stayed away from a group of buffalo in the mud of the isthmus. A well-disguised giraffe startled us when he cantered off ahead of us. I saw the tracks of hyenas. We found the strange nest of the hamerkop.

As we returned, we had the most unexpected encounter. We were only half a mile from camp and just about to cross a small clearing when I put my hand up to stop Sarah and pushed her back into the bush, motioning her to silence.

The rhino was a big male, foraging on dappled yellow grass under the fever trees, upwind and completely oblivious to us. We watched him for half an hour. He seemed to be alone, and had clearly met our kind before as he had a bright orange marker on his right ear. Three tick birds balancing on his back moved only to avoid low branches as he grazed. He gradually worked his way inland from us and eventually we felt it safe enough to cross the clearing and head back to camp.

We kept the fire smouldering, lay out in the sun and had an occasional swim. We were there only for each other. We did not know where we were and no one else mattered. There were no other humans to observe us.

Sarah simmered. She was aroused, playful and passionate - a woman in heat. Her thirst for sex was unquenchable. I teased her and squeezed her and the lightest touches made her twitch, gasp and laugh. There was no modesty left in either of us. I loved her. She was past her first youth and had probably never been a great beauty in the classic sense. She was too tall. Her breasts were too big and probably lower than they had been. There was more of a tummy than is fashionable. But she was in her sexual prime and she had been through a drought. She excited me more than any woman ever had before. She prowled around me all day, a tanned seductive tease with no underwear, allowing glimpses of curves, creases and recesses I had only to reach out to explore. Her lips were incredibly soft. Her nipples were constantly erect. There was a damp patch on the khaki shorts that the sun failed to dry all day.

Late in the afternoon she snoozed on the rug. The refrigerator battery had run down and the beer was warm. A voyeuristic old baboon watched from the fork of a tree fifty yards away. The sky was turning pink. The otter returned to our log, bringing his mate, and they started to play, jostling each other and sliding down the smooth trunk into the water. This was too good for Sarah to miss, so I woke her gently, put my finger to my lips and pointed.

There was a high-pitched squealing sound from across the water. The otters checked their play and disappeared. Then we saw them. A herd of elephants emerged from the reeds on the opposite bank and started to bathe in the water. There were about twenty of them, mostly fully grown, but with some juveniles and babies. They rolled playfully, crushing the papyrus, squirting water and stirring up mud. Waves spread out, raising and lowering the lily pads and lapping the shores near our bathing spot.

She clutched my arm. It was a memorable sight and I felt my heart beating faster. 'You kept your promise,' she breathed.

The huge animals regrouped and, after a bit of jockeying, headed diagonally across our line of sight, almost submerged in the pink water. They emerged from the reeds onto the bank not a hundred yards from the camp, and with a lot of commotion started to feed amongst the trees, gradually working their way towards us. I left the rug and threw whole branches on the fire. The dry leaves ignited in a flash of flame. The baboon disappeared.

The lead elephant was only twenty yards away and had seen fire before. She did not seem unduly perturbed, but stopped feeding. Little eyes evaluated me from above the yellow tusks and the ears swung back and forth. There was a general milling about in the bush, and at one point I thought they were simply going to pass the camp and continue in the same direction. They thought better of this, however, wheeled and started heading off down the bank away from us. Feeding resumed and their noise gradually subsided, although we could hear the occasional crack of a branch breaking.

I felt a chin on my shoulder and arms around my waist. 'Thank you,' she said. 'Next time make it a little less scary.'

There was plenty of wood left, and I built up the fire. We jointly prepared a feast. An insect orchestra played in the bush. The *Simonsig*, our best bottle of wine, was opened. I singed my arm getting the roast potatoes, and we were forced to move the table back from the blaze. She raised her glass. 'To *Geraldine*,' she said. 'She found us and brought us here.'

We went to bed early. She was insatiable. Warm lips teased me.

'If you manage to get anything more out of me,' I said severely, 'I'll tie a pair of your blue cotton knickers on the radio antenna and not remove them until we get to Cape Town.'

'It will be fun trying,' she said.

Much later the flames subsided. I kneeled astride her thighs and massaged her long brown back with hand lotion. The cream mixed with the perspiration and clotted in the downy fold of her back. I felt the muscles relax under my hands. She was slurring her words and almost asleep.

'When I am a very old man,' I prophesied, 'on warm days they will wheel me out on to the porch. I will be able to sit in the sun and dream. And I will smile a toothless smile and remember this as the most wonderful day of my life.'

There was a long silence and I thought she might be gone.

'Perhaps I will be there too,' she said, the words almost inaudible.

CHAPTER 34

Dust devil and Giant Eland. (Taurotragus Derbianus)

The moon was nearly full and, although there was much splashing in the lagoon, no beasts disturbed us in the night.

I was up early, as *Geraldine* needed attention. The engine oil was at the 'max' line and the brake fluid reservoir completely full. I spread a tarp on the ground, wriggled underneath on my back, loosened each of the five level plugs with a crescent wrench and inserted my little finger into orifices to check the levels. All showed a trace of honey-coloured oil.

Two bare feet appeared. I reached out and left a greasy handprint on one ankle. 'Come out and play,' she said, peering at me under the differential. 'But behave yourself if you want coffee.'

You didn't tell me about these leaks. Come under here and fix them.'

Voetstoots, voetstoots, remember?'

'Please. I need a rag. There's an old tee shirt in the side pocket of my pack. White. No Armani label.' Silence for a few minutes. 'I'm sure it's there,' I called. The tee shirt was thrust under a moment later. I wiped down the transfer case dipstick. Full.

I wriggled out, folded the tarpaulin, went for a quick swim and cleaned up. The water was appreciably higher than it had been the day before. The stubble was getting out of hand, so I shaved.

As she bathed, I stole a pair of the blue panties from her pack and tied them firmly halfway up the antenna with one of the nylon cable ties from the toolbox.

We stowed the Land Rover and poured buckets of water over the ashes of our fire. Steam rose and the hot rocks sizzled. We left no trace of our visit.

The engine started happily. The ammeter swung into the charge area to replenish the fridge battery. The oil pressure was a reassuring fifty.

We swayed down the sandy slope between the reeds. Water inundated a considerable area of the track out, but nowhere was it more than a foot deep, and we ploughed through in low range without difficulty. At the fork, I disengaged the free wheeling hubs. Sarah did not want to drive, so I steered us northeastward over the plain, leaving the green belt of forest behind us. We were exactly halfway through our holiday.

The track ran in an almost direct line across sparse grassland that was flat and dry. It was too hot to keep the windows shut, and we were travelling too slowly to get any breeze. The surface alternated between hard and soft sand, and the soft areas became increasingly common. I stopped to re-engage the hubs after one particularly nasty stretch.

A fitful wind from the south raised dust devils - miniature tornados - that swirled across the plain parallel to us. There were no large trees, only isolated patches of dry acacia scrub. There were areas where the thin grass had been burned off, but there seemed to be no pattern to this, and it was a mystery as to how the fires had started. Sand worked its way past a torn gaiter and up through chinks in the floor, settling on our clothes and skin. Frequent forks in the tracks headed off for no apparent reason. There were no signposts, and in most cases I made a choice based on minimal change in direction. Twice I stopped to take a compass bearing before selecting a track.

There was no sign of human habitation, and the only animals we saw were a herd of dirty zebra migrating south and a solitary eland that lumbered off as we approached. Twice we skirted the margins of dry pans. Tire tracks showed previous travellers had crossed the desiccated surface, but I did not want to take the slightest chance of getting stuck. The temperature gauge hovered just below the red area.

Almost exactly at noon, the front tank ran dry and I switched to the rear. We had covered only a hundred and ninety miles since filling the tank. The slow pace and heavy going accelerated fuel consumption. An hour later I noticed the steering was pulling to the right, stopped and found one of the front wheels was going flat. I changed the tyre.

Sarah had barely spoken since we broke camp. A headache, she said, to explain her silence, but somehow the atmosphere had changed. Something was making her withdraw from me, and after the intimacy of the last two days, this was difficult to accept. A touch that would have drawn a corresponding response the day before was ignored, and once, when I looked her in the eyes, she averted her face. This was far more troubling than a flat tyre, as I did not know how to deal with it.

A pair of hooded vultures circled the truck and swooped down to watch us from a grass-covered dune. I bolted the high-lift jack into its bracket, clamped the offending wheel on the bonnet, cleaned my hands with paste cleaner, got back in the driver's seat and slammed the door.

'Have you any idea where we are?'

It was not the question itself that was so offensive but the tone it was delivered in. There was a degree of exasperation and a hint of blame. It was unfair. The decisions made to get us to this point had been joint decisions. The risks had been discussed. She was as familiar with our limited map as I was and fully capable of making the same calculations I was making. This was the sort of question my ex-wife would have asked.

'Not exactly,' I said shortly, and it was the truth. Navigation in flat country with a limited map and a compass is about fifty percent science and fifty percent gut feel. I had kept an eye on the odometer and had a good idea how many miles we had covered parallel to the river. The track we were following had left the forest approximately in the direction of the dotted line shown on our map. I was keeping track of the miles covered since the forest and was making allowances for the sand. Using a ruler and pencil, I had transferred the scale (which was in kilometres) from the margins of the map to the vague dotted line, and I had mentally ticked off our progress by dividing our odometer mileage by five-eighths. The *pans* we had bucked around were shown on the map as an extension of the delta, and gave me additional reassurance that we were headed in the right direction. Granted, here were multiple tracks not shown on our little map, but according to my calculations we would hit the Chobe River long before our fuel ran out. We had plenty of water and a reliable vehicle. My confidence level was high, and although I was concerned about fuel, I was not alarmed.

I knew something about women but - as was soon to transpire - not as much as I thought. 'Are you feeling okay?' I asked.

Sarah broke the silence. 'I should never have come here,' she said.

The statement negated the experience of the past week. A feeling of dread blossomed in my gut: I had dug fast and filled a deep well of affection for this woman who, I now was forced to accept, did not seem to feel the same way.

'We've done the right thing. It's been a great trip so far. We must go on; we can't be more than a hundred miles from Chobe. If we go back, we have barely enough fuel to get to Savutu, and that water was rising pretty fast. Those *dongas* we crossed will all be flooding.'

She did not argue, and I started the motor. We went another hundred yards and stalled. Sarah made an exasperated sigh. I knew what the cause was immediately. The two and a quarter engine has a block-mounted fuel pump that is a long way from the rear tank. If you stop with a hot engine, heat from the block warms the pump sufficiently to cause it to cavitate. I opened the bonnet and packed damp paper towels around the pump to cool it off. Sarah got out and went behind an acacia thicket. She came back and sat on the step on the shady side of the truck, looking miserable. She did not show any interest in what I was doing. 'I can hear an engine,' she said flatly.

Two vehicles were coming towards us, well separated. Distortion in the air made them seem wider than they were. The lead vehicle was a newish Toyota diesel four by four, fitted with a snorkel. The second was a battered ex-military Ford five-ton lorry. The Toyota had three white men in it and the truck three black. There were guns in the Toyota. The twisted horns and glazed eye of a Kudu bull poked out from behind the cylindrical water tank mounted behind the cab of the lorry.

I went over as the whir of a motor drove the window down. A gust of cool air-conditioned air flowed past my face and the unmistakable reek of Cape brandy. They were drinking from plastic cups.

The driver, a florid man with a grey beard and a pockmarked nose, had a large stomach and a frayed collar to his shirt. The other two were designer dressed and looked like advertisements for Abercrombie and Fitch. They all got out. 'Man, it's hot for this time of year,' the big one said. He eyed *Geraldine*. 'That's an old Landy to bring out here in the *Gramadoelas* - who you with? I'm Rudy Rossow. This is Steve Putalski and this is Dave di Pietro. They flew in from Jacksonville, Florida, two days ago.'

We shook hands. 'I'm Giles Jackson,' I said. 'And this is Sarah Oakes.'

Sarah did not stand up. 'Hi,' she said listlessly. A minute later she got up and walked around to the other side of the Rover, effectively out of sight.

'We just had a flat,' I said. 'The fuel pump got too hot. I'm cooling it off.'

'They do that,' said the big man. 'I'll fix your flat for you. Henry's a *fundi*. Henry!' he yelled.

The three black men tumbled out of the truck and were introduced as Henry, Adam and Boesman. They dismounted the wheel and located the offending thorn in minutes. The auger bit into the tyre and a compressor whirred on the truck.

As they worked, we talked. 'Cute truck,' said the tall one.

'GB - England,' said the short one. 'You guys come a long way. Travellin' alone? You huntin'?'

'No,' I said. 'We're by ourselves and we don't have a gun.'

I fetched my map, laid it out on the hood of the Toyota and addressed the guide. 'Obviously you know your way around. We want to get through to the park. Can you show me exactly where we are and suggest a route?'

He lit a cigarette and put it in his mouth while he hitched up his pants. Screwing up his eyes, he peered at the map in the bright sun. 'Need my glasses,' he muttered and pulled them from his shirt pocket. 'Where are we? This is a pretty small scale. I'd say we were about here. Hang on.' He sat in his driver's seat and read the coordinates off a GPS. 'Closer to here.' His nicotine-stained finger indicated the area where I had deduced we were.

He pulled a roll of dirty 50,000:1 maps from a locker and sorted through them. They were the ones that I had been unable to locate in Cape Town. 'Right on the corner of this one,' he said. The track was clearly marked, and there were others crudely added with a ballpoint pen and coordinates. Species of animals and dates were scrawled in, but whether these were observations or kills I did not ask.

''Bout twenty miles from here you cross a big *pan*,' he said. 'Bone dry - hasn't filled for years - you can drive it no problem. Right in the middle, five tracks meet. You can't miss the place. There's a heap of old tyres stacked there - you can see them for miles. You take the second track on the right. When you pull off the *pan*, you go through an area of really dense anthills so you will know it's the right track. After about two hours, you start dropping down and hit the drain. It's got water in it but it's not too deep. There are all sorts of places to cross and the sand is pretty firm. You'll find the track heading east on the other side and a couple of hours later you hit the park. They don't exactly encourage people coming in from this side, so go straight to the office and level with William there - he's a good type.'

I thanked him. It looked pretty straightforward. 'Seen any lions?' asked the tall one.

'No,' I said truthfully. 'I haven't even heard them.'

'Lots where you're going,' said the hunter. 'Water in the drain attracts 'em. They come out of the park. Camp on this side. They may not have crossed yet. Out of my territory.' The last words were tinged with regret.

'Any crocs in the drain?' I asked.

He looked at me with red eyes and sucked the last stub of his cigarette.

'Probably,' was all he said.

They waited while I started our engine. I gave them a thumbs-up sign. I had volunteered to pay for the tyre repair, but he'd just laughed. He leaned out of the window and called to Sarah. 'Cheer up, missus - he's not that bad-lookin', and he's got you on the right road.' The Americans grinned and waved. They put up their windows and drove off in a cloud of dust.

The big truck waited a minute. Henry leaned out of the cab. 'Hey, mister,' he said. 'Got any beer?'

I gave them three cold ones. 'Thanks for the help,' I said. The old truck ground its gears and lumbered off, leaving us in a dirty cloud of diesel smoke that dissipated slowly in the hot air.*

'Good to know we're on the right track,' I said, patting her knee. Pulling her legs out of reach, she closed her eyes and leaned against the door pillar.

We drove across the sandy pan without talking at all. The long silence had lost intimacy; hostility was palpable. The pile of tyres first appeared as a mirage but then inverted itself and became real. I turned right and two hours later found the flood channel.

The water did not seem to be running in any particular direction, and looked deep. There was a fringe of trees along the sandy bank, and animal tracks in the mud. It was late to attempt a crossing, and Sarah was so out of sorts that I decided to stop. We camped under a group of trees. The stripped down shell of an old Land Rover Series I lay on its side at the edge of the clearing. There was an untidy litter of cans and bottles. There were flies. Compared with our previous camp, it was not a pleasant place.

---

* Six months after this meeting, outfitter 'Roer' Rossow disappeared and an extensive search of his licence area failed to find him. Some suspicion fell on his employees, who claimed to have waited eight days for him to show up at a rendezvous point north of the delta.

The mystery of this disappearance was solved eight months later during the dry season, when the pilot of a light aircraft spotted the wreck of his Toyota. It appeared that the vehicle had been driven at high speed into a baobab tree and then rolled down a steep bank into heavy bush. The remains of Mr. Rossow were found near the site, considerably dispersed by animals.

CHAPTER 35

It seemed safer taking my chances with the hyena.
(Spotted Hyena, Crocuta crocuta)

Sarah helped me put up the awning but said she was not feeling hungry. I lit a fire and heated a big pot of water for her to wash. Given the atmosphere, I didn't feel like eating much myself, so I took a beer and went for a walk.

The muddy margins of the water suggested the level was dropping. The channel was roughly a hundred yards wide, and the banks had a steep gradient. I looked for ruts made by previous vehicles making the crossing, but there was no obvious *drift*. There was so little rain here that the bush was criss-crossed with tyre tracks, many of them very old. There were no signs of elephant. The fresh prints in the mud were mostly antelope. There were old tracks, but no signs that lions had been in the area recently.

The most likely looking crossing was where a crude wooden cross was nailed to a tree on the opposite bank. I took off my boots and went in. The water deepened quickly to about two feet and then levelled off. I waded all the way across. Halfway it reached a maximum depth of three feet, which was about the limit I wanted to tackle with *Geraldine*. There were no rocks, but the bottom had a sticky consistency I didn't like. I tried alternative spots a hundred yards north and south, but they were no less deep and seemed even muddier.

I sat down on the bank, pulling *steekgras* burrs from my socks. The air was still and the heat oppressive. A dove made its repetitive soothing call. Impala and waterbuck came down to the water on the opposite bank, watchful but not unduly so as they lingered near the water, another indication that there were no lions in the vicinity.

There was no urgency to get back to camp; with my companion's mood so black, I preferred to be alone. I couldn't fathom her irritation with me. I reflected wryly that I seemed to be getting the same treatment that had caused the split between her and Gert du Plessis. I wondered if Gert had been her lover, too. From what Angela had said, I thought not, but I found myself suddenly feeling almost sick at the thought. I had never met the man, but after talking to him on the telephone I felt an instinctive dislike for him. I realized that I could accept Hal Mathews as a previous lover but not Gert du Plessis. There was a double standard somewhere here. Gert was a young tough guy. And what about the Australian welder? He was also a young stud. How many others had there been on the road down Africa? With the swelling feeling of jealousy came the miserable knowledge of just how important she had become to me and how devastated I'd be if she rejected me.

I was yanked from my thoughts by a loud splash. I'd missed the reptile's strike. Dusk was gathering and one of the impala had strayed too deep into the water. There was a great splashing and struggling. The animals scattered except for the brown form flailing the water with its hooves. It could not have been a very big crocodile or the end would have been swifter. It took thirty seconds before the doomed animal was drawn below the surface and the water returned to calm.

I laced my boots and went back to camp.

'There's supper there if you want it,' she said. It was spaghetti with some sausage chopped in. The stereo was silent. There seemed little point in opening the last bottle of wine.

'Thanks,' I said, helping myself. 'Have you had some?'

'A little, I'm not hungry.'

'How are you feeling?'

'Rotten.'

I got myself another beer. 'There are crocodiles here,' I commented. 'Stay away from the river.'

She did not seem interested. I didn't talk about my wading exercise.

The stack of wood was barely adequate for the night and I was uneasy about predators. It was too late to collect more. If we had visitors, we would have to withdraw into the truck.

I lit the lamp. She did not undress completely and zipped her sleeping bag shut with determination. I made my bed against the opposite wall and lay down, leaving the bag open in case I needed to get up fast in the night.

Sleep eluded me. I was worried about the water crossing in the morning. Sarah was obviously still awake and restless in her sleeping bag.

'Will we get to Victoria Falls tomorrow?' The voice was unfriendly.

'We will if I can get us across this creek,' I said. 'Look. Something's bugging you. Is it something I've done?'

Silence. I gave up. 'Did Sam Loos ever suggest you fit *Geraldine* with a snorkel when he outfitted the truck?'

'How the hell do you know Sam Loos?'

'Mark Franklin told me you took *Geraldine* to him.'

'The old writer? I never met him but he gave me good advice. You talked to him? How do you know him?'

'We write for the same magazine.'

'You really have been snooping, haven't you? First Hal Mathews and the Wilds, now Mark Franklin and Sam Loos. Who else did you get your information from?'

I didn't like the direction this was heading and chose the least harmful course. 'I had a drink with Tony Morganter.'

'What!' She bolted upright. 'Good grief! You discussed my private life with him, too.'

'He told me about your adventures in Ethiopia together. He likes you a lot and wonders why you never wrote to him. You were both brave and you saved the life of that woman. After I heard his story, I really wanted to meet you.'

'How did you find out I liked opera?'

'A guy in London told me. He was going to travel with you and fitted the CD player.'

'Adam Williamson,' she said. 'That little prick. What a snake he turned out to be. How the hell do you know him?'

'His name was on your carnet. I found him on the Internet.'

'This is incredible,' she said. 'I've been working away in Cape Town and you've been busy digging around in my life - obsessed with me. Just how did you get hold of my carnet?'

'From the RAC.'

'It must be important. You could have written me a letter. Instead, you've been systematically stalking me. Who do you work for? What do you want? I don't believe this crap about working for Land Rover. You're a liar.'

'Your lawyer was not forwarding letters. He absolutely refused.'

'You know why? Because of men. Hal insisted on the clean break and it would have torn me apart if he had changed his mind. Then has a little drink with you and tells you all about it. Did he go into the details?'

No answer seemed the safest bet.

'And then my husband. He's destroying my life - *that's* it! You work for him, don't you? He's paid you to track me down. The bastard - '

'I didn't know you still had a husband. You told me - '

'I suppose that jerk Williamson told you about Angela and Gert?'

'He did,' I said. 'Tony Morganter also told me a bit about them.'

'What! You tracked them all down? You're sick. There's nothing to find out that's worth all this trouble. What did they tell you about me?'

'I had dinner with Angela,' I said. 'She told me about her trip to Cairo with you. And I did speak to Gert on the 'phone from Cape Town. There's nothing sinister in all of this. We do want to buy *Geraldine*. The money's in your bank by now.'

'I bet you fucked her,' she sneered. 'Angela fucks every man she meets. She's got the roundest heels in Europe. She spent more time on her back going to Cairo than we did driving. She must have had thirty different men in ten weeks.'

I did not deny it, and knew my silence was an admission of guilt.

'Shit,' she said. 'I thought I liked you. I can't understand why you're running around stalking me and prying into my life. I realized what you were up to when I found a photo of myself when I pulled that shirt out of your pack this morning. Are all men perverts, or is it just my luck to attract ones who are? If all you wanted was to buy the stupid Land Rover, you wouldn't have persuaded me to come here. And you jumped into bed with that tart. When? About two weeks ago, I'll bet, before you came here. And then I made love to you. You acted like a lovely, gentle, kind man, put on this big "trust me" act and I fell for it.'

Her voice rose hysterically. 'What was yesterday about? I don't understand your game plan. I'm not another Angela. You've violated me. Then you tie my panties to your truck so every alcoholic bushwacker in Botswana knows what you've done. I'm nobody's trophy. Not his. Not yours.'

What had seemed harmless and fun before was being turned on me. I went on the offensive. 'Look here,' I said. 'I can explain that photo. I admit I slept with Angela. Maybe she does like to screw around and I knew that when I did it. I'm human. She's an attractive woman and I enjoyed her company. No one lost anything. It was a rush. I don't even know why I'm even admitting this to you. I didn't know you then. You can't compare what we shared yesterday to a one-night stand with Angela!'

'It shows a certain lack of discrimination,' she said sarcastically. 'Was all that body piercing and the tattoo a turn-on? I hope you used a condom.'

'We did,' I said, annoyed. 'This is ridiculous. We're both adults. You've had an affair with a married man. You're thirty-five and an experienced woman. And now I learn that you're still married as well. Who's being deceived here? And talk about one-night stands! What about that ruddy Australian welder guy in Uganda? I gather you had him twenty-four hours after you met him. And I'll bet there were others. What about Luke, the doctor in Zomba? You stayed at his place. He's HIV positive, for Christ's sake. And what about that Afrikaaner du Plessis ? What was that box of condoms in your first-aid kit for?'

'You are an absolute creep,' she said, her voice trembling and icy. 'Are you working for the government or some garbage tabloid? I had no idea just how much you found out about me in your slimy way. Well. I've news for you. No matter how deep you dig with those people, you'll never figure out my real problem. Go to hell. Stay on your side of the tent. When we get out of this tomorrow, I'm going to fly home. Or take a bus. I don't want to spend another bloody minute in your company.'

She threw herself down with her back to me. Immediately I regretted some of the things I'd said, but there was no taking them back.

I heard a noise outside. I took the flashlight and caught the gleam of the big hyena's eyes just beyond the fire. I threw a log at him and he snarled and loped off. I retrieved the log and placed it on the fire. There was no point in going back into the tent. It seemed safer taking my chances with the hyena.

I fetched my sleeping bag and put it over my shoulders. I settled into one of the camp chairs with a hefty stick handy and resigned myself to a long night. The moon climbed, an almost perfect disc with a coterie of millions of stars mirrored on the still water. A worried baboon on the opposite bank barked and was reassured by his companions.

There was silence in the tent. Last week I had thought I knew Sarah inside and out. How wrong I'd been. Here I was, thinking that things were going well between us, and then the sky had fallen. Nothing I had discovered about her prepared me for the venom of this attack. What was going on? Why would her husband have people tracking her, and what the hell would the government be interested in? Which government? And tabloids? Who *was* she? What was her 'real problem'? Nothing made any sense. I was in over my head.

A rustling in the bushes showed only a *ratel* on his evening rounds. High clouds drifted across the face of the moon. At two in the morning I stoked the fire for the last time and went to sleep on the ground.

CHAPTER 36

Up an embankment and into a clump of prickly pear...

At dawn the level of the water was deeper. There was no movement from the tent.

I took a latex glove from the first-aid kit and punched holes in the tips of all five fingers. I opened the bonnet, marked the base of the distributor with a pencil, then lifted out the whole unit, disconnecting wires from the spark plugs as I did so. I threaded the five high-tension wires through the holes in the fingers of the glove and snapped the wrist around the body just above the neck. I put the distributor back on the engine and reconnected the wires. I removed the fan belt after slackening off the generator.

The old wreck in the bushes supplied me with four feet of rusted exhaust pipe. I joined this to *Geraldine's* exhaust using a spare upper radiator hose and a couple of jubilee clamps. I tied the pipe to the roof ladder with a bungee cord.

The wading plug needed to be screwed into the bell housing. I laid the recovery strap, the snatch block and the leather gloves out on the back seat. I unrolled the first six feet of winch cable and tied the hook to the spare wheel mount.

Sarah got up while this was going on, but neither asked what I was doing nor made any move to help. She made coffee, poured me a cup and, when asked, helped put away the awning. She collapsed her *thermarest*, kneeling on it and rolling it in such a way that air was forced from the vent, then rolled up both pad and bag in a neat cylinder and strapped them to her pack. The inference was obvious.

I doused the ashes of the fire. The engine sounded strange

without the fan, and there was a different note to the exhaust. I drove us down to the water's edge and lined us up with the cross on the opposite bank.

'It's going to be pretty deep,' I said. 'If the motor stops, we may be here for a long time. I'd like you to drive, going very slowly in low-range second. Whatever you do, don't rev the engine. If she starts to bog down, I'm going to jump out and push. If we get halfway and the engine is still running, we'll be okay because I can get the winch cable onto that tree. I took the fan belt off so the water won't splash too much.' No response other than a nod.

I selected low range and walked around to the other door. Sarah slid across into the driver's seat. She nosed *Geraldine* down into the water. The saturated sand made the ride seem heavy and unresponsive, but the tyres bit well and we made good progress, pushing a small wall of water ahead of us. A flock of ducks scattered. In the centre of the stream the water started coming in the doors, but I had expected that. Waves fanned out in all directions. As we approached the opposite bank, the upward slope became steeper and I felt her floundering. Twenty yards from the bank, our forward progress slowed. We were bogging down. Spinning the wheels would simply dig us in deeper.

I pushed open the door, jumped into the water and splashed aft. Some subconscious memory of rugby caused me to put my shoulder against the galvanized corner capping and heave. This, perhaps combined with the lack of my weight on board, was all that was required. The truck lurched forwards and surged up the bank, leaving me spread-eagled in the mud with the side of my shorts torn by the roof ladder.

Before, there would have been humour in the situation, but the black cloud hanging over our expedition precluded it. 'Shut it off,' I yelled up to her. I walked fifty yards to where the water was clean and undisturbed. I stripped and washed the mud off, emptied my boots and rinsed my clothes. Barefoot, in damp shorts and carrying the boots, I went up to the truck. 'Nice driving, thanks,' I said. She remained mute and shifted to the other seat.

After taking off my makeshift exhaust extension, I replaced the fan belt, restarted the engine and wound in the winch cable. I went under the chassis and removed the wading plug. I tied my shirt to the roof rack. In doing so, I noticed the unrecognizable, frayed and dirty bit of cloth on the antenna and cut it off with my knife. I threw my boots in the back and drove barefoot down the obvious dusty track east.

Two hours later, a big sign requesting all travellers to report to the ranger station marked the park border.

Thirty miles farther on we came to the camp. There was an impressive lodge-style building with vast areas of thatched roof. Guests lounged in plastic chairs while waiters hovered. A fleet of excursion vehicles had rows of open seats. Hippos yawned in a pool, surrounded by manicured green grounds. I pulled up a little distance from the reception area.

The park offices were contained in a small compound a few hundred yards from the lodge. I put on my damp shirt and wet boots. I walked through a grove of *mopani* to get to the offices.

The woman in uniform behind the reception desk looked me

over. 'I've come to check in,' I said. 'We just came in on the track from the west.'

She pulled out a ledger from under the counter.

'How did you cross the spillway?' asked a voice from out of sight around a corner of the office. A small man in uniform appeared with a cup of coffee in his hand.

'Drove,' I said. 'We almost had to winch up the bank.'

'I saw you pulling in,' he said. 'The muddy old Land Rover. What route did you take to get here?' I explained as best I could.

'Pretty wild down there. You must have seen a lot of game.'

'We did. Including a black rhino. I was surprised. Male. Orange tag on his right ear.'

'So that's where he is,' he said. 'We lost him six months ago. Could you show me the location on a map?'

He took me back into the office. Maps covered the walls. 'That's the park,' he said. 'We need something more south.' He rummaged in a cabinet and spread out another map on his desk. 'This should do it.'

It was confusing looking at the large-scale map and it took me ten minutes to confidently select where we had camped.

'That's a hunting concession in there,' he said. 'I hope some idiot doesn't shoot it. I'll warn them. Some of these foreigners will shoot anything that moves.'

'The rate the water was coming up that island will be pretty well cut off by now.'

'Thanks for letting me know, anyway,' he said.

We talked about conservation for another fifteen minutes.

The woman relieved me of my park fees and I headed back to the lodge.

The Land Rover was locked and there was no sign of Sarah.

A small Mercedes Benz bus had drawn up to the reception area, and a driver with white gloves was sliding luggage into a locker under the deck. Amongst the elegant suitcases was a brown pack with a tidy bedroll secured on top. I looked up and saw her face behind the tinted window.

A cardboard sign in the windscreen read "Victoria Falls". I pushed a red button and the door folded open with a hiss. It was cool and air-conditioned inside. The bus was full of older affluent-looking white people. She was sitting three rows from the front next to a wizened old guy wearing a Cardinals baseball cap. She had changed into clean clothes.

'Please don't do this,' I said.

'It's no good, Giles. I've booked a flight to Cape Town tomorrow. I'm sorry it didn't work out. Please go. I gave your keys to the concierge.'

A tear trickled down her cheek from behind the dark glasses. There was silence amongst the other passengers. A large woman made a sympathetic clucking noise.

'This is crazy.' My voice sounded too loud. 'Let's talk about it. We can't finish like this.' She sat rigid with her arms folded, staring out of the window.

The driver got in and started the engine. I could see him looking at me in his driving mirror. He said something into a microphone.

A man got on the bus. He had a name tag which read 'William

Wilson, Day Manager'. 'Excuse me, sir,' he said. 'You will have to get off. This bus is leaving.'

The doors closed with a sigh. The diesel rattle changed to a purr and the coach swung out from under the thatched porch into the sun.

Wilson was not overly hospitable. 'The lady gave me this to give to you, sir,' Wilson said, handing me a white envelope heavy in one corner. 'Would you please move your vehicle.'?

I stood in the driveway, conscious of my filthy shirt, torn pants and wet boots.

Across an immaculate lawn was an outdoor bar. I sat down at an empty table. A group of waiters tittered in a corner but no one came to take an order. I waited ten minutes. I opened the envelope. Car keys. The note said 'I'm sorry, but it would never have worked.'

I strode up to the bar. 'If you don't bring me a beer in thirty seconds - ' I said threateningly.

The manager was waiting and he had two large men with him. I got no beer and found myself firmly propelled out into the parking area.

I drove right through the park. If there were any animals about, I did not see them. Two hours later I passed out of the north gate. I had just enough petrol to get to Kasane. I filled both tanks and headed for the Zimbabwe border, arriving at Kazangula post just as the gate was closing for the night. They would not let me through.

I ended up camping in a commercial site crowded with young people who partied late into the night. I had a cold shower and cleaned up as best I could. When I went back to the truck, I found the backpack with my clothes was missing.

Geraldine was first in the lineup at customs in the morning. They made a bit of a fuss about my not being a listed driver on the carnet, but, for a fee, a 'temporary permit' was arranged, although nobody gave me any paperwork.

I gunned the old truck eastward across the plain, ignoring the imploring waves of locals looking for rides. The temperature gauge hovered on the red line as the old engine revved far beyond the limit its designers had intended. After forty miles of this, the worn spare tyre blew out on a cattle grid, and I had a sickening battle with the steering wheel that took me clear across the road, through a ditch, up an embankment and into a clump of prickly pear.

The jack handle was stowed behind the passenger seat and, after stomping down as much of the pear as was strategically necessary, I reached in to retrieve it. My hand closed on something soft and warm - the small zip-up green bag that she used as a purse. Mints, lip balm, sunscreen, a gold-capped vial of *Sisley* perfume. A simple Rolex watch. An international telephone calling card. A small pocket calendar with today's date circled showing the full moon and a note. 'Middle of bridge. Moonrise 9.38.' A doodle of two stick figures holding hands. A suede jewellery pouch held a simple twisted gold band and a pair of diamond earrings that blazed when I held them in the sun.

CHAPTER 37

We sat on the terrace and he ordered a Campari for himself and a pint of beer for me.

The early flight from Victoria Falls to Johannesburg had already left, but there was a second one about to depart.

She was not in the line of tourists. I watched them walk across the apron with too much hand luggage. A solitary Chinese carried a large carved crocodile made from soft wood blackened with shoe polish. The shoe polish had come off on his hands and stained his shirt.

I approached the check-in desk, where the attendant was attempting to placate an obese Englishman whose bags had not arrived on the incoming flight. As she called Johannesburg, he sized me up. 'Hopeless,' he said. 'You take your life in your hands flying with this mob and then some joker steals your luggage.' To the woman: 'What do you mean, "tomorrow"? You told me that yesterday. What am I supposed to wear, for Christ's sake?' He realized the futility of further remonstration and stomped off.

I smiled at the attendant as pleasantly as I could. 'Hello. I was hoping to say goodbye to my friend, Sarah Oakes, but she didn't seem to be boarding the flight. I must have got the day wrong.'

Almost invariably airlines will not disclose information about their passengers. No such scruples seemed to have filtered down to the employees of Air Zimbabwe. She picked up a printed list. 'Oakes,' she said. 'No Oakes.'

'Damn. She must be flying under her married name, and I

don't remember it.'

'That's funny. There was a no-show this morning, a Sarah....'

A policeman in uniform joined her behind the desk. He looked me up and down.

'Passport,' he said with his hand out. He looked at my picture in the scruffy Canadian passport and handed it back without comment, but continued to look at me speculatively.

The attendant looked at the policeman and adopted the official line. 'We do not disclose passenger information, sir. I'm sorry.'

Victoria Falls had changed, and not for the better. Souvenir sellers were everywhere, as always, but there was also a bewildering array of activities on offer, from bungee jumping to booze cruising. The area surrounding the waterfall had been fenced off, and the entrance to this 'park' would only accept hard currency. Grey-haired matrons in bright pants wandered the forest trails complaining about the mist. The falling water, the bright rainbows and the graceful bridge remained unchanged. None of the hotels would admit that Sarah was or had been a guest. Once I thought I spotted her walking, but when I closed in I found it wasn't her.

A wasp buzzed against the inside of the windshield. I sat in the driver's seat for half an hour with my forehead pressed on the upper rim of the steering wheel and the contents of her purse spread out on the seat beside me. Nothing made any sense. Why was the government involved? Which government? - and who was she, such that a tabloid would be interested in her affairs? She had said, "Well, I've news for you. No matter how deep you dig with those people, you'll never figure out my real problem."

The falls thundered a few hundred yards away. I felt sick. I wondered if she was suicidal. A body falling into the gorge would never be found.

Three hours later I was back at the Land Rover, soaked. I had explored every spray-drenched viewpoint and peered over the edge of every dizzying precipice.

There was one more flight out. I returned to the airport, changed a small amount of money and watched the boarding process. There was no sign of Sarah. Two policemen were observing me as I left.

I started back towards the town only to be flagged down by a white man holding a leather Gladstone bag and standing next to a disabled taxi. 'Do you mind taking me into town?' he asked. I waited while he paid the driver. English. He climbed into the passenger seat and I let in the clutch.

'Thanks awfully,' he said. 'The gear lever broke off. Would you believe it?'

'You must have been on the SAA flight that just came in.'

'Yes, I'm from London. I took a flight through Jo'burg.'

'Welcome to Zimbabwe - what's left of it. Have you been here before?'

'Several times. I sell works by Michael N'komo and Joshua Mabele. They're both based here and becoming very popular.'

Suddenly he gasped and grabbed the edge of the parcel shelf with both hands. I glanced sideways at him. He was pale and had a most unusual expression on his face. I pulled over to the verge. 'Are you okay?'

'I'm okay. But I just realized something. I've been in this Land Rover before. I didn't recognize it, as it's been repainted - '

'You have? When?'

'Last summer. It belongs to a woman I know - a Sarah.'

'Oakes,' I said.

'Marsh,' he corrected. 'You must be Giles Jackson. There's a bit of a hunt on for you, although you probably don't know it. We've spoken on the phone before. I'm Adam Williamson. You can carry on - I'm all right. Where is she, anyway?'

'Adam Williamson! The gallery owner. What the hell are you doing here?'

'Partly business. I told you - '

'Partly?'

'Well, personal reasons, too. Look, it's a godsend meeting you. We have to talk.'

I drove into town confused. Who the hell could be hunting for me - Melvin Noor? How the hell was he connected to this well-dressed young man in the passenger seat?

'Victoria Falls Hotel,' Adam said. 'Left at the next corner. Come in and have a drink.'

'I'm not really dressed for that,' I protested.

'Screw them. They won't throw you out if you're with me. You'll add local colour - the other guests will love it.' We parked in the hotel parking lot and were challenged by the attendant. 'Yes, my friend,' said Adam, 'we do want to park here, and I have a bag in the back.'

We sat on the terrace and he ordered a *Campari* for himself and a pint of beer for me. 'I love your backwoods appearance,' he said. 'What's been going on?'

'Adam, you were very helpful to me on the phone, but you obviously didn't tell me everything you knew. What the hell are you doing here, and who's looking for me?'

'Giles, it's true. When we talked, I wasn't exactly honest with you. However, I think meeting you like this is divine providence. You may be able to help me sort something out. Let me cut directly to the quick. Sarah's husband and I are lovers. We've been together for thirteen years.'

I nearly spilled the beer into my lap.

'But she's been married for ten years. She told me. They split up three years ago because he had an affair.'

'Married ten years exactly,' he said. 'Today's their anniversary. But I question your use of the word "affair". In my books, he and she have been having the affair. I was there first. In fact, he had an affair with me during his first marriage - that's why it broke up. We have a long commitment to each other. Look, we own a flat together - he financed my gallery. He's everything to me: inspiring, challenging, the pivotal figure in my life. He's so appreciative of beauty and art. You don't realize it, but you've met him. He's gorgeous, and I assume you don't know what an incredible lover he is.' He gave me an arched look.

'The family business has made millions yet he's extraordinarily generous. He's been a socialist since Oxford and always a champion of the underdog. A sort of modern Cadbury. Tony Blair persuaded him to get into politics. Have you heard him speak - he's mesmerizing.

'Mind you, he has his dark side. He's manipulative, unforgiving and jealous. He can be very dangerous if you cross him. He wouldn't listen to me when he married Sarah. He told me he just wanted her as a front. He's got this irrational fear that if he comes out, the world will come to an end. Stupid, really. So many people know anyway. And of course she found out. I was a little indiscreet, I suppose. She never discovered my identity, though.'

Stunned by these revelations and completely at a loss, I focused on what I knew.

'But why were you planning to travel Africa with her?'

'I never planned to go to Africa at all. I'm not too proud of my role in this - it was all pretence so Peter could find out what her plans were. Worked a treat. We even got a boffin from the MOD to install a transponder in her vehicle. Fooled you, too. When you called, I only phoned back on the off chance you might know where she was. You see, Peter lost her in Ethiopia last year. Transponder went dead. Consulates all over Africa were alerted, but they're a bunch of career slobs who couldn't find a turd in a hot tub. Peter was with me when I called you. You weren't exactly honest with me, either. "Interview her about her experiences," you said. "My editors are particularly interested in that angle"; "intrepid women heading off into the blue with Land Rovers." Utter bullshit. Your pal Melvin Noor hired you to buy her chariot, not probe her brain.'

I wasn't certain how to reply to that. Could he know that my feelings for the woman had eclipsed my interest in the vehicle?

'I really hoped we'd seen the last of her when she started screwing her boss. Peter had a private dick on that and even got photos. Then the old gaffer has a stroke, and the next minute she's driving off to Africa in a clapped-out Land Rover. Peter went berserk. She was out from under his control, calling the shots. He would never accept that. Extraordinary woman. In the brief time I got to know her, I could see why he fell for her. Very smart, and she'd be quite sexy without the boobs. Where is she, anyway?'

'Damned if I know, I've lost her,' I said. 'We had a flaming row, and she took off on a bus yesterday. To here, as it turns out. I've spent all day looking for her, but she's disappeared.'

'I wouldn't worry too much. Her tantrums are famous; even Peter admits defeat. But she's probably here somewhere. I know that he is, and there's no smoke without fire. Our travel agent told me he'd flown to Lusaka. He's probably over there on the Zambian side' - he gestured in the direction of the river. 'He's not allowed in Zimbabwe - some diplomatic thing. Come to think of it, she's probably over there in a hotel with him and they're fucking each other's brains out.' He added the last statement morosely.

We both took sips of our drinks. It was not a pleasant image, and too easy to conjure up.

'Is it he who's looking for me?' I asked, hurting.

'Not directly,' he said. 'He learned from his pal Melvin at a committee meeting last week that you had found her in Cape Town. He sicced the consulate on to you to establish exactly where.

'Blow me down if didn't she call him last Wednesday out of the blue. Told him she was going to Victoria Falls but was backing out of an anniversary date they'd made, romantic meeting this evening on the bridge here as the full moon rose - he'd joked about it months ago.

'I was sitting next to him when she called, and I could hear her voice. Calm and confident. She'd made up her mind to divorce him, had no intention of meeting him here, and was heading off into the *bundu* with you. I was all but doing cartwheels around the living room. He just exploded. I've never seen him so mad. He shouted that if she didn't show up as planned, he'd make her life a living hell and she could kiss an easy settlement goodbye. I won't go into details about what he said he would do to you. Lie low or prepare to join a celibate order on a Greek island. He was foaming at the mouth, Giles. Until she called, he had absolutely no intention of going to Africa, of course. We had a dinner party planned.

'When he loses control, he freaks out totally. She hung up on him and the next minute he was on the phone to Ted at the foreign office getting him to put out an all points alert for the two of you in Botswana. Then he turned on me - his voice was chilling - "what are you grinning about, you turkey?" he said. He'd never been violent towards me before, but I tell you, I was terrified. I locked myself in the bathroom. He rampaged around the flat for a while and then went out, slamming the door - I haven't seen him since. He didn't even tell his security detail where he was going.'

It suddenly hit me who he was talking about.

'For Christ's sake! Why have you followed him here?'

'Giles, I think he's crazy enough to do something really

stupid. He hates losing control. I love him but I know he has a Svengali-like hold on me - and on Sarah, too, I suspect. I've never determined what the medical term is that applies to him. A type of schizophrenia, or maybe a bipolar or mood disorder. If Sarah has managed to break her string, I think he will go off the rails. The reality is that I'm the only one who has a hope of getting through to him. In a crisis, he thinks he's perfectly rational and stops taking his medications. He left them behind, and I've got them with me.'

'Look,' I said, my stomach churning. 'I'm not on your wavelength, it's not my scene, but you've been up front with me. What can I do to help Sarah?'

'Giles, he's only damaging himself by hanging onto Sarah. I'm not overstating my fears in the least by telling you that he may kill himself and Sarah too. Get Sarah out of here - if she hasn't seen him yet, don't let her confront him.

'I may be a fool, but my instinct tells me this will be the seminal event that forces him to accept that there's no point in continuing his charade. He is gay and one hell of a player on the world stage. The tabloids will have orgasms, *The Mirror* will use their largest font, *The Times* will make an editorial comment and *The Economist* will ignore it completely. The unwashed masses will titter, but they'll accept it. We will live happily ever after. Sarah can seduce an alternative and stock a kindergarten if she feels like it.'

'But I have no idea where Sarah is - ' I started to say when he looked over my shoulder and cringed.

'Holy shit! Look what the cat puked. Fred Bigglesworth. Fucking paparazzi! No! Don't turn round - he hasn't seen me.' He dumped a ten-pound note on the table and disappeared through the nearest door. I waited thirty seconds and looked around. Apart from a group of inoffensive pensioners, the patio was empty.

I was shaken. It had never occurred to me that Sarah was in any danger other than from herself, and the thought of her being used by Peter Marsh was sickening. I left my beer and found a washroom. I splashed myself with cold water, hardly recognizing the wild-haired, ashen-faced reflection in the gilded mirror.

Outside, the sun was setting, turning the 'smoke that thundered' to the colour of candyfloss. I drove back towards the bridge and parked. I sat on a bench and tried to apply logic to the situation.

Adam's story made some sense of her comments about paparazzi and the government being involved, but did nothing to assist me in finding her unless - of course! - she had changed her mind and planned to show up on the bridge at moonrise that evening. In which case---

My planning was interrupted by the large tourist from the airport who ambled up to *Geraldine*. 'Your vehicle, mate?'

I nodded.

'You drove this all the way from England?' he enthused. 'That must be quite a trip. By yourself, are you?'

He was wearing shorts too tight for him and his spindly legs glowed white in the dusk. Humpty Dumpty with lank black hair and reeking of stale tobacco. The lens cap was off his impressive camera. Under the circumstances, a pest.

'Ja,' I said in my best Afrikaans, and decided to clean the windows and check the engine oil.

'"*Ja*," you drove all the way from England or "*Ja*," you're alone?' he asked pleasantly. 'Like a cigarette?'

'*Nee Dankie,*' I said, hoping he would go away. I cleaned up the interior and dumped the litter into an overflowing rubbish bin. A troop of monkeys immediately sorted through my detritus, looking for snacks. He took their picture.

'Cute,' he said. 'You're Giles Jackson, aren't you?'

"Jan van der Merwe," I said, "from Thabazimbi."

'You're Giles Jackson, mate. That was an interesting enquiry you were making at the airport, and I've been watching you all afternoon inspecting the bottom of this waterfall. Have you dropped something? Your name cropped up in a conversation I overheard the other day in London. Colonial fellow, rushing around Africa chasing a certain woman. And you write for a magazine - I picked up a copy at Heathrow. Your mug shot's on top of your column and one of your colleagues, old fellow Mark Franklin, gave me the goods on you - a knock-off Indiana Jones.'

'*Ek kan jou nie verstaan nie.*'

'Come off it,' he said. 'I'm Fred Bigglesworth. I just saw you all pally with Adam Williamson.' He made a limp wrist gesture. 'The bird you were looking for at the airport roosted in his hotel last night. So did I, but she gave me the slip. Must be a convention going on around there. I ran the registration on this vehicle and guess who it belongs to? I'm sure you've done a lot of interesting things with this Land Rover and some more interesting than others, if you get the drift. Now she's done a runner, has she? If you wanted to share some of your experiences with me, I'll make it worth your while. About five hundred quid, perhaps? You could get yourself new pants and a haircut.'

'Get lost!' He laughed and flashed his camera at me. 'Think about it, Mr. Jackson. You're going to be in the story anyway. You might as well be the star and get paid for it - "Minister's Wife a Tiger in the Bush." I can see the headline now..'

The stores had closed for the day and it was too late to buy any clothes or get a haircut. If there were going to be a party, the uninvited guest would be the most uncouth. It was nine when I locked the doors and walked towards the bridge.

CHAPTER 38

'I was chatting with Fred Bigglesworth earlier this evening, and he's very interested in traffic on this bridge tonight.'

The immigration officer at the border on the Zimbabwe side was tall and obviously a Matabele. I told him I was crossing for dinner. He stamped my passport and yawned. 'Do something for me,' I said, speaking in Sindebele. 'There's a fat white Englishman called Bigglesworth following me. Woman problem. I'd like a quiet evening. Here's twenty US for you. Stop him following me and there's another twenty when I come back...' The banknote disappeared in a flash.

The road through the forest was damp and poorly lit. There was no traffic. Lights twinkled on the Zambian side as I walked out onto the bridge. Four hundred feet below, the Zambezi swirled.

I recognised him immediately, leaning over the railings on the upstream side under a solitary lamp near the bungee jump. He was perfectly turned out in khaki slacks, desert boots and a Barbour jacket. A wave of elation swept over me. He was here and she was not. No reconciliation had taken place.

'Good evening, minister.' The dull undulating sound of falling water made it difficult to talk normally.

He took a long pull on a cheroot. 'Giles Jackson, I presume. We meet again. You *are* looking a little worse for wear.'

I made no response.

'Where is my wife?'

'I have no idea.'

'She told you I would be here?'

'No.'

'What did she tell you?'

'We've never discussed you.'

'I find that hard to believe. How else would you know that I would be here?'

'Adam Williamson told me where to find you.'

'Ah, Adam.' A deep intake of breath. 'What connected him to me?'

'You live together. It's no big secret.'

'Goddamn, Adam.' He looked at his watch. 'And what is your purpose here?'

'I have no plans.'

'Have you made love to my wife?'

'How can you have any claim to Sarah as a wife when you've been with Adam Williamson for thirteen years?'

'If you don't understand me, let me rephrase the question. Have you fucked Sarah?'

'You know she's set on divorcing you. It's over. Nothing you do here will make her change her mind.'

'Just who do you think you are? She's married to *me*.'

'That's nothing but a piece of paper, you arrogant bastard. You don't own her. She's a free woman. If she was continuing to play your game, you wouldn't be here waiting for her.'

He looked at his watch again and his tone changed to cocktail party smooth. 'We came here on our honeymoon, you know. Just like her parents did. She had a *wonderful* time. This little anniversary rendezvous was her idea.'

'And despite her call last week, you expect her to show up? Get real.'

'Why not? I give her a long leash, and when I tug she comes. She's had plenty of opportunities to stray. What's different now? The way we conduct our marriage has been convenient for both of us. I didn't object to her fling with Harold Mathews - a married man mind you - and she certainly wasn't a paragon of virtue on her way down Africa. She probably satisfied some lucky buggers in Cape Town. Then she gets involved with you. Bottom feeding in my opinion. Two years ago we agreed that neither of us would do anything rash until our tenth wedding anniversary. That's tonight. I'm confident she will show up. I'm as far as one can climb up the social heap; she's not going to do any better. There's never been much fuss about us in the papers. She's never played a significant role in my career. After the last blow-up, she disappeared and sulked, but her absence has scarcely been noticed. She has a certain propensity to histrionics. The ethnic chic had an appeal to voters, but it's run its course.' He laughed cynically. 'I just found out about the business school. A degree from an African university will pull in a few extra votes in my constituency, but I'm a shoo-in anyway.'

'So you're prepared to let her go?' My voice must have expressed relief.

He flipped the stub of his cheroot into the abyss. Sparks spiralled down until the spray extinguished them. 'Long way down, isn't it.' His tone was threatening. 'If she were to disappear tonight, the locals will assume it was a suicide. And you, Mr.

Jackson, are such a nonentity that it's unlikely anyone would report you missing.'

Christ, I thought. *Adam's right. The man's crazy. I wonder if he's armed.* I stepped back from the railing.

'I wouldn't count on that,' I said. 'I was chatting with Fred Bigglesworth earlier this evening, and he's very interested in traffic on this bridge tonight.'

That got his attention. 'Bigglesworth, eh? Nice company you keep. I can deal with him.'

A gust of wind blew a patch of mist up the gorge from the east, and I realized I was lightly dressed and cold. He sneered. 'Look at yourself, Jackson. You're a tramp. A part-time hack - writing for a yobbish magazine. Dependent on handouts - like the one I gave you - fifteen minutes of my time discussing rural byways. A bush mechanic living in a rented shack. I know you're not even legally in England. I could have you chucked out next week if I chose. I probably will - you're a minor annoyance. And you think you can ride off into the sunset with Sarah! Dream on.'

A rind of moon showed over the horizon, illuminating the anger in his face and stance. The solid slab of water curling over the lip of the precipice was suddenly phosphorescent as it plunged into the gorge below.

I moved closer, standing over him. 'I don't know the complete story,' I said, 'but you suckered her into marrying you. You needed her to enhance your political career and manipulated her for years while you led a double life. Well, she's smartened up, minister. When you wind in your leash, you'll find nothing on her end. We are lovers.'

His face was ashen in the unkind light, his jaw clenching in spasms, but no words came out. The confidence of the tycoon and powerful politician had dissipated. A string of spittle ran from his jaw to the collar of his jacket. He was obviously a sick man, but I felt no sympathy for him. He and I had both lost the same woman. My shirt might be filthy, but it held a trace of Sarah's perfume. However badly she and I had parted, I had treated her honestly and he had not.

His face contorted as he struggled to regain control. 'You fucking bastard!' He screamed and lunged at me. I sidestepped easily and he stumbled, grasping the lamppost to arrest a fall. I kept my distance, alert and wary of a second attack. He muttered under his breath, and I was conscious of his body shaking as he let go of the post and braced himself against the balustrade. As I stood, dwarfed by the immensity of the plunging Zambezi and drenched in the light of the rapidly rising moon, it crossed my mind that I could be rid of him in an instant by pushing him over the edge. I came close to doing so, but the moment passed.

The steel beneath my feet trembled slightly to the rhythm of footsteps. I glanced behind me. Somebody was approaching, wrapped in one of the hooded plastic capes the locals sell to tourists. Peter Marsh regained his composure completely and straightened up.

'Ah, she's here. Get lost, Jackson! Go play with your Land Rover.'

The order was given with such confidence it was like a physical blow.

The moon, now a perfect disk well clear of the horizon, illuminated every bolt and rivet of the rusty bridge.

The posture of the approaching figure was wrong. It was deferential, almost apologetic, and belied the possibility that this was the woman who had conquered a continent, split logs with a big axe and walked with me unarmed through the Okavango bush.

I faced Marsh again.

'You're in for a very long wait,' I said, with more self-assuredness than I felt. 'In my experience, Sarah doesn't change her mind.

I turned to address the hooded figure. 'Good evening, Adam,' I said pleasantly. 'He's all yours.'

CHAPTER 39

The farm complex was a mile from the road.
It was a sorry sight.

The immigration officer had his hands behind his head and his feet on his desk. In a cell behind him, clasping the bars and looking like a deflated dinghy, was Fred Bigglesworth*.

'Jackson. Vouch for me. Get me out of here.'

'Why should I? You're going to write a story that includes Sarah and me.'

'On my mother's grave. I won't mention you. That's my word. Blighter took my passport and camera.'

I shook the officer's hand. 'Magnificent specimen you have there.'

'He tried to take my picture. That's contrary to subsection 278B of the Customs and Immigration Act. We could hold him a week. I let the thin one go even though they seemed to know each other.'

I looked at the clock on the wall. 'Let him out onto the bridge, in five minutes, say, at 10.15 exactly. He's probably good for a hundred. I don't care what you do with him when he comes back, but please don't confiscate his camera.' I slipped him a fifty. 'Nice work; I really appreciate it.'

I turned to Fred. 'On your mother's grave?'

'I swear, mate, I swear.'

I gave him a thumbs up and left.

The service station was open and I topped up. In Zimbabwe no motorist passes a functioning garage without refuelling. With both

---

* *Winston Babela has been promoted within the Zimbabwe Customs and Excise Authority and can no longer be found behind a desk at Victoria Falls.*

tanks full, I could make it to the South African border. An elderly black man operated the pump and washed the windows. I gave him the small change.

There were no women on the streets as I made one last circuit of the town. I took the road south towards Bulawayo. The moon went behind the clouds near Hwange, but I drove steadily on using a light foot. There was no traffic. The occasional animal ran across the road or stood paralysed by my lights. I played *La Bohème* several times over, as it matched my mood. Emotions conflicted. Elation, fear, despondency. Most of all, there was a profound sense of loss, made all the more poignant by the red plaid rug folded on the empty passenger seat. Somewhere near the Bembizi River, I was tired enough to pull off the road into the bush and go to sleep.

I read the *Bulawayo Chronicle* over an early lunch. It had little to offer in the way of international news. I did not seem to have missed anything important.

Little had changed since my last visit. The town still had the relaxed feel I recalled from my youth, with broad streets and colonial architecture.

At a trading store, I purchased some cheap shirts, socks and shorts.

I took the spare wheel to a garage. 'Two hours,' they said. 'Provided the power stays on.'

My old high school was still there. Boys were practicing rugby on the broad fields. A stained-glass window in the cathedral was broken.

At three I collected the spare wheel and got back on the road.

It seemed a pity to bypass the village and the farm without stopping to look. Twenty miles from town, I swung off the main road.

The village was much as I remembered it. The primary school was there, with the hard earth playground ringed by eucalyptus. The roof of Patel's General Store was rustier, and a '*No Blend*' sign hung on the sole petrol pump. A concrete bridge had replaced the culvert that used to overflow during summer thunderstorms.

The entrance to the farm had changed. The imposing stone pillars and concrete sign reading 'Jacksland Farm' - of which my father had been very proud - were still there. But the gates were falling off their hinges, and pampas grass was taking over the driveway. Clearly nobody farmed here any more. Where once were lucerne and maize fields with paddocks for horses was now a wild profusion of invasive plants.

A tractor came round the bend pulling a disc harrow. The machine was an old one with a homemade corrugated iron awning. The engine sounded loose and defeated. The driver was an elderly white man; I waved at him, and he stopped on the verge eyeing the Land Rover.

'You're a long way from home,' he observed.

'This was home once,' I said. 'I was a kid here on this farm. I'm the last Jackson, as a matter of fact. What's going on here now?'

'You must have been away a long time,' he said. 'That place was expropriated by the government about eight years ago. Belongs to a big man in the cabinet. Shona fellow. We don't see much of him and he don't do much for us.' He was direct and outspoken, and made no attempt to conceal his contempt.

'Will it be all right if I go in and take a look around?'

'Be my guest,' he said. 'No one's going to bother you. There's a caretaker, but he's on the bottle. Drop in for a beer when you're done. My place is a couple of kilos down the road on the left. It's called *Willowbrook*. Bailey's the name. Chris Bailey.' He started the tired motor and drove on. The tyres on the harrow were completely bald.

I forced open the gates and drove *Geraldine* down the overgrown avenue between the oleanders. Brush flattened ahead of me and sprang up behind. A faint footpath followed the drive, but no vehicle had driven here for many months. Termites had destroyed some of the electric poles, and the wires were gone.

The farm complex was a mile from the road. It was a sorry sight. Windows empty of glass, doors missing and sections of the iron roof twisted. A rusting barbed wire fence marked the defensive perimeter. I pulled up near the house. A smashed birdbath lay in the dry fishpond. Yellow lantana had exploded up the walls*.

Smoke rose from the compound, and I walked down to clear things with the caretaker. Squash, pumpkins and maize flourished. A young Matabele woman nursed a baby and tended a cooking pot. Two small children played in the concrete yard. Chickens pecked. A lean yellow dog growled but did not stir from the dust where he lay in the sun.

---

* All buildings on Jacksland Farm were completely destroyed by a veldt fire in 2004. The property is now completely uninhabited.

There was no response when the woman called into the little house. In the gloom, I could make out a man sprawled on the bed with a bottle nearby.

They were desperately poor. There were no mats on the floor, and the covering on the bed was torn and ragged. The stump of a candle protruded from a broken bottle. A faded picture of Christ in a wooden frame was the only decoration. There was a bicycle with a hopelessly bent front wheel.

I thought of the unused food in my refrigerator. I beckoned to the woman, who tucked her breast into her blouse, put the baby on her hip and followed me to the Land Rover. I gave her a box with the bruised softening fruit, most of the cans of condensed milk and the other supplies I would not need. Gratitude and embarrassment showed in her face.

Exploring this lost world brought childhood memories vividly to mind. The house was gutted and anything of value gone. Faded wallpaper sagged; china plumbing was smashed; the tin chimney lay in the weeds outside. Orchard and kitchen garden were overgrown. The grapevines, that my grandmother had planted, spread their tentacles twenty years beyond the twisted arbour where my father used to enjoy his evening Scotch.

The disconnected crank rod of the windmill rapped against the angle iron of the tower as it swung - a rusty pendulum in the afternoon breeze. The yard stand pump remained; still working, the cast iron handle burnished from fifty years of use. The damp earth under the spout was printed with the hooves of goats and the bare feet of adults and children. Only one in the family had shoes;

attested to by the worn cloverleaf of a *Vibram* sole. There was a depressing litter of plastic containers and rusty paraffin cans in the encroaching bush.

The tobacco shed had collapsed. A diesel generator, the sound of which had dominated my childhood, was rusty, vandalized and useless. Along the path to the empty dam, anthills rose in the paddocks. Concrete footings and a few lengths of rusty pipe showed through the weeds. I tripped over the rotted frame of a *bakkie*. It was infinitely sad. My grandparents and my parents had loved this land. They were dead, and Africa was reclaiming two generations of sweat and toil.

Back behind the house where *Geraldine* was parked under the peppercorn tree, I unpacked my sleeping bag and was unrolling the awning when two strong arms encircled me from behind. 'I was beginning to think you would never come,' she said.

She drank beer as I cooked supper and reminisced about my childhood. Tension, the legacy of our argument, lingered.

She ate hungrily, even helping herself to the tail of *boerewors* left on my plate. She did not respond to the invitation of a touch on her cheek. Intimacy was obviously not on the menu. She had kissed me after giving me the hug, but it was the kiss of a casual acquaintance. It was as if she was rejoining her tour group and I was merely the guide. I was certain that she had no idea of the emotional roller coaster her disappearance had created and which I had been riding for the past forty-eight hours.

She stretched. 'Thank you, I needed that. Any chance you could heat me one of those big bowls of water? You wouldn't want to share the tent with me like this.' Conversation remained inconsequential, and once the pot heated she took it behind *Geraldine* to wash out of my sight. By the time I'd finished the chores, washed myself and shaved, she was already in her sleeping bag facing the back wall of the tent.

It crossed my mind that my treatment of Peter Marsh might not meet with her approval.

I was unsure where to place my sleeping bag, but she rolled over, propped her head on her hand and said. 'Put it here, Giles. We need to talk.'

We lay together in silence for a few minutes. The lamp hissed and the old windmill made an occasional muffled clank.

'What *is* that noise?'

'Broken windmill.'

'It was doing that last night too...'

'You were here? I had reason to believe that you were expected at the Falls last night.'

An intake of breath. 'How did you find out?'

'I met a man on a bridge.'

'Peter?'

Yes. Do you want to talk about it?'

To be honest, no.'

'You dumped me and went to meet him.'

'I'm not exactly a class act, am I? How do you know?

'I found your toilet bag in *Geraldine*. Then I ran into someone you know.'

'Who?'

'Adam Williamson.'

'Adam who? – Oh -That little creep! - What the heck is he doing here?'

'He's your competition. Peter's lover.'

Her eyes widened in shock and I could see her chest heave. I thought she was going to be sick. I put my arms around her. After at least four clangs from the windmill she let out a long breath. 'My God! - That explains a lot, doesn't it? I'll bet he was spying for Peter, and that's where that transponder came from.' She broke free of my embrace, sat up and clasped her knees. She was wearing a grey tee shirt with a yacht club logo. 'It's pathetic how stupid I've been. Just how long has he been Peter's lover?'

'Thirteen years, he told me.'

Shit.' She dropped back down on her pillow and stared at the awning above.

You didn't meet with Peter. Why not? Where've you been?'

She twisted a lock of hair around her finger. 'After that bus dropped me off, I checked into the Victoria Falls Hotel. I was a mess. I'd cried most of the way there.

I had an endless shower, slept for a few hours, awoke ravenous and ordered a snack in the bar. A fat slob tried to pay for my meal and followed me back to my room. I recognized him, a tabloid hack from London. He's hung around me before.'

Fred Bigglesworth.'

Is there anything you don't know?'

Try me.'

'I spent the night thinking about our wonderful time together and how it ended. I realized you may have become a bit obsessed with me before we met, but, looked at in retrospect, it was a compliment. You'd proved to me that you weren't sick or dangerous. You didn't bully me or become the least bit pushy. You were sympathetic, resourceful and fun. I was attracted to you despite the conflict in my head. And when it did seem right to make love with you, it was truly magical. I lost myself completely over those two days.' Her voice was soft and reflective, and she reached for my hand.

'Peter tried to make a pact with me the day I last saw him. He said then, that if I gave him another eighteen months, he would give up his lover and we would get together again. Just the two of us in a normal marriage. Dogs, children, the works. We were to meet last night - our tenth anniversary - on the bridge. It was the night of the full moon.' She turned to me with a wry look. 'Hopelessly romantic, I know, but that was part of his charm. One day I'll try to explain Peter to you, but it won't be easy.'

'You don't have to explain him to me now, Sarah. I think I understand already.'

'When we met at the Mount Nelson Hotel and you suggested taking a safari together and visiting Victoria Falls, it was an outlandish proposition from a total stranger. But it also seemed like divine providence. Fate was playing her hand. And I felt I could trust you. I even felt I could level with you, and you could escort me to the meeting. But the plan unravelled because, try as I might, I couldn't stop comparing you with him and, believe me, there cannot be two more disparate men on the planet.

'I made the decision to call him from that border post. It was the first time we had talked since New Year's Eve two years ago - the night of the millennium. He claimed he had completely lost track of me, was still in love with me, and was planning to be at Victoria Falls as arranged. I told him I was going to be in Victoria Falls but that there was no point in him coming there. I didn't want to see him; I wanted the divorce, and was never going back into the sham he called marriage. He was foul to me and demanded to know where I was, so I told him I was in Botswana with you. He called me a slut. Apparently you interviewed him once. He insisted I meet him as planned, and said he would be waiting for me. He continued to berate me, and I hung up on him.

'After the wonderful time you and I shared, I realized it was over with Peter. You killed my wanting him forever, and I feared the consequences of a confrontation with him on that bridge.'

I put my arms around her again and held her close. She was warm and wonderfully solid. I felt her relax in my arms.

'You and I may never be a long-term proposition, but you've focused my mind. You obviously care for me and accept me the way I am. Even after I wobbled a bit, you made it clear to me that you wanted us to continue. I'm not apologizing. If you want to maintain harmonious relationships with your women friends, don't carry surreptitious photos of them nearly naked around in your pack. And don't make uncouth victory displays with their underwear. All I will admit to is that was I was jealous of that pathetic Angela.'

'Why did you come here?'

'There was a very good chance you would come here; you told me you would like to see your childhood home again. I remembered the name of the farm and I knew it was near Bulawayo. To avoid that creep, Bigglesworth, I got up really early in the morning and checked out. There was a taxi dropping staff off at the hotel. I just got in. "Airport?" the driver asked, and I said, "Bulawayo." He took me to a market area where there were lots of minibuses and got me on the right one.

'It was crazy. I was jammed in with twelve other people for hours. I was confident that I was in Bulawayo before you. I went into a co-op place where the farmers brought stuff, and right away one of the men said he knew where Jacksland farm was and drew me a map. "Don't get too excited, though," he warned me. "There's nothing there anymore."

'At the supermarket I bought a bottle of water and a packet of chocolate biscuits. A taxi dropped me outside the farm. It was about five when I got here and hid in the bushes by the fruit trees over there.

'It was a long night. It didn't rain, but it was cold towards morning. I had so little water that I got up in the last of the moonlight, went to that pump and tried to work it. It was awfully loud and it's difficult to work a big pump and drink at the same time, but I managed, and also refilled my bottle. I freaked out when a dog started barking. I went back to my hiding spot, pretty shaken. Then I heard a drunk singing and talking to himself. He passed within feet of me, and the reality of how stupid I was to be here alone hit me.

'Bloody stupid. But I'm also an idiot. I should have recognized your footprints by the pump.

'I thought about you the whole time, speculating where you were, if you had been turned back at the border or had gone home via Botswana.'

'Will you take off this tee shirt?'

'Okay, how's that? I waited all day for you, and I decided to stay until noon tomorrow. If you hadn't shown up by then I would have given up.

'I hunkered down in the bushes all day, and prayed the dog wouldn't sniff me out. A woman worked in the garden. Nobody else came; then I heard the engine and knew it was *Geraldine*. I was going to rush out, but something held me back. I laid low and saw you give the woman food. I stole one of your beers while you walked down through the fields.'

She snuggled closer. 'Keep on doing that... By the way, I've forgiven you for Angela, and I figured out she gave you the picture of me. You were wrong about Gert du Plessis and Luke Chikale. You are just going to have to forgive me for that Australian. It was a moonlit night...'

A deep, sleepy laugh. 'I'm not laughing at you; I'm laughing at myself. I must be the only tourist who stayed a night at that hotel and never saw the waterfall.'

FINAL WATCHER

Cape Dutch Farmstead 1712.

On the Cape Peninsula, is a famous vineyard. Huguenot refugees planted the first vines here the year William of Orange died.

Mountain water is diverted along a system of *leiwater* channels to feed the cabernet grapes. The produce of these vines, in simple dark bottles, is sold to connoisseurs in many lands.

A two-hour summer drive from Cape Town, over a winding pass, will bring you here, and you may lunch, with a bottle of wine, in the shadow of venerable oaks.

The farmhouse is over two hundred years old. It is a gabled building of serene proportions floored with yellow wood. It is now an exclusive small hotel, and if you wish to stay here in the summer, you must book many months ahead.

The ownership of this establishment can be traced to a corporation in Gauteng whose directors employ thousands in industries ranging from beer to diamonds. Wisely, they leave the running of the hotel to a man in his sixties who was born in the valley, speaks four languages and has no high school education.

In winter there are fewer guests. Frost rimes the high peaks and berg winds blow down the *kloofs*.

On a crisp clear morning, a man telephoned asking for accommodation for that evening. The manager accepted the reservation and allocated an upstairs room.

The guests arrived shortly after noon. A tall striking couple, on whom it was difficult to place an age; certainly the man was a few years older than the woman. Their dusty vehicle looked distinctly out of place between the Mercedes and BMWs in the stable yard. 'Wash it,' he ordered the protesting gardener. 'We clean every customer's car. No exceptions.'

The guests declined lunch. In the late afternoon, the manager saw them walking hand in hand towards the mill. They visited the cellars and the cooper's shop. They sat on the arch of the bridge as the last rays of the sun painted the peaks of the Waterberg amber.

They were undemanding, and he liked them. At dinner he gave them a good table. They ordered one of the cheaper wines, and, as he was about to open it, he saw the man lean across the table and kiss the woman tenderly. He selected a better bottle and delivered it. 'I think you will like this instead,' he said. 'It is a Twee Jonge Gezellen from '93, and a gift of the house.'

The woman wore a white dress such as one can purchase in the dusty small towns of the Karroo. Between her breasts hung a curious silver pendant shaped in the form of an elongated Maltese cross. The man's khaki was casual and the military jersey a little small for him. They were talking about South America.

After dinner they sat close together on the leather sofa with legs stretched towards the fire. The man accepted a brandy. She rested her head on his shoulder.

The man was saying, 'It seems far too early, to be discussing this, but what if it's a girl? *Geraldine*? Do I have any say in this?'

She laughed. 'I think one *Geraldine* in a family is enough.'

They had an early breakfast. The Land Rover raised a vortex of oak leaves as it departed down the avenue in the morning sun.

444

EPILOGUE

In late 1999 the American corporation Ford purchased the English company Land Rover Limited from B.M.W. of Germany. Under Ford ownership, nothing came of the plan - outlined in this story - to redesign the Defender model.

In 2008 Ford sold Land Rover Limited to Tata of India. The company now named Jaguar Land Rover has flourished under Tata ownership and several new and innovative vehicles have been introduced - however the Defender model has soldiered on virtually unchanged.

In 2011 Tata issued a press release stating that manufacture of this iconic vehicle is to be discontinued at the end of 2015 and replaced by something called 'A Modern Interpretation'. This announcement was greeted with some dismay.

At the time of publication of this book, Geraldine is fifty-eight. years old and continues her adventures.

ACKNOWLEDGEMENTS

Writing Stalking Geraldine would have been difficult without the help of a number of generous people. These include:

Old Africa hand Neil Podmore who once broke a Bedford lay shaft in the Ngorogo Crater. Zimbabwean ex-pat and 6 cylinder fanatic Philip Goodall who has shovelled the Maun sand track. Overland Expedition Fundi Paul Marsh. Cartoonist Tom Grogg on whom I inflicted the first draft of this yarn. Oenophile Jamie Cowel who drives one of Geraldine's siblings. Gerry Hogan who knows how to pummel a manuscript and editor Cathy Morton who inserted most of the commas. Clinical Counsellor Suzanne Kyra who yelled 'Publish' and diagnosed the sickness of my putative parliamentarian and Psychologist Gordon Cole who put aside his Guitar to prescribe treatment. My ever optimistic daughter Shelley Wood who not only gave constructive criticism and encouragement but slept on the ground in Hwange National park despite the lions and the missing perimeter fence. My publisher William Gelbert who loves beautiful books. Author Marina Sonkina whose work is an inspiration. Thanks too, to the many people who helped us on our African travels, allowed us to camp in their *bomas* and reassured us we were mad but not completely crazy.

CPSIA information can be obtained
at www.ICGtesting.com
Printed in the USA
LVOW10s1615210317
527965LV00007B/885/P